Objective

ELECTRICAL ENGINEERING

for

Diploma Engineers

DRDO, BHEL, DMRC, Railways &
Other Engineering (Diploma) Competitive Examinations

G K Publications (P) Ltd
gateway to knowledge

CL MEDIA (P) LTD.

Typeset by : *CL Media DTP Unit*

Printed at : Repro Knowledgecast Limited, Thane

Administrative and Production Offices

Published by : **CL Media (P) Ltd.**
KH No. 1027, Ramnagar, Salempur, Rajputana, Roorkee (U.K.)-247667

Marketed by : **G.K. Publications (P) Ltd.**
H-205, Sector-63
NOIDA - 201307 (U.P.)
☎ (0120) - 4267181, 82, 84
Telefax : 4267183

For product information :
Visit ***www.gkpublications.com*** or email to ***gkp@gkpublications.com***

Contents

Basic Electricals

ALTERNATING QUANTITY

In an electrical circuit direct current flows continuously in one direction only and if the applied voltage and circuit resistance are kept constant, the magnitude of current flowing through the circuit remains constant over time. However, when current flowing varies in magnitude and direction periodically, it is called *alternating current*. Thus an alternating quantity (either current or emf) is one which periodically passes through a definite cycle, each consisting of two half cylces, during one of which the current or emf around the circuit varies in one direction and during the other, in the opposite direction.

Equations of Alternating Voltage and Currents.

Alternators produce an emf which is for all practical purposes is sinusoidal. The equation for the emf generated versus time is given as

$$e = E_{max} \sin \omega t$$

where, e = instantaneous emf

E_{max} = maximum emf

ωt = angle through which the armature has turned from neutral.

Taking frequency as *f* hertz (cycles per second),

$$\omega = 2\pi f,$$

$$\therefore \qquad e = E_{max} \sin 2\pi ft$$

Waveform.

Shape of the curve of the voltage or current when plotted against time as base is called *waveform*. The waveform of induced emf in an alternator differs slightly from that of sine wave but for calculation purposes it is treated as such. The advantage of doing so is that calculations become simple.

Alternation and cycle.

When a periodic wave, such as sinusoidal wave, goes through one complete set of positive or negative values, it completes one alternation and when it goes through one complete set of positive and one complete set of negative values it is said to have completed one cycle.

Periodic time (T).

The time taken in seconds by an alternating quantity to complete one cycle is called *periodic time*.

Frequency (f).

The number of cycles completed per second by an alternating quantity is called *frequency*.

In SI system, frequency is expressed in hertz (pronunced as hurts).

Periodic time or time period is reciprocal of frequency.

$$i.e. \qquad T = \frac{1}{f} \qquad or \qquad f = \frac{1}{T}$$

In a multipolar machine having P poles and running at a speed of N rpm, frequency of generated emf

$$f = \frac{PN}{120}$$

Amplitude.

The greatest value, positive or negative, which an alternating quantity attains during one cycle is called the amplitude of the alternating quantity.

AC AMPERE.

The value of an alternating current is not based on its average value but is based on its heating effect.

AC ampere is that current, which when passed through a given resistance for a given time, produces same heat as produced by flow of one ampere of direct current through the same resistance for the same time.

Instantaneous value.

Alternating current or voltage changes from instant to instant. The value of alternating current or voltge at any particular instant is called **instantaneous value**. Instantaneous value of an alternating quantity can be determined either from the curve or from an equation of the alternating quantity.

Maximum value.

The greatest value, positive or negative, which an alternating quantity attains during one complete cycle is called its **amplitude or maximum or peak crest value.**

Average or Mean Value.

The average or mean value of an alternating current is expressed by that steady current which transfers across any circuit the same charge as is transferred by that alternating current during the same time.

Since in the case of a symmetrical alternating current (i.e. one whose two half cycles are exactly similar whether sinusoidal or non sinusoidal) the average or mean value over a complete cycle is zero hence for such alternating quantities average or mean value means the value determined by taking the average of instantaneous values during one half cycle or one alternation only. However, for unsymmetrical alternating current (such as half-wave rectified current), the average value means the value determined by taking the mean of instantaneous values over the complete cycle.

The average values for perfect sinusoidal, half-wave rectified, full-wave rectified, rectangular and triangular wave alternating currents are 0.636, 0.318, 0.636, 1 and 0.5 times the maximum value respectively.   The average or mean value is only of use in connection with processes where the results depend on the current only, irrespective of the voltage, such as electro-plating or battery charging.

Rms or effective value.

It is that steady current or voltage which when flows or applied to a given resistance for a given time produces the same amount of heat as when the alternating current or voltage is flowing or applied to the same resistance for the same time.

The effective or virtual value of alternating current or voltage is equal to the square root of the mean of the squares of successive ordinates and that is why it is known as root-mean-square (rms) value.

The root mean square of effective values for perfect sinusoidal, half-wave rectified, full wave rectified, rectangular and triangular wave alternating currents are 0.707, 0.5, 0.707, 1 and 0.578 times the maximum value respectively.

Equation for the instantaneous values of emf is given as

$$e = E_{max} \sin \omega t = E_{max} \sin 2\pi ft$$

Hence

(*i*) maximum value of an alternating emf is given by the coefficient of the sine of the time angle.

(*ii*) frequency is given by coefficient of time t divided by 2π

i.e. $$f = \frac{\text{Coefficient of time } t}{2\pi}$$

Similarly we can also find the maximum value and frequency of the current from the equation of instantaneous values of current.

Form factor.

It, is defined as the ratio of effective value to the average or mean value of a periodic wave.

Mathematically,

$$\text{Form factor} = \frac{\text{effective value}}{\text{average value}}$$

The values of form factor for perfect sinusoidal, half-wave rectified, full-wave fectified, rectangular and triangular wave alternating currents are 1.11, 1.57, 1.11, 1 and 1.16 respectively.

Peak factor.

It is very essential in connection with determining the dielectric strength since dielectric stress developed in any insulating material is proportional to the maximum value of the voltage applied to it.

Peak or crest or amplitude factor of a periodic wave is defined as the ratio of maximum or peak to the effective or rms value of the wave.

i.e   Peak factor, $$K_p = \frac{\text{maximum value}}{\text{effective value}}$$

The values of peak or crest factor for perfect sinusoidal, half-wave rectified, full-wave rectified, rectangular and triangular wave alternating currents are $\sqrt{2}$, 2.0, $\sqrt{2}$, 1 and $\sqrt{3}$ respectively.

Phase and Phase angle.

Phase of an alternating current means fraction of the time period of that alternating current that has elapsed since the current last passed through the zero position of reference. The phase angle of any quantity means the angle the vector representing the quantity makes with the reference line (which is taken to be at zero degrees or radians).

Phase difference.

When two alternating quantities are considered simultaneously, the frequency being the same, they may not pass through a particular point at the same instant. One may pass through its maximum value at the instant when the other passes through the value other than its maximum one. These two quantities are said to have a phase difference. Phase difference is always given either in degrees or in radians.

The phase difference is measured by the angular distance between the points where the two curves cross the base or reference line in the same direction.

The quantity ahead in phase is said to lead the other quantity while the seond quantity is said to lag behind the first one.

If I_1 is taken as reference vector, then two currents can be expressed as

$$i_1 = I_{max} \sin \omega t, \quad \text{and} \quad i_2 = I_{2max} \sin (\omega t - \phi)$$

The two quantities are said to be in phase with each other if they pass through zero values at the same instant and rise in the same direction. But the two quantities passing through zero values at the same instant but rising in opposite directions, are said to be in phase opposition, i.e. phase difference is 180°. When the two alternating quantities has a phase difference of 90° or $\frac{\pi}{2}$ radians they are said to be in quadrature.

NETWORK ANALYSIS

Network analysis consists in finding the response (or output) when stimulus (or input) and the network components are given

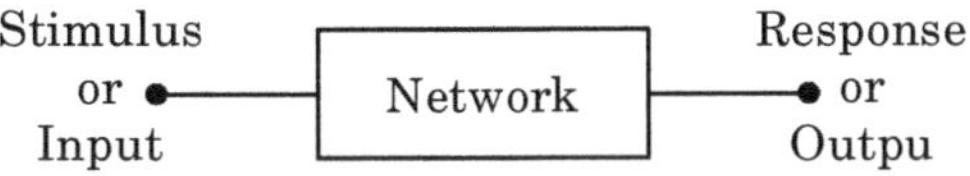

Fig. Factors involved in network analysis

DIRECT METHOD.

Here the network is left in its original form and the currents and voltages in different elements of the network are determined using a standard method of analysis such as loop analysis or node analysis. In addition use is made of Kirchhoff's laws and different network theorems such as superposition theorem, compensation theorem, reciprocity theorem etc. Such a direct approach is generally used in case of relatively simple networks.

Kirchhoff's laws.

There are two laws given by Kirchhoff namely Kirchhoff's current law and Kirchhoff's voltage law.

(i) **Kirchhoff's Current Law (KCL) :** It states that in any electrical circuit,the algebraic sum of current meeting at a point (or node) is zero.

If we take the current component convergent (entering) at the node as positive and current component divergent (leaving) at the node as negative, then KCL implies that : *at any zunction (node) in electrical circuit, the sum of current components entering the junction equals the sum of the current components leaving the junction.*

This statement is true for any point because there can not be continued accumulation of charges or continued depletion of charges. Symbolically we may write,

$$\Sigma \pm j = 0$$

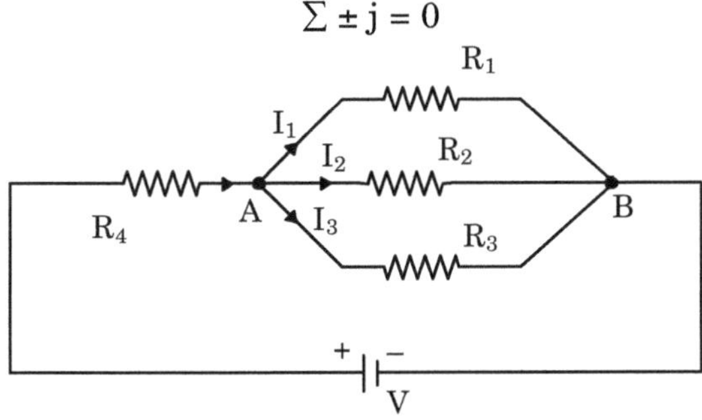

Above figure shows a simple electrical network with one energy source V. At node A, current I enters the node while currents I_1, I_2 and I_3 leave the node A.

Obviously then as per KCL,

$$I + (-I_1) + (-I_2) + (-I_3) = 0$$

or $\quad I = I_1 + I_2 + I_3$

In the circuit of figure, directions of current components. In a complicated network, we do not know the actual directions of all current components at any specific node. In that case, we arbitrarily assign directions to the current components and analyze the network to find the values of these current components. If the value of any current component comes out to be positive, then its actural direction is the same as the assigned direction. On the other hand, if any current component is found to be negative, then its actual direction. On the other hand, if any current component is found to be negative, then its actual direction is opposite to assigned direction.

(ii) **Kirchhoff's Voltage Law (KVL) :**

It states that : *the algebraic sum of potential rises (or potential drops) in any set of branches forming a closed circuit or loop is always zero.*

Symbolically we may write,

$$\Sigma \pm v = 0$$

The validity of kVL is quite obvious. Thus starting from any node, as we travel along a closed path and come back to the same node, the net voltage drop or the net voltage rise must be sero

Use of sign + or – : In the above equation, plus sign may be used for voltage rise and minus sign may be used for voltage drop (alternatively opposite notation may be used). Thus while we move along the closed path along the current in any branch, there results a voltage drop across the resisitor R and a – sign may be used as shown in Fig. (*a*). Thus voltage rise from A to B is (–jR). On the other hand, if we travel opposite to the current in any branch, there results a voltage rise and + sign may be used as shown below in Fig. (*b*). Thus voltage rise from A to B is + *j*R.

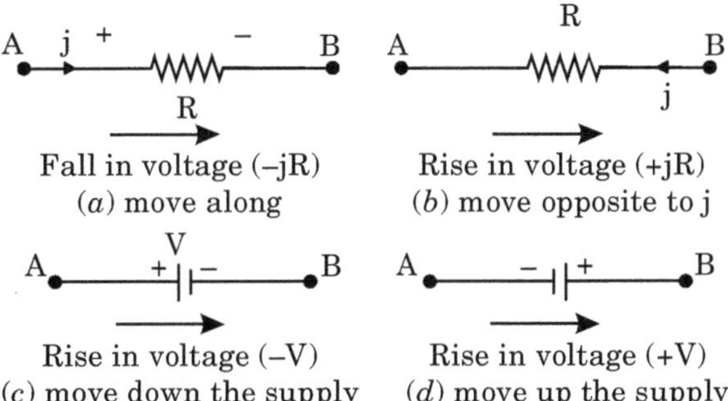

As an illustration, consider the loop ABCD in the network of figure and travel along ABCDA in this loop.

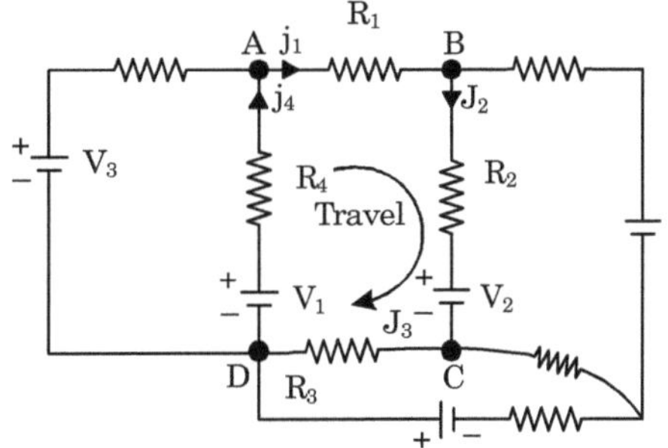

Then

$j_1 R_1$ is a voltage fall and hence negative

$j_2 R_2$ is a voltage fall and hence negative

$j_3 R_3$ is a voltage rise and hence positive

$j_4 R_4$ is a voltage fall and hence negaitve

V_2 is a voltage fall and hence negative

V_1 is a voltage rise and hence positive

Then application of kVL gives

$$- j\,R_1 - j_2\,R_2 + j_3\,R_3 - j_4\,R_4 - V_2 + V_1 = 0$$

or $\quad V_1 - V_2 = j_1\,R_1 + j_2\,R_2 - j_3\,R_3 + j_4\,R_4$

Note : Kirchhoff's laws are applicable to both dc and ac circuits.

ELECTRO-MAGNETIC INDUCTION

The phenomenon whereby an emf and hence current is induced in any conductor which is cut across or is cut by a magnetic flux is called *electro-magnetic induction*.

Faraday's laws of Electro-magnetic induction.

Faraday's first law :

This law states that, when the flux linking with the coil or circuit changes an emf is induced in it or whenever the magnetic flux is cut by the conductor an emf is induced in the conductor.

Faraday's second law :

This law states that, magnitude of emf induced is directly proportional to the rate of change of flux linking the coil.

i.e $\qquad$ induced emf $\propto N \cdot \dfrac{d\phi}{dt}$

where $N \dfrac{d\phi}{dt}$ is product of number of turns and rate of change of linking flux and is called rate of change of flux linkage.

Lenz's law.

The law states that, direction of induced emf is such that the current produced by it sets up a magnetic field opposing the motion or change producing it.

$\therefore \qquad$ Induced emf, $e = - N \dfrac{d\phi}{dt}$

INDUCED EMF.

EMF can be induced by changing the linking flux in two ways:

1. Dynamically induced EMF.

This is induced by moving a conductor in a uniform magnetic field and emf produced in this way is known as dynamically induced emf.

When a conductor of length l metres is moved in a magnetic field of strength B wb/m² with a velocity v m/s in a direction perpendicular to its own length and at an angle θ to the direciton of magnetic field, the induced emf will be given as

$$e = B\,l\,v \sin\theta \text{ volts}$$

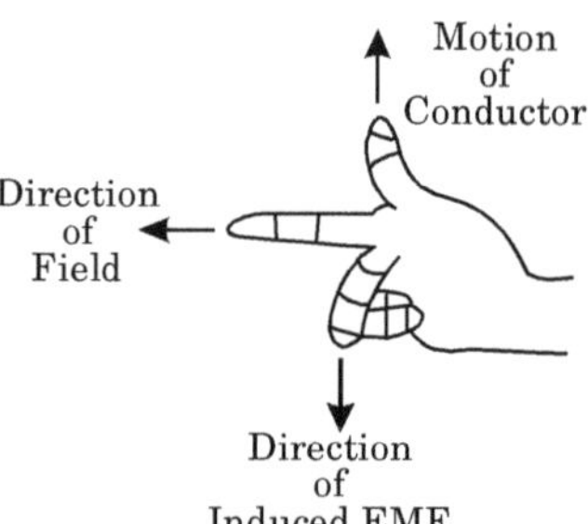

The direction of this induced emf is given by Fleming's right hand rule. If thumb, fore-finger and middle finger of right hand are held mutually perpendicular to each other, fore-finger pointing into the direction of the field and thumb in the direction of motion then middle finger will point in the direction of the inuced emf.

2. Statically induced emf.

Increasing or decreasing the magnitude of the current producing the linking flux. In this case there is no motion of the conductor or of coil relative to the field.

TYPE OF STATICALLY INDUCED EMF .

(i) Self induced EMF.

When the current flowing through the coil is changed, then flux linking with its own winding changes and due to the change in linking flux with the coil, an emf called self induced emf is induced.

Since according to Lenz's law, any induced emf acts to oppose the change that produces it, a self induced emf is always in such a direction as to oppose the change of current in the coil or circuit in which it is induced. This property of the coil or circuit due to which it opposes any change of the current in the coil or circuit, is called *self-inductance*.

Self induced emf in a solenoid of N turns, length l metres, area of cross-section a square metres and of relative permeability μ_r when the current flowing through the solenoid is changed is given as

$$\text{Self induced emf, } e = - \frac{N^2 \mu_r \mu_o a}{l} \cdot \frac{di}{dt}$$

The quantity $\dfrac{N^2 \mu_r \mu_o a}{l}$ is a constant for any given coil or circuit and is called *coefficient of self-inductance*. It is represented by symbol L and is measured in *henrys*.

$$\therefore \quad \text{self induced emf, } e = -L\frac{di}{dt}$$

$$\text{where, } L = \frac{N^2 \mu_r \mu_o a}{l} \text{ henrys}$$

(ii) Mutually induced EMF :

The phenomenon of generation of induced emf in a coil by changing the current in the neighbouring coil is called the *mutual induction* and emf so induced is called mutually induced emf.

The mutually induced emf in a solenoid B of N_2 turns, placed nearby another coil A of N_1 turns, length l metres, area of cross-section a square metres and of relative permeability μ_r when the current flowing through coil A is changed is given as

$$\text{Mutually induced emf, } e_m = \frac{N_1 N_2 \mu_r \mu_o a}{l} \cdot \frac{di}{dt}$$

assuming that whole of the flux produced due to flow of current in coil A is linking with coil B.

The quantity $\dfrac{N_1 N_2 \mu_r \mu_o a}{l}$ is called *coefficient of mutual induction of coil B with respect to coil A*. It is represented by symbol M and is measured in henrys.

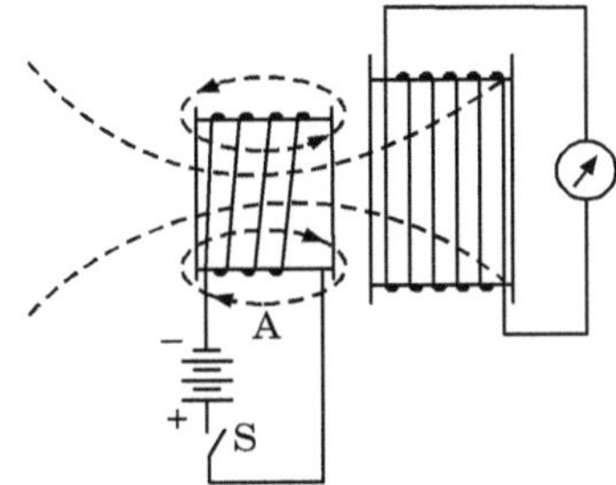

$$\therefore \quad \text{Mutually induced emf } e_m = -M\frac{di_1}{dt}$$

$$\text{where, } M = \frac{N_1 N_2 \mu_r \mu_o a}{l} \text{ henrys.}$$

COEFFICIENT OF COUPLING.

When two coils are placed near each other, all the flux produced by one coil does not link the other coil, only a certain portion (say K) of flux produced by one coil links with the other coil, K being less than unity. K is called *coefficient of coupling*.

The coefficient of coupling between two coils having self inductances L_1 and L_2 respectively and mutual inductance M is given as

$$K = \frac{M}{\sqrt{L_1 L_2}}$$

When coils are tightly coupled, *i.e.* when flux due to one coil links with the other coil completely, then coefficient of coupling, K is unity. If flux due to one coil does not link with the other coil at all, then value of coefficient of coupling is zero.

INDUCTANCES IN SERIES AND PARALLEL.

(i) Inductances in series.

When coils are connected in series such that their fluxes (or mmf) are additive i.e. in the same direction, then equivalent inductance of the combination is given as

$$L = L_1 + L_2 + 2M$$

where L_1 and L_2 = coefficients of self induction of coils A and B respectively

M = coefficient of mutual induction.

When coils are connected in series in such a way that their fluxes (or mmfs) are subtractive, *i.e.* in opposite directions, then equivalent inductance is given as

$$L = L_1 + L_2 - 2M$$

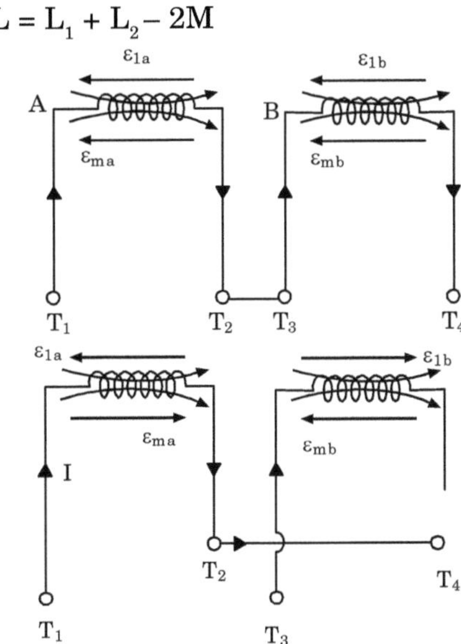

(ii) Inductances in parallel.

When two coils of self inductances L_1 and L_2 and mutual inductance M are connected in parallel, then equivalent inductance of the combination is given as

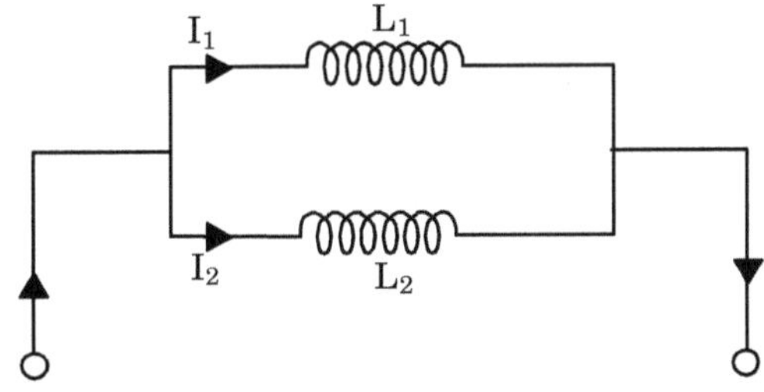

When mutual flux helps the individual flux, then

$$L = \frac{L_1 L_2 - M^2}{L_1 + L_2 - 2M}$$

When mutual flux opposes the individual flux, then

$$L = \frac{L_1 L_2 - M^2}{L_1 + L_2 + 2M}$$

OBJECTIVE TYPE QUESTION

1. The terminals across the source are .... if a current source is to be neglected.
   (a) open-circuited
   (b) short-circuited
   (c) replaced by a capacitor
   (d) replaced by a source resistance

2. An active element in a circuit is
   (a) Current source   (b) Resistance
   (c) Inductance   (d) Capacitance

3. A bilateral element is
   (a) Resistor   (b) Inductor
   (c) Capacitor   (d) all of these

4. The circuit having same properties in either direction is called
   (a) bilateral circuit   (b) unilateral circuit
   (c) irreversible circuit (d) reversible circuit

5. Kirchhoff's laws are valid for
   (a) linear circuits only
   (b) passive time invariant circuits
   (c) non-linear circuits only
   (d) both linear and non-linear circuits

6. Kirchhoff's laws are not applicable to circuits with
   (a) distributed parameters
   (b) lumped parameters
   (c) passive elements
   (d) non-linear resistances

7. Kirchhoff's current law is applicable only to
   (a) electric circuits
   (b) electronic circuits
   (c) junctions in a network
   (d) closed loops in a network

8. Kirchhoff's voltage law is concerned with
   (a) IR drops   (b) battery emfs
   (c) both (a) and (b) (d) none of these

9. According to Kirchhoff's voltage law, the algebraic sum of all IR drops and emfs in any closed loop of a network is always
   (a) negative
   (b) positive
   (c) zero
   (d) determined by emfs of the batteries

10. The algebraic sign of an IR drop primarily depends upon the
    (a) direction of flow of current
    (b) battery connections
    (c) magnitude of current flowing through it
    (d) value of resistance

11. Maxwell circulating current theorem
    (a) utilises Kirchhoff's voltage law
    (b) utilises Kirchhoff's current law
    (c) is a network reduction method
    (d) is confined to single loop circuits

12. The insulation on a current carrying conductor is provided to prevent
    (a) current leakage   (b) shock
    (c) both (a) and (b)   (d) none of these

13. EMF of a zinc-carbon cell is about
    (a) 1.2 V   (b) 1.5 V
    (c) 1.75 V   (d) 2.2 V

14. The emf of primary cell depends upon the
    (a) physical dimensions of a cell
    (b) nature of electrolyte
    (c) both (b) and (c)
    (d) none of these

15. The internal voltage drop of a voltage source
    (a) is independent of load current supplied
    (b) depends upon internal resistance of the source
    (c) does not influence the terminal votlage
    (d) does effect the emf of the source

16. A voltage source of emf E volts and internal resistance r ohms will supply, on short circuit, a current of
    (a) $\dfrac{E}{r}$ amperes   (b) zero
    (c) infinite   (d) E × r amperes

17. When two batteries of unequal voltages are connected in parallel, the emf of the combination will be equal to the
    (a) emf of the large battery
    (b) emf of the small battery
    (c) average of the emfs of two batteries
    (d) none of these

18. At the centre of a current carrying single turn circular loop, magnetic field is

   (a) $B = \dfrac{\mu l}{2R}$ (b) $\dfrac{\mu l}{.2\,\pi R}$

   (c) $B = \dfrac{\mu l}{4\pi R^2}$ (d) none of these

19. The magnitude of force acting on a current carrying conductor placed in a magnetic field is independent of

   (a) flux density.

   (b) length of conductor.

   (c) cross-sectional area of conductor.

   (d) current flowing through the conductor.

20. The direction of mechanical force experienced on a current carrying conductor placed in a magnetic field is determined by

   (a) Fleming's left hand rule.

   (b) Fleming's right hand rule.

   (c) Helix rule.

   (d) Cork screw rule.

21. In Fleming's left hand rule thumb always represents direction of

   (a) current flow   (b) induced emf

   (c) magnetic field   (d) mechanical force

22. If a current carrying conductor is placed in a magnetic field, the mechanical force experienced on the conductor is determined by

   (a) simple product   (b) dot product

   (c) cross product   (d) any of these

23. The force experienced by a current carrying conductor lying parallel to a magnetic field is

   (a) zero   (b) $B\,I\,l$

   (c) $B\,I\,l\sin\theta$ (d) $B\,I\,l\cos\theta$

24. An electric field is parallel but opposite to a magnetic field. Electrons with some initial velocity enter the region of the fields at an angle θ along the direction of the electric field. The electron path will be

   (a) straight   (b) helical

   (c) circular   (d) elliptical

25. The field at any point on the axis of a current carrying coil will be

   (a) perpendicular to the axis.

   (b) parallel to the axis.

   (c) at an angle of 45° with the axis.

   (d) zero.

26. The magnetic flux inside the exciting coil

   (a) is the same as on its outer surface.

   (b) is zero.

   (c) is greater than that on its outside surface.

   (d) is lower than that on the outside surface.

27. If the two conductors carry current in opposite directions there will be

   (a) a force of attraction between the two conductors.

   (b) a force of repulsion between the two conductors.

   (c) no force between them.

   (d) none of these

28. If a straight conductor of circular cross-section carries a current, then

   (a) no force acts on the conductor at any point.

   (b) an axial force acts on the conductor tending to increase its length.

   (c) a radial force acts towards the axis tending to reduce its cross-section.

   (d) a radial force acts away from the axis tending to increase its cross-section.

29. mmf of magnetic circuit is analogous to

   (a) current   (b) emf

   (c) resistance   (d) power

30. Unit of reluctance of magnetic circuit is

   (a) AT/m   (b) webers/m

   (c) AT/weber   (d) H/m.

31. Property of a material which opposes the production of magnetic flux in it is called

   (a) mmf   (b) reluctance

   (c) permeance   (d) permittivity

32. Unit of mmf is

   (a) AT   (b) weber/ampere

   (c) Henry   (d) AT/m

33. Conductance is analogous to

   (a) reluctance   (b) mmf

   (c) permeance   (d) inductance

34. An air gap is usually inserted in magnetic circuits to

   (a) prevent saturation

   (b) increase in mmf.

   (c) increase in flux.

   (d) increase in inductance.

35. Permeability is reciprocal of
(*a*) reluctivity
(*b*) susceptibility
(*c*) permittivity
(*d*) conductivity

36. The magnetic reluctance of a magnetic circuit decreases with
(*a*) decrease in cross-sectional area.
(*b*) increase in cross-sectional area.
(*c*) increase in length of magnetic path.
(*d*) decrease in relative permeability of the magnetic material of the circuit.

37. A ring shaped coil with fixed number of turns of it carries a current of certain magnitude. If an iron core is threaded into the coil without any change in coil dimensions, the magnetic induction density will
(*a*) increase
(*b*) reduce
(*c*) remain unaffected
(*d*) unpredictable

38. The ratio of total flux (flux in the iron path) to useful flux (flux in the air gap) is called
(*a*) utilisation factor
(*b*) fringing factor
(*c*) leakage factor
(*d*) depreciation factor

39. According to Faraday's law of electro-magnetic induction an emf is induced in a conductor whenever it
(*a*) lies in a magnetic field.
(*b*) lies perpendicular to the magnetic field.
(*c*) cuts the magnetic flux.
(*d*) moves parallel to the direction of magnetic field.

40. "In all cases of electromagnetic induction, an induced voltage will cause a current to flow in a closed circuit in such a direction that the magnetic field which is caused by that current will oppose the change that produces the current", is the original statement of
(*a*) Lenz's law.
(*b*) Faraday's law of magnetic induction.
(*c*) Fleming's law of induction.
(*d*) Ampere's law.

41. The emf induced in a coil due to relative motion of a magnet is independent of
(*a*) coil resistance
(*b*) magnet not visible
(*c*) number of coil turns.
(*d*) pole strength of the magnet.

42. When a single turn coil rotates in a uniform magnetic field, at uniform speed the induced emf will be
(*a*) alternating   (*b*) steady
(*c*) pulsating   (*d*) none of these

43. Principle of dynamically induced emf is used in a
(*a*) choke   (*b*) transformer
(*c*) generator   (*d*) thermo-couple

44. The direction of dynamically induced emf in a conductor can be determined by
(*a*) Fleming's left hand rule.
(*b*) Fleming's right hand rule.
(*c*) Helix rule.
(*d*) Cork screw rule.

45. Principle of statically induced emf is used in
(*a*) transformer   (*b*) motor
(*c*) generator   (*d*) battery

46. Magnitude of statically induced emf depends on the
(*a*) coil resistance
(*b*) flux magnitude
(*c*) rate of change of flux
(*d*) none of these

47. The property of a coil by which a counter emf is induced in it, when the current through the coil changes, is called
(*a*) self inductance
(*b*) mutual inductance
(*c*) capacitance
(*d*) none of these

48. If in an iron cored coil the iron core is removed so as to make the air-cored coil, the inductance of the coil will be
(*a*) more   (*b*) less
(*c*) the same   (*d*) none of these

49. Lower the self inductance of a coil
(*a*) more will be the weber-turns.
(*b*) more will be the emf induced.
(*c*) lesser the flux produced by it.
(*d*) smaller the delay in establishing steady current through it.

50. When an electric current is passed through a bucket full of water, lot of bubbling is there. The electric current is

(*a*) ac.

(*b*) dc

(*c*) pulsating

(*d*) none of these.

51. The most important advantages of using electrical energy in the form of ac is

(*a*) the construction cost per kw of ac generator is lower than that of dc generator

(*b*) conductor of smaller x-section is required in case of ac in comparison to dc for carrying the same current.

(*c*) less insulation is required in case of ac.

(*d*) transformation of voltage is possible in case of ac only.

52. The frequency of an alternating quantity is the number of

(*a*) direction reversals in per second.

(*b*) cycles completed per second.

(*c*) cycles completed per minute.

(*d*) all of these

53. The time period of periodic time T of an alternating quantity is the time taken in seconds to complete

(*a*) one cycle

(*b*) one alternation

(*c*) any of these

(*d*) none of these

54. Average value of an unsymmetrical alterating quantity is calculated over the

(*a*) whole cycle

(*b*) half cycle

(*c*) unsymmetrical part of the waveform

(*d*) none of these

ANSWERS

1. (*a*)	**2.** (*a*)	**3.** (*d*)	**4.** (*a*)	**5.** (*d*)	**6.** (*a*)	**7.** (*c*)	**8.** (*c*)	**9.** (*c*)	**10.** (*a*)
11. (*a*)	**12.** (*b*)	**13.** (*b*)	**14.** (*d*)	**15.** (*b*)	**16.** (*a*)	**17.** (*a*)	**18.** (*a*)	**19.** (*c*)	**20.** (*a*)
21. (*d*)	**22.** (*c*)	**23.** (*a*)	**24.** (*b*)	**25.** (*b*)	**26.** (*a*)	**27.** (*b*)	**28.** (*c*)	**29.** (*b*)	**30.** (*c*)
31. (*b*)	**32.** (*a*)	**33.** (*c*)	**34.** (*a*)	**35.** (*a*)	**36.** (*b*)	**37.** (*a*)	**38.** (*c*)	**39.** (*c*)	**40.** (*a*)
41. (*a*)	**42.** (*a*)	**43.** (*c*)	**44.** (*b*)	**45.** (*a*)	**46.** (*c*)	**47.** (*a*)	**48.** (*b*)	**49.** (*d*)	**50.** (*b*)
51. (*d*)	**52.** (*c*)	**53.** (*a*)	**54.** (*a*)						

■■

TYPE OF DC MOTORS

Similar to dc generators, the dc motors may also be put into the following three categories on the basis of field excitation:

1. *Shunt motor* – field winding in shunt with the armature
2. *Series motor* – field winding in series with the armature
3. *Compound motor* – one fielding winding in series with armature and another in shunt

1. Shunt Motor.

Field winding is placed in shunt with the armature. This winding draws a separate current I_{sh} from the mains. The field winding consists of a large number of fine wires on each pole. Usually windings on all the poles are connected in series.

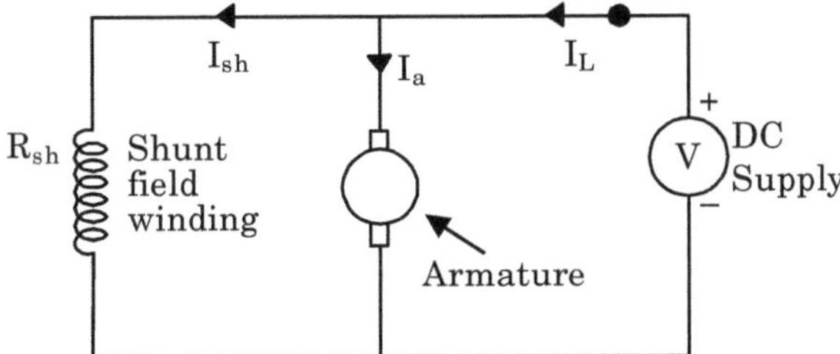

2. Series Motor.

The field winding is placed in series with the armature. Thus the armature current I_a itself flows through the field windings. Series field winding consists of a few turns of thick copper wire on each pole and all these windings on different poles are connected in series.

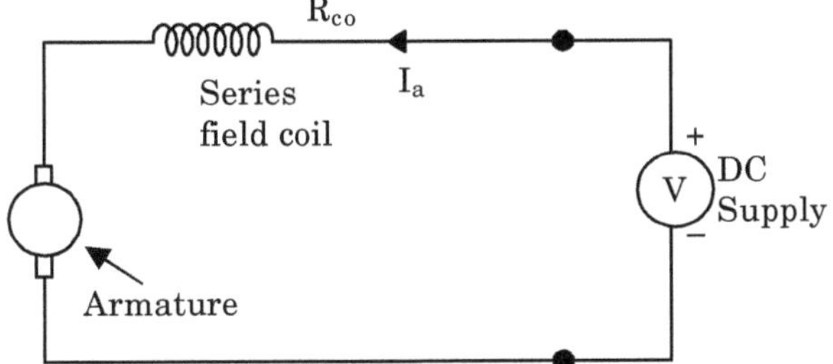

3. Compound Motor.

Compound motor uses two field windings. The series winding is placed in series with the supply and the armature shown in figure. It consists of a few turns of thick copper wire on each pole, all connected in series. The shunt winding is placed in parallel with the armature as shown in figure. The shunt field

winding consists of a large number of fine wire on each pole, all connected in series.

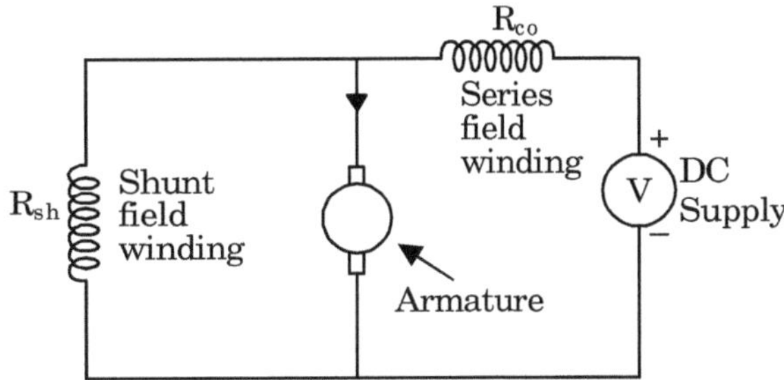

PRINCIPLE OF WORKING OF A DC MOTOR

A dc motor is a machine which converts dc power into mechanical power. Its operation is based on the principle that when a current carrying conductor is placed in a magnetic field, the conductor experiences a mechanical force. The direction of this force is given by Fleming's left hand rule and the magnetic force F is given by

$$F = BI\,l \text{ newtons.}$$

Construction of a dc motor is basically similar to a dc generator. Hence the same dc machine may be used either as a dc generator or a dc motor. Finally like dc generator, dc motors are also series wound, shunt wound and compound wound.

Production of Torque in a dc Motor. Figure shows a part of a multiple dc motor. When the field magnets are excited and current is sent through the armature conductors, then the conductors experience a force tending to rotate the armature. Let the armature conductors under north pole carry current in the direction normal to the surface of paper in figure and pointing into the paper as shown by the crosses. Similarly let conductors under south pole carry current in the direction normal to the surface of paper and pointing out as shown by the dots. Application of Fleming's left hand rule gives the direction of the force exerted on each conductor.

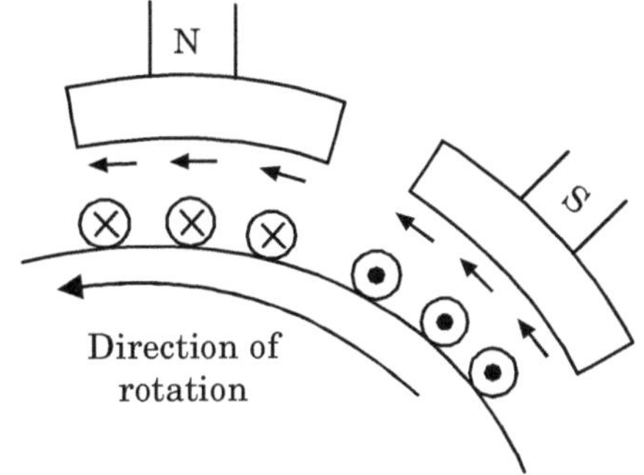

This direction is anticlockwise as shown by the small arrows placed above each conductor. This force exerted on armature conductor tends to rotate the armature in the anticlockwise direction as shown in figure. These forces on conductor add up to produce the driving torque, which causes rotation of the armature.

Function of Commutator. Function of commutator in a dc motor is the same as in dc generator. Thus it reverses the current in each conductor as it passes from one pole to another. This results in a continuous and unidirectional torque.

BACK EMF

In a dc motor, as the armature rotates, its conductors also rotate and cut the flux of the poles. Hence as per laws of electromagnetic induction, emf is induced in the conductors. As per Fleming's right hand rule, the direction of this emf is opposite to the applied voltage. Hence this emf is called the counter emf or *back emf* V_b. Obviously then the applied voltage V has to drive armature current I_a in the presence of opposing back emf V_b. The power required to overcome this opposition is $V_b \cdot I_a$.

Magnitude of back emf may be calculated using the same emf equation as used for dc generator.

$$\text{Back emf} \qquad V_b = \frac{\phi NZ}{60} \cdot \frac{P}{A} \text{ volt}$$

where ϕ N, Z, P and A have the same meanings as in dc generator.

Presence of back emf makes a dc motor self-regulating i.e. it makes motor to draw the armature current just sufficient to develop the torque needed by the load. Back emf among other factors, depends on the armature speed. If speed is high, V_b is large and armature current I_a being equal to $(V - V_b)/R_a$ is small. On the other hand, if speed is low, back emf V_b is small and armature current is large resulting is larger torque. Thus we find that like a governor, the back emf makes a motor self regulating, permitting it to draw the current just necessary for torque needed.

DC GENERATOR

Function. A dc generator is an electromagnetic machine, which converts mechanical energy into dc electrical energy.

Principle. Whenever magnetic flux is cut by a conductor, an emf is induced in the conductor as per Faraday's law of electromagnetic induction. This voltage so induced is basically an a.c. voltage. It is made unidirectional with the help of commutator and brushes. This emf causes flow of current in the external circuit if the circuit is closed.

Essential Parts of a DC Generator

(*i*) Magnetic field created by electromagnet

(*ii*) Conductors housed in armature slots

(*iii*) Motion of conductors cutting the magnetic field

(*iv*) Commutator and brushes to collect the voltage and convert it into unidirectional voltage.

Difference in the Structures of DC and AC Generators. In a dc generator, magnetic field is stationary and the conductors move through the field. In an a.c. generator, conductors are stationary and the magnetic fields move.

SPLIT RING LOOP GENERATOR

Fig. (a) gives the basic structure. A single turn rectangular coil ABCD rotates about its own axis within the magnetic field created by either permanent magnet or an electromagnet. The two terminals of the coil are connected to split rings made out of a conducting cylinder cut into two halves or segments insulated from each other by a thin sheet of an insulating material typically mica. Coil terminals are joined to these segments on which rest the carbon or copper brushes as shown in Fig. (a) These brushes collect the voltage induced in the coil and to apply it to the external load resistor R_L. The magnets are called the field magnets since they create the magnetic field and similarly call the rotating coil as the armature.

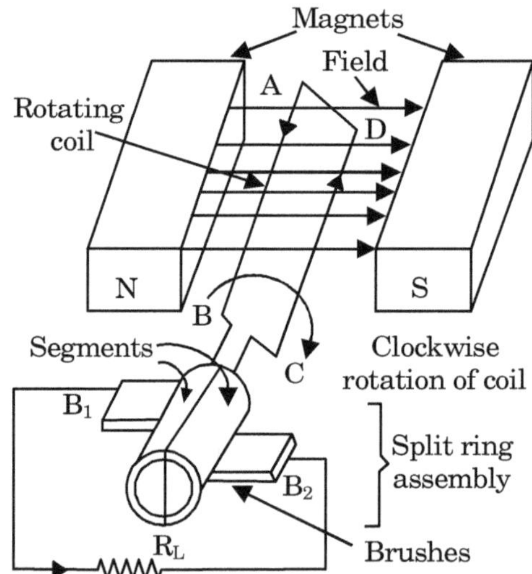

(*a*) Split ring loop generator

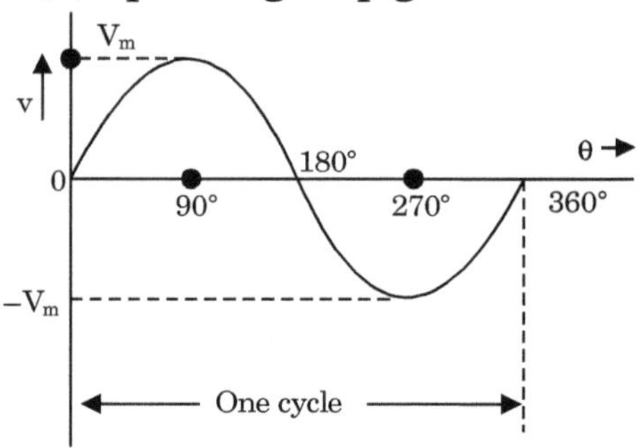

(*b*) Variation of induced emf v with angle θ coil

Smoothening of Output Voltage and Current. Output voltage waveform is not smooth and involves large variations. This defect may be overcome to a large extent by dividing the commutator ring into 4 parts connected to the coil terminals. For output voltage to be quite smooth, a brush is connected to a segment for only one-fourth revolution i.e. for 90 degrees.

Classification of Transformers base on Construction

Transformers may be classified into the following three types depending on the type of laminated core:

1. *Core type transformer* with single magnetic circuit
2. *Shell type transformer* with double magnetic circuit
3. *Berry type transformer* with distributed magnetic circuit

1. **Core Type Transformer.** Fig(a) shows the general shape of core type transformer. The core is built up of iron or alloyed steel sheets or laminations assembled to provide a continuous magnetic path with minimum air gap. Laminated structure is used to reduce the eddy current losses. Average thickness of sheet is 0.35 mm for a frequency of 50 Hz. Laminations are insulated from each other by a thin coat of varnish or oxide layer. Fig (b) shows a typical method of arranging the core strips. Here the joints in alternate layers are staggered in order to avoid the presence of narrow gap right through the cross-section of the core. Such a joint is called an *imbricated joint.*

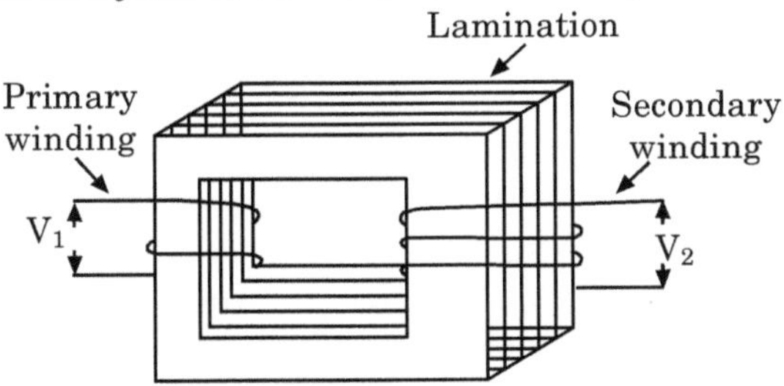

(a) Core type transformer

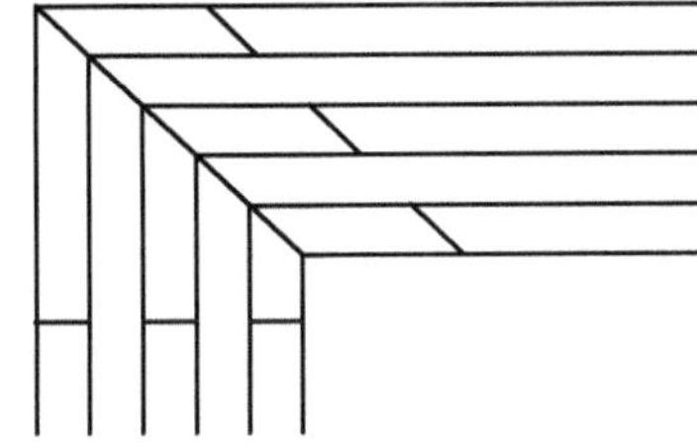

(b) Imbricated joints

In small size transformers, core has rectangular cross-section. However, in large transformers, it is preferred to use an approximately circular cross-section since such a section has the smallest perimeter for a given area and hence it requires less copper in the form of wire, than the rectangular section. In very large transformers, strips may be used in packets with duct in between. These ducts help in ventilation.

In the simplified diagram of Fig (a) the primary and the secondary windings are placed on the opposite limbs of the core. However, in practice, the two windings are interleaved to reduce leakage flux. Thus half of the primary winding and half of the secondary winding are placed on each limb either side by side or concentrically with high voltage winding surrounding the low voltage winding with insulation in between the layers and heavy insulation between the windings.

2. **Shell Type Transformers.** Figure shows the section of the laminated core. This section has double magnetic circuit. Shell type transformerdiffers from the core type in that it has two magnetic circuits instead of one. Both the primary and secondary windings are placed on the central limb. Further in core type transformer, the two winding ususally multilayered, almost fully surround the core while in shell type transformer, the two outer section of the core almost fully surround the windings.

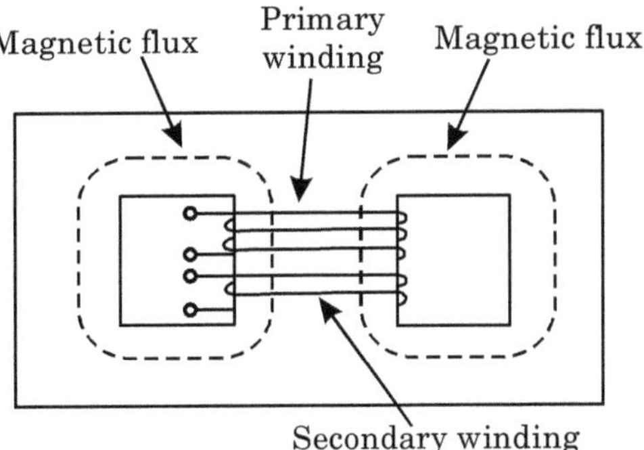

3. **Berry type transformer.** It is basically shell type transformer but in this case, the core consists of laminations arranged in groups, which radiate out from the centre.

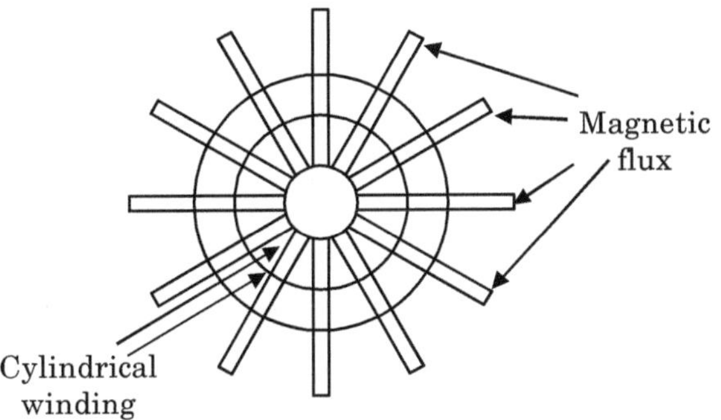

Berry type transformer

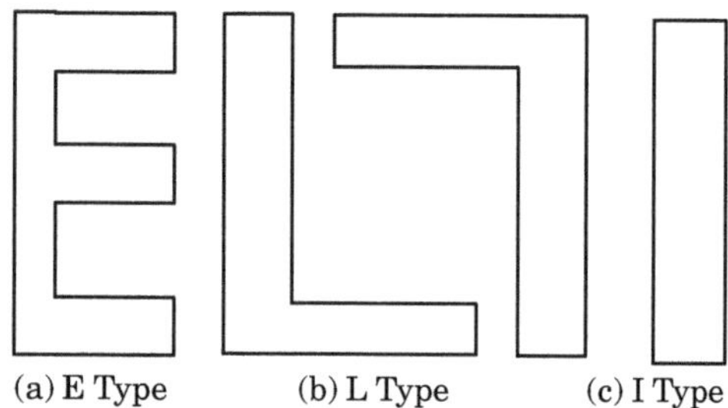

(a) E Type   (b) L Type   (c) I Type

Shapes of Laminations. Individual laminations in all types of transformers are usually cut in the form of long strips of E, L and I shapes

Placement of Windings . The primary and the secondary windings may be either of

(i) *cylindrical or concentric type* or

(ii) *sandwich type*

Fig. (a) shows coaxial windings while Fig. (b) shows sandwich type windings where primary and secondary windings are placed side by side. The concentric type windings are used mainly on core type transformers while *sandwich type* windings are used mainly on shell type transformers.

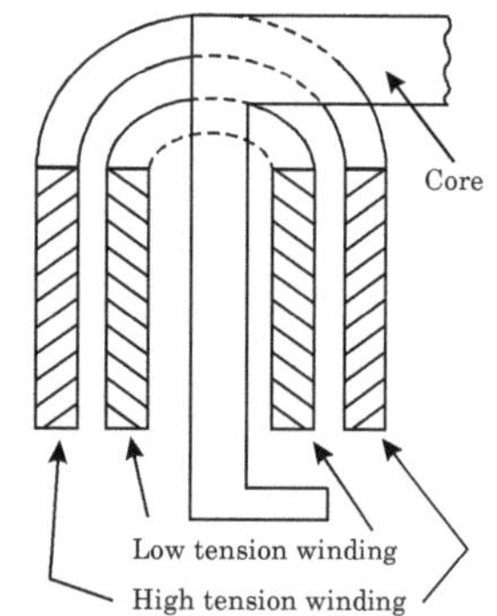

(a) Concentric or cylindrical type windings

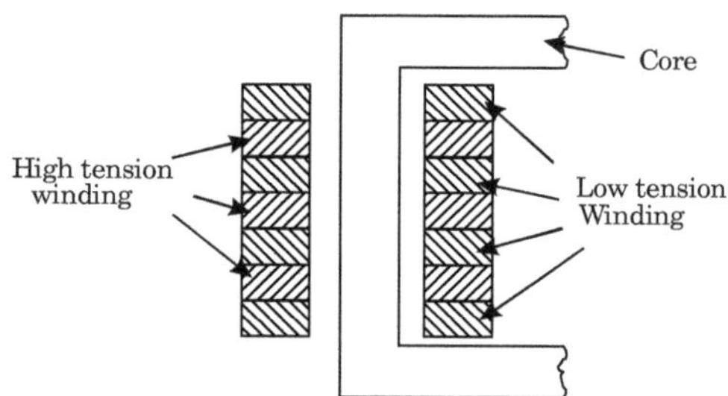

(b) Sanswich type windings

CONSTRUCTION OF A PRACTICAL DC GENERATOR

Basic structure of a commercial dc generator consists of following basic parts:

1. **Field System**
   (i) Metallic frame or yoke
   (ii) Pole cores and pole shoes
   (iii) Field coils or pole coils
2. Armature core
3. Armature winding
4. Commutator
5. Brushes and bearings

Out of these, the yoke, pole core and pole shoes, and armature core constitute the magnetic circuit while the pole coils, armature winding, commutator and brushes form the electrical circuit.

IMPORTANT TERMS CONCERNING ARMATURE WINDING

Pole Pitch. It is generally defined as the number of armature slots per pole. Thus if there are 4 poles and 48 conductor slots, then pole pitch is 48/4 = 12.

Conductor. By conductor is meant the metallic wire housed in the conductor slot in the armature and in which the emf is induced.

Coil Pitch (Coil Span)Y_s. It is the distance between the two sides of a coil measured in terms of armatures slots.

If the coil pitch is equal to the pole pitch, the winding is said to be *full-pitched*. In such a case, coil span is 180° electrical degrees and the coil sides lie under opposite poles. Then the induced emfs in the coil sides are in phase and additive and maximum emf is induced in the coil, being equal to twice that in each coil side. Thus if there are 4 poles and 40 slots, the coil span is 40/4 = 10 slots.

If the coil pitch is less than the pole pitch, the winding is said to be *fractional pitched*. In such a coil, the emfs induced in the two coil sides are not in phase and do not fully add up. Output emf of the coil, being the vector sum of emf's of the two coil sides, is less than that obtained in full-pitched coil. In commercial dc generators, coil pitch as low as 0.8 of pole pitch is used to cause saving in copper of the end connections and for improving commutation.

Pitch of a Winding (Y). This the distance (in terms armature slots) around the armature between two successive conductors which are directly connected together or the distance between the beginning of two consecutive turns.

Back Pitch (Y_B) . It is the distance (in terms of armature slots), which a coil advances on the back of the armature. Thus if element 1 is connected on the back of armature to element 7, then $Y_B = 7 - 1 = 6$.

Front Pitch (Y_F). It is the number of armature conductors spanned by a coil on the front or the commutator end of an armature. Thus if element 7 is connected to element 3 on the front end of the armature, then the front pitch $Y_F = 7 - 3 = 4$.

Resultant Pitch (Y_R). It is the distance between the beginning of one coil and the beginning of the next coil to which it is connected.

Commutator Pitch (Y_C) . It is distance (in terms of commutator bars or segments) between the segments to which the two ends of a coil are connected.

Single Layer Winding. It is the armature winding in which only one conductor or one coil side is placed in each armature slot. These are not used popularly.

Multilayer Winding. It is the armature winding in which two or more conductors or coil sides are placed in each armature slot, usually in two layers.

LAP AND WAVE WINDINGS

The lap and wave windings differ regarding the arrangement of the end connection at the front or commutator end of armature.

Features of Common to Lap or Wave Windings

(*i*) Front pitch and back pitch are each approximately equal to the pole pitch i.e. windings should be full pitched.

(*ii*) Both front and back pitches should be odd, otherwise it is difficult to place former wound coils properly on the armature.

(*iii*) Number of commutator segment is equal to the number of slots because the front ends of conductors are jointed to the segments in pairs.

(*iv*) The winding must close upon itself.

Lap Winding. In lap winding, the finishing end of one coil is connected to a commutator segment and to the starting end of the adjacent coil situated under the same pole and so on till all the coils have been connected. Fig.(*a*) gives the arrangement for single turn coils. The name lap winding is used because the winding doubles up or laps back with its succeeding coils.

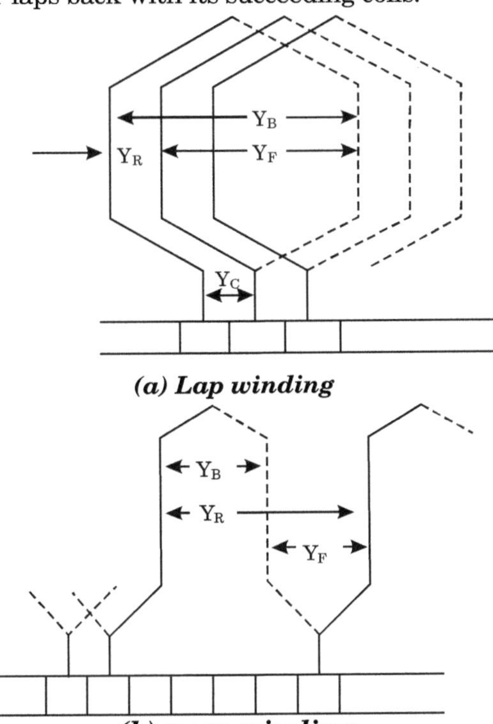

(a) Lap winding

(b) wave winding

Wave Winding. In wave winding, a conductor (or coil side) under one pole is connected at the back to a conductor, which occupies an almost corresponding position under the next pole. Fig (*b*) shows the arrangement for single turn coils.

Relative Performance of Lap and Wave Windings

Merits of Wave Winding.

(*i*) More emf than lap winding for a given number of poles and armature conductors. Thus for the same emf, wave winding requires smaller number of conductors resulting in lower winding cost and more efficient utilization of space in armature slots.

(*ii*) Equalizing connections are necessary.

Limitation of Wave Winding. It is suitable for low current high voltage (600 volts) generators.

Merit of Lap Winding. Since it uses more number of parallel paths, it is useful for large current, low voltage generators.

Armature Resistance R_a. It is the resistance between the armature terminals and includes the resistance of armature conductors and brushes. It is generally small and depends on

(*a*) Number and size of armture conductors

(*b*) Type of armature winding

(*c*) Contact resistance between carbon brushes and the commutator.

TYPES OF DC GENERATOR

DC generators are generally classified according to the method used for field excitation. Thus dc generators may be classified as:

1. **Separately Excited Generator.** In this generator, the fieldelectromagnet is energized from an external independent source such as a battery or a separate small dc generator called the exciter.

2. **Self Excited Generator.** In this generator, the current through the field electromagnetic is supplied from the generator output itself. Self excited generator may be put into three categories depending on where the field coil is placed in series, in parallel or both.

   (*i*) **Series Wound Self-excited Generator.** In this generator, the field windings are placed in series the armature conductors . As a result, the entire armature current I_a flows through the field coil and the load. Since the field windings carry the full load current, they consist of only a few turns of thick wire or strips having low resistance.

   (*ii*) **Shunt Wound Self Excited Generator.** In this generator, the field windings are placed in shunt, i.e. in parallel with the armature conductors with the result that the full generator voltage gets applied across the windings. The shunt field winding uses large number of turns of fine wire. The coil resistance is, therefore, high. As a result only a small part of armature current flows through the field windings.

(iii) Compound Wound Self Excited Generator. In this generator, there are two sets of field windings on each pole, one in series and the other in parallel with the armature.

Compound wound generators may be of two types :

(a) Short Shunt Compound Wound Generator. The shunt coil is placed directly across the armature while series coil is placed in series with the load.

(b) Long Shunt Compound Wound Generator. The shunt coil is placed in parallel with both armature and the series coil.

In a compound wound generator, the shunt field is stronger than the series field. When the series field aids the shunt field, the generator is said to be commutatively compounded. On the other hand, if series field oppose the shunt field, the generator is said to be differentially compounded.

EFFICIENCY OF GENERATOR

Out of the total input mechanical power, a part is lost as iron losses and friction losses. The balance power constitutes the electrical power $V_g I_a$ developed in the armature as shown in figure. Out of the total electric power developed in armature, a part is loss as copper losses while the balance of electric power is available at the output.

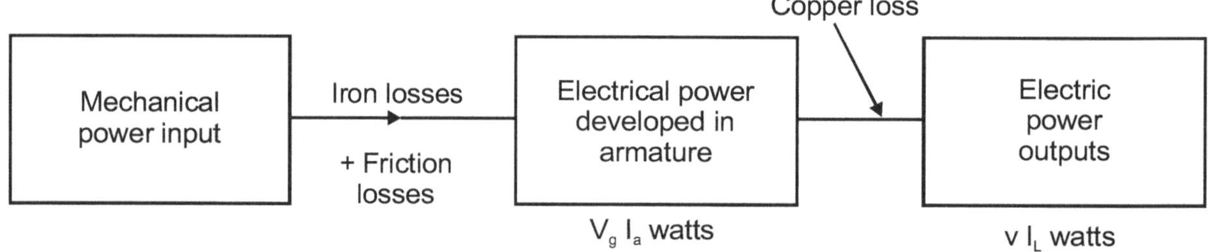

Power losses in a dc generator

Mechanical Efficiency : η_m = Electrical power generated in armature = $\dfrac{V_g I_a}{\text{output of driving engine}}$

Electrical Efficiency : $\eta_e = \dfrac{\text{Electrical power at the output}}{\text{Electrical power generated in armature}} = \dfrac{VI_L}{V_g I_a}$

Overall Efficiency or Commercial Efficiency :

$$\eta_c = \frac{\text{Electrical power at the output}}{\text{Mechanical power input to Machine}} = \frac{VI_L}{\text{output of driving engine}}$$

Evidently $\eta_c = \eta_m \times \eta_c$. In a good quality generator, overall efficiency may be as high as 95%.

DC GENERATOR CHARACTERISTICS

Following are the important characteristics of a dc generator :

(i) Open Circuit Characteristics V_g - I_f. This curve plots open circuit or no load generated emf V_g against field current I_f at a constant armature speed. This characteristic is basically the magnetization curve of the material of the electromagnets. The shape of this characteristic is practically the same for all generators whether self excited or separately excited.

(ii) Internal or Total Characteristic (V_g - I_a). This plots the emf V_g actually induced in the armature (after allowing for the magnetizing effect of armature reaction) against the armature current I_a. When the generator is supplying load to the external circuit, the total flux gets reduced due to the armature reaction. Hence actually generated emf V_g is less than the emf V_{go} generated under no load condition.

(iii) External Characteristic (V_L – I_L). It plots the terminal voltage V_L against load current I_L. This characteristic is also called the *performance characteristic* or the *voltage regulation characteristic*.

OBJECTIVE TYPE QUESTIONS

D.C. MACHINES

1. Carbon brushes are used in electric motors to
(a) prevent sparking during commu-tation
(b) provide a path for flow of current
(c) brush off carbon deposits on the commutator
(d) none of these

2. Interpoles in dc motors are used for
(a) increasing the speed of motor
(b) reducing sparking at the commu-tator
(c) decreasing the counter emf
(d) converting armature current to dc

3. The air gap between stator and armature of an electric motor is kept as small as possible
(a) to get a stronger magnetic field
(b) to improve the air circulation
(c) to reach a higher speed of rotation
(d) to make the rotation easier

4. Small dc motors upto 5 HP usually have
(a) 2 poles
(b) 4 poles
(c) 6 poles
(d) 8 poles

5. A dc motor can be easily identified by
(a) yoke
(b) size of conductor
(c) commutator
(d) winding

6. In dc motor, the rotor is
(a) welded to the shaft
(b) keyed to the shaft
(c) soldered to the shaft
(d) bolted to the shaft

7. In a dc motor, pole shoes are fixed to the magnet core by
(a) set of screws
(b) key
(c) soldering
(d) welding

8. The armature of a dc motor is laminated
(a) to reduce hysteresis loss
(b) to reduce eddy current loss
(c) to reduce the cost of core
(d) to reduce the mass of the armature

9. The value of diverter resistance for a series dc motor is of the order of
(a) 0.1Ω
(b) 2Ω
(c) 20Ω
(d) 400Ω

10. A shunt motor is fitted with a field regulator for speed control. For constant torque load, the speed will be minimum when the resistance of the regulator is
(a) 0Ω
(b) infinite
(c) about 10Ω
(d) about 100Ω

11. The resistance of the field regulator of a dc shunt motor is of order of
(a) 0.1Ω
(b) 1Ω
(c) 10Ω
(d) 100Ω

12. The dc compound motors are generally
(a) cumulative compound
(b) differential compound
(c) level compound
(d) none of these

13. The resistance of the starter of a 220 v, 5 HP dc shunt motor is of the order of
(a) 0.01Ω
(b) 0.1Ω
(c) 1Ω
(d) 10Ω

14. In a dc motor, unidirectional torque is produced with the help of
(a) brushes
(b) commutator
(c) end plates
(d) both (a) and (b)

15. The back emf of a dc motor
(a) adds to the supply voltage
(b) regulates its armature voltage
(c) helps in energy conversion
(d) usually exceeds the supply voltage

16. In a dc motor, the ratio of back emf to supply emf is an indication of its
(a) efficiency
(b) speed regulation
(c) starting torque
(d) running torque

17. The mechanical power developed by the armature of a dc motor is equal to
(a) power input minus copper loss
(b) armature current multiplied by back emf
(c) armature current multiplied by supply emf
(d) power input minus mechanical losses

18. The armature torque of a dc motor is a function of its
   (a) field flux alone
   (b) armature current alone
   (c) speed alone
   (d) both field flux and armature current

19. The shaft torque of a dc motor is less than its armature torque because of
   (a) copper losses   (b) mechanical losses
   (c) back emf   (d) rotational losses

20. Under constant load condition, the speed of a dc motor is effected by
   (a) field flux alone
   (b) armature current alone
   (c) back emf
   (d) both armature current and field flux

21. If the load on a dc shunt motor is increased, its speed decreases primarily due to
   (a) increase in its flux
   (b) decrease in back emf
   (c) increase in armature current
   (d) decrease in brush drop

22. If the load current and flux of a dc motor are held constant and voltage applied across its armature is increased by 10 per cent, its speed will
   (a) decrease by about 10 per cent
   (b) remain unchanged
   (c) increase by about 10 per cent
   (d) increase by 20 per cent

23. If the field circuit of a loaded shunt motor is suddenly opened
   (a) it slows down
   (b) it would draw extremely high armature current
   (c) its speed becomes dangerously high
   (d) torque developed by the motor would be reduced to zero

24. If the pole flux of a dc motor approaches zero, its speed will
   (a) approach zero
   (b) approach infinity
   (c) not change
   (d) approach a stable value between zero and infinity

25. As the load on a dc shunt motor is increased, its speed
   (a) increases proportionately
   (b) remains constant
   (c) increases slightly
   (d) reduces slightly

26. A large series motor is never started without some load on it, otherwise
   (a) it draws very heavy current
   (b) it develops excessive speed and get damaged
   (c) there results heavy sparking at the brushes
   (d) circuit gets open circuited

27. When load is removed, which of the following dc motors will run at excessively high speed ?
   (a) shunt motor
   (b) series motor
   (c) cumulative compound motor
   (d) differential compound motor

28. Speed of a dc motor may be varied by varying
   (a) field current
   (b) applied voltage
   (c) resistance in series with armature
   (d) any of these

29. In a dc motor, maximum power is developed when supply voltage is equal to
   (a) $\dfrac{1}{2}$ back emf   (b) $\sqrt{2}$ back emf
   (c) 2 back emf   (d) $\dfrac{1}{\sqrt{2}}$ back emf

30. The speed of a series wound dc motor
   (a) can be controlled by shunt field regulator
   (b) can not be controlled by diverter
   (c) increases as flux decreases
   (d) increases as armature circuit resistance increases

31. The speed of a dc motor is
   (a) always constant
   (b) directly proportional to back emf
   (c) directly proportional to flux
   (d) inversely proportional to the product of back emf and flux.

32. The highest speed attained by a dc shunt motor at rated flux is
   (a) infinity
   (b) higher than no load speed
   (c) equal to the no load speed
   (d) lower than the no load speed

33. The speed of a dc shunt motor is required to be more than full load speed. This may be achieved by
   (a) increasing the armature current
   (b) decreasing the armature current
   (c) increasing the excitation current
   (d) reducing the field current

34. If the speed of a dc shunt motor increases, the back emf
   (a) increases
   (b) decreases
   (c) remains unchanged
   (d) first increases and then decreases

35. For a dc motor operating under condition of maximum transfer of power, the efficiency of the motor is
   (a) 100%   (b) about 90%
   (c) 75%   (d) less that 50%

36. DC motors are considered most suitable for the applications in
   (a) fans   (b) water pumps
   (c) traction   (d) flour mills

37. Which of the following dc motors will have least percentage increase in input current for a given percentage increase in torque ?
   (a) series motor
   (b) shunt motor
   (c) separately excited motor
   (d) cumulatively compound motor

38. Which dc motor will have highest precentage increase in input current for a given percentage increase in torque ?
   (a) series motor
   (b) shunt motor
   (c) cumulatively compound motor
   (d) separately excited motor

39. In a dc series motor, the shaft torque is less than the armature torque due to
   (a) eddy current losses (b) stray losses
   (c) hysteresis losses   (d) copper losses

40. If the load current and flux of a dc motor are kept constant while the voltage applied across the armature is increased by 4 per cent, the speed of the motor will
   (a) remain unchanged (b) decrease by 4%
   (c) increase by 4%   (d) increase by 16%

41. If the applied voltage to a dc shunt motor is halved and the load torque doubled, the armature current will be
   (a) unaltered   (b) zero
   (c) doubled   (d) halved

42. A dc motor is preferred to an ac motor for the application in
   (a) low speed operation
   (b) high speed operation
   (c) variable speed variation
   (d) fixed speed operation

43. The starting resistance of a dc motor is usually
   (a) infinitely large   (b) large
   (c) about 100Ω (d) small

44. If 220 V dc series motor is connected to a 220 V ac supply, then at will
   (a) not run
   (b) burn out
   (c) run smoothly
   (d) run with less efficiency and high sparking

45. Which of the following dc motor has approximately constant speed ?
   (a) series motor
   (b) shunt motor
   (c) cumulatively compound motor
   (d) differentially compound motor

46. The back emf of a dc motor depends on
   (a) field flux   (b) shape of conductors
   (c) type of slip rings   (d) brush material

47. The back emf of dc motor depends on
   (a) armature speed N
   (b) field fllux ϕ
   (c) number of armature conductors
   (d) all of these

48. The air gap between the stator and armature of a dc motor is kept small in order to
   (a) facilitate high speed operation without vibration
   (b) produce strong magnetic field
   (c) reduce noise
   (d) improve cooling

49. In a dc machine prominent and noisy blue and green sparks indicate
   (a) excessive brush wear
   (b) winding fault
   (c) worn out insulation
   (d) none of these

50. In a dc machine dull yellow spark indicates
(*a*) winding fault
(*b*) excessive brush wear
(*c*) excessive noise
(*d*) none of these

51. If the back emf of a dc motor suddenly vanishes
(*a*) the motor will run faster
(*b*) the motor will start hunting
(*c*) the efficiency of the motor will increase
(*d*) the motor will burn out

52. If the supply voltage to a shunt motor is increased by 25%, which of the following will decrease ?
(*a*) starting torque   (*b*) full load speed
(*c*) full load current   (*d*) none of these

53. In dc motor, which of the following part can withstand the maximum rise in temperature ?
(*a*) armature winding
(*b*) field winding
(*c*) commutator winding
(*d*) slip rings

54. A dc shunt motor has external resistance R_1 in the field circuit and resistance R_2 in the armature circuit. The starting armature current for the motor will be minimum when
(*a*) R_1 is minimum and R_2 is maximum
(*b*) R_1 maximum and R_2 is minimum
(*c*) both R_1 and R_2 are maximum
(*d*) both R_1 and R_2 are minimum

55. Two dc series motors are coupled. One motor runs as generator and the other as motor. The friction losses of the two machines will be equal when
(*a*) both operate at same voltage
(*b*) both have same back emf
(*c*) both have same speed
(*d*) both have same excitation

56. Two dc series motors are mechanically coupled. One machine runs as motor and the other as generator. The iron losses of the two machines will be identical when
(*a*) both have the same excitation
(*b*) both have the same speed
(*c*) both have the same back emf
(*d*) both operate at the same voltage

57. The brush voltage drops in dc motors in / of the order of
(*a*) 2 V   (*b*) 10 V
(*c*) 20 V   (*d*) 40 V

58. When the direction of power flow reverses, a differentially compoun-ded motor becomes
(*a*) differentially compounded generator
(*b*) cumulatively compounded generator
(*c*) a shunt generator
(*d*) a series generator

59. When the direction of power flow reverses, a cumulatively compounded motor becomes
(*a*) a differentially compounded generator
(*b*) a cumulatively compounded generator
(*c*) a shunt generator
(*d*) a series generator

60. Frog leg winding is
(*a*) same as simplex winding
(*b*) same as duplex winding
(*c*) combined lap and wave windings on a single rotor
(*d*) duplex wave winding on a single rotor

61. In a compound dc motor, the shunt field winding as compared to series winding will have
(*a*) more turns of smaller diameter
(*b*) less turns of larger diameter
(*c*) more turns of larger diameter
(*d*) less turns of smaller diameter

62. The flux is maximum in following unit of a dc motor
(*a*) yoke
(*b*) leading end of pole shoe
(*c*) trailing end of pole shoe
(*d*) any of the above

63. In dc motor, the amount of flux leakage depends on
(*a*) length of air gap
(*b*) shape of the magnet core
(*c*) flux density used in core and teeth
(*d*) all of these

64. In a dc motor, the flux leakage coefficient is typically
(*a*) 0.5 to 0.7   (*b*) 0.8 to 1.0
(*c*) 1.1 to 1.3   (*d*) 1.4 to 1.6

65. The direction of rotation of a dc motor can be reversed by reversing the connection to
(*a*) armature   (*b*) series field
(*c*) shunt field   (*d*) any of the above

66. The current flowing in conductors of a dc motor is
(*a*) ac   (*b*) dc
(*c*) ac as well as dc   (*d*) transient

67. Torque of a motor is
 (a) force in N-m acting on the rotor
 (b) product of tangential force on the rotor and its radius
 (c) the electrical power in kW
 (d) power given to the load

68. The output power of any electrical motor is taken from
 (a) the armature
 (b) the conductors
 (c) the coupling mounted on the shaft
 (d) the poles

69. Which of the following statements about a series motor is correct
 (a) It can run easily without load.
 (b) It has poor torque.
 (c) It has an almost constant speed.
 (d) Its field winding consists of small number of thick wires.

70. Which of the following dc motors has the least reduction in speed from no load to rated load ?
 (a) shunt motor with commutating poles
 (b) series motor with commutating poles
 (c) series motor without commutating poles
 (d) compound motor without commuta-ting poles

71. The speed of a series dc motor at no load is
 (a) zero (b) medium
 (c) high (d) tending to infinity

72. The speed of a dc series motor decreases if the flux in the field winding
 (a) remains constant (b) increases
 (c) decreases (d) none of these

73. By putting a variable resistance (diverter) across the series field in a dc series motor, speed above normal can be obtained because
 (a) armature current decreases
 (b) flux gets reduced
 (c) line current gets decreased
 (d) none of these

74. The direction of rotation of a dc series motor can be reversed by interchanging
 (a) the supply terminals only
 (b) the field terminals only
 (c) the supply and the field terminals
 (d) none of these

75. The armature reaction in a dc motor is attributed to
 (a) the effect of magnetic field set up by field current
 (b) the effect of magnetic field set up by armature current
 (c) copper losses in the armature
 (d) the effect of magnetic field set up by back emf

76. When an electric traian is moving down a hill, the dc motor acts as
 (a) dc series motor
 (b) dc shunt motor
 (c) dc series generator
 (d) dc shunt generator

77. If the armature current of a dc motor is increased keeping the field flux constant, then the developed torque
 (a) increases proportionately
 (b) decreases in reverse proportion
 (c) remains constant
 (d) increases proportional to the square root of current

78. The armature current drawn by a dc motor is proportional to
 (a) the speed of the motor
 (b) flux required in the moor
 (c) torque required
 (d) voltage applied to the motor

79. In a dc motor if the brushes are given a backward shift, then
 (a) commutation improves and speed decreases
 (b) commutation is uneffected and speed increases
 (c) commutation improves and speed increases
 (d) commutation worsens and speed decreases

80. A dc shunt motor is driving a constant torque load with rated excitation. If the field current is reduced to half, then the speed of the motor will become
 (a) half
 (b) slightly more than half
 (c) double
 (d) slightly less than double

81. A dc shunt motor is driving a mechanical load at rated voltage and rated excitation. If the load torque becomes double, then the speed of the motor

(a) increases slightly

(b) decreases slightly

(c) becomes double

(d) becomes half

82. A dc series motor is running with a diverter connected across its field winding. If the diverter resistance is increased, then the speed of the motor

(a) decreases/increase

(b) increase

(c) remains unchanged

(d) becomes very high

83. A dc series motor is running at rated speed. If a resistance is placed in series, the speed of the motor

(a) increases

(b) decreases

(c) remains unchanged

(d) increases very much

84. In a dc shunt motor, field excitation is kept at maximum value during starting to

(a) increase acceleration time

(b) reduce armature heating

(c) prevent voltage dip in the supply mains

(d) decrease starting torque

85. If the field circuit of a dc shunt motor running at rated speed gets open circuited, then immediately thereafter the speed of the motor would tend to

(a) decrease   (b) increase

(c) remain unchanged (d) increase excessively

86. Two dc series motors connected in series are driving the same mechanical load. If now the motors are connected in parallel, the speed becomes

(a) slightly more than double

(b) slightly less than double

(c) slightly more than half

(d) slightly less than half

87. The back emf Vb of a dc motor

(a) opposes the applied voltage

(b) assists the applied voltage

(c) does not influence the applied voltage

(d) none of these

88. All d.c. machines are characterized by

(a) electric brushes   (b) armature

(c) commutator   (d) magnetic poles

89. Armature voltage control is suitable if d.c. machine is driven at constant

(a) torque   (b) magnetic field

(c) speed   (d) current

90. Current normally used to excite synchronous and d.c. generators is

(a) D.C.   (b) A.C. single phase

(c) A.C. two phase   (d) A.C. three phase

91. In all electric machines, basic action taking place is

(a) motor action   (b) generator action

(c) both (a) and (b)   (d) all of these

92. In case of a motor

(a) only motor action takes place

(b) motor action precedes generator action

(c) generator action precedes motor action

(d) both take place precedes simultaneously

93. All rotating machines are basically

(a) D.C. machines

(b) A.C. machines

(c) electro-mechanical convertors

(d) heat converters

94. All machines have the structure such that

(a) armature is rotating and field is fixed

(b) field is rotating and armature is fixed

(c) either (a) or (b)

(d) none of these

95. All electrical machines have poles with

(a) a hetro-polar structure

(b) a horse shoe structure

(c) (a) above (b)

(d) none of these

96. Maximum number of brushes which can be used in a machine is

(a) 2

(b) 4

(c) 6

(d) number of poles in the machine or 2

97. Which of the following motors has high starting torque?
(*a*) D.C. shunt motor
(*b*) Induction motor
(*c*) D.C. series motor
(*d*) A.C. series motor

98. What is the standard direction of a motor?
(*a*) clockwise
(*b*) anti-clockwise
(*c*) none of these
(*d*) either (a) or (b)

99. Left hand rule is applicable to
(*a*) motor
(*b*) generator
(*c*) transformer
(*d*) mercury are rectifier

D.C. MOTOR

100. Effect of armature flux on the main flux in a d.c. motor is that
(*a*) it inclines lines of force through the air gap such that they do not remain radial.
(*b*) it makes distribution of the flux density across both sections unequal
(*c*) both (a) and (b)
(*d*) none of these

101. Speed of d.c. series motor at no load is
(*a*) infinity
(*b*) 3000 rpm
(*c*) 1500 rpm
(*d*) zero

102. Function of the commutator in a d.c. machine is
(*a*) for easy speed control
(*b*) to improve commutation
(*c*) to change a.c. to d.c.
(*d*) to change alternating voltage to direct voltage

103. If back e.m.f. suddenly disappears in a d.c. motor
(*a*) nothing will happen
(*b*) windings will burn due to high armature current
(*c*) motor will start acting as a generator
(*d*) motor will stop

104. Direction of rotation of a d.c. series motor can be changed by interchanging
(*a*) voltage terminals
(*b*) field terminals
(*c*) both (a) and (b)
(*d*) none of these

105. If a d.c. motor is connected across a.c. supply, the motor will
(*a*) run at normal speed
(*b*) run at lower speed
(*c*) burn
(*d*) run continuosly but for sparking at brushes

106. Voltage applied across the shunt motor has to
(*a*) overcome the back emf
(*b*) supply armature ohmic drop
(*c*) supply fied ohmic drop
(*d*) both (*a*) and (*b*)

107. If back emf of a d.c. motor is doubled while its speed is also doubled, then torque developed by the machine will
(*a*) remain same
(*b*) become four times
(*c*) double
(*d*) becomes half

108. If field of d.c. shunt motor is opened, then
(*a*) current in the armature will increase
(*b*) it will run at its normal speed
(*c*) speed of motor will be reduced
(*d*) speed of motor will be high

109. For a series motor, field flux is
(*a*) constant
(*b*) proportional to armature current
(*c*) proportional to temperature
(*d*) inversely proportional to armature current

110. Field flux is constant in
(*a*) series motor
(*b*) compound motor
(*c*) shunt motor
(*d*) none of these

111. Dummy coil in a d.c. machine is used to
(*a*) eliminate reactance voltage
(*b*) eliminate armature reaction
(*c*) for mechanical balance of armature
(*d*) none of these

112. Four point in d.c. motor is used
(*a*) to decrease the field current
(*b*) to increase the field current
(*c*) not to affect the current through hold on coil even if any change in field current takes place
(*d*) none of these

113. Torque speed characteristic of a series motor is
(*a*) linear
(*b*) parabola
(*c*) rectangular hyperbola
(*d*) none of these

114. Shunt motor has
(*a*) widely varying speed
(*b*) constant speed
(*c*) low speed at high loads and high speed at low loads
(*d*) low speed at low loads and high speed at high loads

115. In series-paralled control method when two d.c. series motors are connected in series, speed of the set is
(*a*) same as in parallel
(*b*) rated speed of any of the motors
(*c*) half of the speed of the motors
(*d*) one fourth of the speed of the motors

116. Torque produced by series combination of two d.c. series motor is
(*a*) four times the torque when they are connected in parallel
(*b*) equal to the torque when they are connected in parallel
(*c*) twice the torque when they are connected in parallel
(*d*) half the torque when they are connected in parallel

117. For most of the application purpose
(*a*) series motor is used
(*b*) shunt motor is used
(*c*) compound motor is used
(*d*) depends on requirement

118. Use of the starter in d.c. motors is necessary becaues
(*a*) to overcome back emf
(*b*) they are not self starting
(*c*) to limit the high intial current by inserting high resistance
(*d*) none of these

119. Speed of the d.c. motor can be varied by
(*a*) varying field current
(*b*) varying armature resistance
(*c*) varying supply voltage
(*d*) either (*b*) or (*c*)

120. As the load is increased, speed of d.c. shunt motor will
(*a*) reduce slightly
(*b*) increase slightly
(*c*) remains constant
(*d*) none of these

121. Field flux of d.c. motor can be controlled to
(*a*) steady speed
(*b*) speeds above rated speed
(*c*) speeds below rated speed
(*d*) speeds above and below rated speed

122. If field current of a shunt motor is changed, then
(*a*) horse power remains constant but torque will change
(*b*) torque remains constant but h.p will change
(*c*) both will change
(*d*) both remains constant

123. Synchronous reactance is defined as reactance
(*a*) due to leakage flux
(*b*) of synchronous machine
(*c*) due to armature reaction of the machine
(*d*) due to armature reaction and leakage of flux both

124. Armature winding of a series motor is excited
(*a*) inductively (*b*) resistively
(*c*) conductively (*d*) none of these

125. Speed of a d.c. motor depends upon
(*a*) armature resistance
(*b*) field flux
(*c*) applied voltage
(*d*) all of these

126. In the field flux method of speed control
(*a*) speeds above normal speed can be attained
(*b*) speeds below normal speed can be attained
(*c*) any speed can be attained
(*d*) none of these

127. Dynamic braking is generally used for
(*a*) series motors
(*b*) shunt motors
(*c*) compound motors
(*d*) all of these

128. Stalling current is the maximum value of
(*a*) field current for which speed is maximum
(*b*) load current for which speed is zero
(*c*) diverter current for which speed is maximum
(*d*) load current for which speed is maximum

129. Torque developed in d.c. motor depends on
(*a*) magnetic field (*b*) armature
(*c*) speed (*d*) both (*a*) and (*b*)

130. Which method of speed control has minimum efficiency?
(*a*) armature control method
(*b*) voltage control method
(*c*) field control method
(*d*) none of these

131. Ward-Leonard method of speed control is basically useful where usually
(a) narrow range of speed control is required
(b) wide range of speed control is required
(c) wide range of sensitive speed control is required
(d) none of these

132. In ward-Leonard system, minimum number of machines required are
(a) two   (b) three
(c) four   (d) five

133. Ward-Leonard method is basically a
(a) field control method
(b) field diverter method
(c) voltage control method
(d) armature resistance control method

134. Disadvantage of ward-Leonard system is
(a) its high initial cost
(b) increased maintenance cost
(c) its low efficiency at light loads
(d) all of them

135. Speed regulation of a d.c. motor can be ideally achieved with
(a) no excitation to the field of the motor
(b) constant excitation to the field of the motor
(c) variable excitation to the field of the motor
(d) A.C. excitation to the field of the motor

136. Disadvantage of the field-control method of speed control is
(a) its low efficiency
(b) that speeds above normal speed can be achieved
(c) that commutation becomes unsatisfactory
(d) none of these

137. If plugging is applied to series motor for a long time, then
(a) motor will burn
(b) motor will stop
(c) it will start revolving in other direction at low speed
(d) none of these

138. In case of regenerative braking, the motor
(a) dissipates energy in armature circuit
(b) dissipates energy in field circuit
(c) both (a) and (b)
(d) supply energy to source

D.C. GENERATORS

1. The operation of an electric motor or generator is based on
(a) the law of electromagnetic induction
(b) interaction between magnetic field and current carrying conductor
(c) interaction between two electric fields
(d) interaction between magnetic field and electric field

2. All rotating electric machines are basically
(a) d.c. machines
(b) a.c. machines
(c) electro-mechanical convertors
(d) machines using electromagnetic induction

3. All rotating electrical machines have
(a) rotating armature and fixed field
(b) rotating field and fixed armature
(c) either (a) or (b)
(d) none of these

4. In any dc generators, the emf generated in the armature is maximum when
(a) rate of change of flux linkage is minimum
(b) rate of change of flux linkage is maximum
(c) flux linkage with conductors is maximum
(d) flux linkage with conductors is minimum

5. All dc machines are characterized by
(a) armature   (b) commutator
(c) magnetic poles (d) electric brushes

6. $V \times B = e$ is the equation of the electrical machines which
(a) is a dc machines
(b) has magnetic poles
(c) works as a motor
(d) converts mechanical energy into electrical energy

7. The function of commutator in a dc machine is
(a) to improve commutation
(b) to change dc voltage into dc voltage
(c) to change ac voltage into dc voltage
(d) to provide easy speed control

8. Under commutation in a dc machine gives rise to
(a) sparking at the leading edge of the brush
(b) sparking at the trailing edge of the brush
(c) no sparking at all
(d) sparking at the middle of the brush

9. In a dc generator, if the brushes are given a small amount of forward shift, the effect of armature reaction is

(*a*) totally demagnetising

(*b*) totally magnetising

(*c*) partly demagnetising and partly cross-magnetising

(*d*) totally cross-magnetising

10. A conductor is rotating within a magnetic field. At which of the following positions do the zero voltages occur ?

(*a*) along the axis of the magnetic field

(*b*) at right angles to the axis of the magnetic field

(*c*) at 45° with the axis of the magnetic field

(*d*) none of these

11. In a dc machine, the laminated parts are the armature core and

(*a*) base   (*b*) yoke

(*c*) shaft   (*d*) pole shoes

12. The commutator in dc machine works as

(*a*) mechanical inverter

(*b*) mechanical rectifier

(*c*) energy converter

(*d*) either (*a*) or (*b*)

13. Which of the following forms an energy converter?

(*a*) piezo-electric effect

(*b*) magneto-striction effect

(*c*) Hall effect

(*d*) all of these

14. Commutation is possible in dc machines

(*a*) only when the field is rotating in the armature

(*b*) only when the armature is rotating in the field

(*c*) either (*a*) or (*b*)

(*d*) none of these

15. Which of the following parts helps the commutation process ?

(*a*) interpoles

(*b*) compensating winding

(*c*) pole shoes

(*d*) all of these

16. Commutation segments in a dc machine are separated by thin layers of

(*a*) synthetic rubber

(*b*) mica

(*c*) paper

(*d*) PVC

17. Commutation in a dc machine may be improved by

(*a*) reducing to number of turns in the armature and segments of commu-tator

(*b*) increasing the resistances of brushes

(*c*) neutralizing the reactance voltage by producing a reverse emf in the coil undergoing commutation

(*d*) all of these

18. In the commutation process in a dc machine, which of the following quantity reverses ?

(*a*) the voltage

(*b*) the current

(*c*) both voltage and current

(*d*) none of these

19. Increase in the number of com-mutator segments of a dc machine results in

(*a*) increase in the total output power

(*b*) decrease in the total output power

(*c*) increase in the magnitude of output voltage

(*d*) smoothening of the shape of output dc wave

20. Each commutator segment is connected to the armature conductor by means of

(*a*) insulator

(*b*) copper lug

(*c*) resistance wire

(*d*) carbon brush

21. Brushes for commutator are made of

(*a*) copper   (*b*) aluminium

(*c*) carbon   (*d*) synthetic rubber

22. In a dc generator, brushes are always placed

(*a*) along geometrical neutral axis (GNA)

(*b*) along magnetic neutral axis (MNA)

(*c*) along bisector of GNA and MNA

(*d*) arbitrarily

23. In dc generators, brushes remain in contact with the conductors which lie

(*a*) under north pole

(*b*) under south pole

(*c*) in the interpolar region

(*d*) arbitrarily

24. In a dc generator, sparking between brushes and commutator surface may be due to

(*a*) overcommutation

(*b*) undercommutation

(*c*) to rapid reversal of current

(*d*) any of these

25. In a dc generator, rapid brush wear may be due to
(a) rough commutator surface
(b) severe sparking
(c) imperfect contact with commutator
(d) any of these

26. In a dc machine commutator, pre-ssure on the brush is usually
(a) less than 1 kg/cm^2
(b) about 3 kg/cm^2
(c) about 5 kg/cm^2
(d) about 10 kg/cm^2

27. Brushes for commutators for 220 V dc generator are generally made of
(a) copper
(b) carbon copper
(c) electrographite
(d) graphited copper

28. Carbon brushes are used in dc machines to
(a) brush off carbon deposits in the commutator
(b) provide a path for flow of current
(c) prevent overheating of armature winding
(d) prevent sparking during commu-tation

29. Commutator of a dc machine acts as a
(a) fullwave rectifier
(b) halfwave rectifier
(c) inverter
(d) controlled rectifier

30. The commutator pitch of a quadruplex lap winding in a dc generator is
(a) 1
(b) 2
(c) 4
(d) 8

31. The maximum number of brushes which may be used in an electrical machine is equal to
(a) number of poles in the machine
(b) 2
(c) 4
(d) either (a) or (b)

32. In a dc generator, sparking at brushes results due to
(a) winding distribution
(b) armature reactance
(c) high constant resistance of the brushes
(d) reactance voltage in coil undergoing commutation

33. Equalizer rings in lap wound armatures are used to
(a) get sparklers commutation
(b) avoid unequal current distribution at brushes
(c) both (a) and (b)
(d) to neutralize the armature reaction

34. Which winding on dc generators is preferred for generating large current ?
(a) lap winding
(b) progressive wave winding
(c) retrogressive wave winding
(d) all winding give similar results

35. Equalizer rings can be used by
(a) lap wound armatures only
(b) wave wound armatures only
(c) both lap and wave wound armatures
(d) none of these

36. The function of equalizing ring in lap wound dc generator is
(a) to avoid short circuit current
(b) to neutralize the armature reaction
(c) to help get sparklers commutation
(d) to increase the efficiency of the machine

37. In a ring wound commutator, the brush width equals the width of
(a) one commutator segment and one mica insulation
(b) one commutator segment and two mica insulations
(c) two commutator segments and two mica insulations
(d) two commutator segments and one mica insulation

38. In a dc machine without any brush shift, the shift of the magnetic natural axes due to armature reaction is
(a) in the direction of rotation for the generator and against the direction of rotation for the motor
(b) in the direction of rotation for both the generator and the motor
(c) against the direction of rotation for both the generator and the motor
(d) against the direction of rotation for the generator and in the direction of rotation for the motor

39. In a dc machine without interpoles, to get improved commutation, the brush shift angle must be
(a) varied with change in load
(b) kept constant
(c) zero degree
(d) none of the above

40. In a dc generator, the polarity of the interpole is
(a) always N
(b) always S
(c) same as the main pole ahead
(d) same as the main pole behind

41. In a dc generator, compared to the air gap under field poles, the interpole air gap is made
(a) larger
(b) smaller
(c) the same
(d) much smaller

42. A dc machine is provided with both interpole winding (IPW) and compensating winding (CPM). With respect to the armature
(a) both IPW and CPW are in parallel
(b) both IPW and CPW are in series
(c) IPW is in series and CPW is in parallel
(d) IPW is in parallel and CPW is in series

43. The function of using compensating winding in dc machines is to neutra-lize the
(a) armature reaction in the interpole zone
(b) armature reaction in the commu-tating zone
(c) armature reaction under the pole faces
(d) cross-magnetizing armature reaction

44. The yoke of a dc generator is made of cast iron because
(a) it is cheaper
(b) it completes the magnetic path
(c) it gives mechanical protection to the machine
(d) all of these

45. The conductors of the compensating winding are housed
(a) entirely in the armature slots
(b) entirely in the slots in the pole faces
(c) partly in armature slots and partly in slots in pole faces
(d) around the pole core

46. The armature mmf waveform in a dc machine is
(a) pulsating
(b) rectangular
(c) triangular
(d) sinusoidal

47. Armature magnetic field in a dc generator produces which of the following effect ?
(a) It demagnetizes or reduces the main flux
(b) It cross-magnetizes the main flux
(c) It magnetizes or reinforces the main flux
(d) Both (a) and (a)

48. In a dc generator, in armature conductor along MNA
(a) maximum current is produced
(b) maximum emf is produced
(c) minimum emf is produced
(d) minimum current is produced

49. A dc shunt generator driven at normal speed in the normal direction fails to build up armature voltage because
(a) the resistance of the armature is high
(b) there is no residual magnetism
(c) the field current is too small
(d) none of these

where ϕ is the flux and N is the speed

50. In a dc machine, the armature mmf is always directed along the
(a) polar axis
(b) brush axis
(c) interpolar axis
(d) none of these

51. In dc machines, armature windings are placed on the rotor because of the necessity for
(a) electromechanical energy conversion
(b) generation of voltage
(c) commutation
(d) development of torque

52. Armature in a dc machine is made of laminated steel instead of wood because it has
(a) low permeability
(b) high permeability
(c) more mechanical strength
(d) more mechanical strength and high permeability

53. Copper losses in armature of dc generator amount to which of the following percentage of full load losses ?
(a) 5 to 10%
(b) 10 to 20%
(c) 20 to 30%
(d) 30 to 40%

54. Stray losses in a dc generator are the same as
(a) mechanical losses
(b) magnetic losses
(c) both (a) and (b) added together
(d) none of these

55. Standing or constant losses of a dc generator are
(a) field losses of shunt generator
(b) armature losses of a compound generator
(c) stray losses
(d) both (a) *and* (b) added together

56. Out of the following four sources of losses in a dc generator which one is minimum ?
(a) copper losses
(b) hysteresis losses
(c) eddy current losses
(d) windage losses

57. Overall efficiency of dc generators is usually of the order of
(a) 60 to 70 %
(b) 70 to 80%
(c) 80 to 90 %
(d) 85 to 95 %

58. DC shunt generator has terminal voltage versus load current characteristic which is
(a) constant
(b) slightly drooping
(c) slightly rising
(d) highly drooping

59. Which of the following type of dc generator gives constant output voltage at all loads ?
(a) shunt generator
(b) series generator
(c) shot shunt compound generator
(d) level compound generator

60. The terminal voltage of dc shunt generator drops on load because of
(a) armature reaction
(b) armature resistance
(c) weakening of the field due to armature reaction
(d) all of these

61. If the load on an overcompounded dc generator is reduced, the terminal voltage
(a) increases
(b) decreases
(c) remains unchanged
(d) may increase or decrease

62. Main reason for break point in the load characteristic of a dc generator is
(a) armature drop
(b) armature reaction
(c) both (a) and (b)
(d) none of these

63. The internal characteristic of generator is the curve between
(a) armature current and generated emf
(b) load current and terminal voltage
(c) field current and no load voltage
(d) armature current and IR drop

64. The load characteristic of a gene-rator is the curve between
(a) load voltage and field current
(b) generated emf and armature current
(c) load current and terminal voltage
(d) load current and voltage drop in armature winding

65. An ideal dc generator has regulation of
(a) zero
(b) 20%
(c) 30%
(d) 40%

66. Equalizer connections are required when paralleling two
(a) bipolar generators
(b) shunt generators
(c) series generators
(d) compound generators

67. In case of parallel operation of compound generators, for proper division of load from no load to full load, it is essential that
(a) the regulation of each armature should be the same
(b) their series field resistances should be equal
(c) their ratings should be equal
(d) none of these

68. Generators are often run in parallel because it
(a) keeps stability of supply
(b) gives facility of repair which results in fewer breakdown
(c) gives facility of an additional unit to be installed as and when required
(d) all of these

69. Two dc shunt generators are operating in parallel. If it is desired to shut down one of the generators

(a) its main switch is suddenly opened

(b) its field current is gradually reduced

(c) the input to its prime mover is suddenly reduced to zero

(d) none of these

70. In dc generator, the principal reasons for delay in the reversal of current is

(a) reactance voltage

(b) the capacitor action with two segments as electrodes and mica as the dielectric

(c) the air gap between the brushes and the commutator surface

(d) none of these

71. The critical resistance of dc generator is the resistance of

(a) field

(b) brush

(c) armature

(d) compensating pole

72. One method of neutralizing the armature reaction in a dc generator is to

(a) shift the brushes in lagging direction of rotation

(b) shift the brushes in leading direction of rotation

(c) interchange the terminals at the brushes

(d) none of these

73. The critical resistance of a dc gene-rator can be increased by

(a) increasing the field current

(b) increasing its speed

(c) increasing the armature resistance

(d) all of these

74. A series dc generator does not build up voltage. The reason is

(a) short circuited terminals

(b) reversed terminal of field winding

(c) reversed terminal of armature winding

(d) disconnected load

75. Residual magnetism is necessary in

(a) self excited generator

(b) separately excited generator

(c) both (a) and (b)

(d) none of these

76. If number of poles in a lap wounded generator is increased by a factor 2, then generated emf will

(a) increase by a factor of 4

(b) remain same

(c) increase by a factor 2

(d) decrease by a factor 2

77. Which of the following accounts for smallest part of full load losses?

(a) magnetic losses

(b) mechanical losses

(c) field copper loss

(d) armature copper loss

78. Stray losses in a d.c. generator are same as

(a) mechanical losses

(b) magnetic losses

(c) windage losses

(d) both (a) and (b)

79. Efficiency of a d.c. shunt generator is maximum when

(a) stray losses are equal to copper losses

(b) magnetic losses are equal to mechanical losses

(c) armature copper losses are equal to constant losses

(d) field copper losses are equal to constant losses

80. Copper loss in armature of d.c. generator accounts for

(a) 0 —10% of full load losses

(b) 10 —20% of full load losses

(c) 20 —30% of full load losses

(d) 30 —40% of full load losses

81. Constant losses of a d.c. generator are defined as

(a) stray losses

(b) field losses of shunt generator

(c) armature losses of a compound generator

(d) both (b) and (c)

82. Equilizer ring in the lap winding of d.c. generator are used to

(a) avoid overhang

(b) avoid noise

(c) avoid harmonics

(d) avoid unequal distribution of current at brushes

83. D.C. generator have normally an over-all efficiency of the order of
- (*a*) 85 — 95%
- (*b*) 75 — 85%
- (*c*) 65 — 75%
- (*d*) 55 — 65%

84. Sparking at the brushes in the d.c. generator is due to
- (*a*) high resistance of the brushes
- (*b*) reactance voltage
- (*c*) armature reaction
- (*d*) quick reversal of current in the coil

85. Armature magnetic field has the effect that it
- (*a*) cross magnetizes it
- (*b*) demagnetizes it
- (*c*) strengthens the main flux
- (*d*) both (*a*) and (*b*)

86. Brushes are always placed along
- (*a*) Geometrical neutral axis
- (*b*) Magnetic neutral axis
- (*c*) perpendicular to magnetic neutral axis
- (*d*) none of these

87. Interpoles in the armature of d.c. generator are used to
- (*a*) neutralize the reactance voltage only
- (*b*) neutralize the reactance voltage and cross-magnetization effect of armature reaction
- (*c*) neutralize demagnetization effect
- (*d*) none of these

88. Function of compensating winding is to neutralize
- (*a*) cross-magnetization effect of armature reaction
- (*b*) demagnetization effect of armature reaction
- (*c*) reactance voltage
- (*d*) all of these

89. Critical resistance of the d.c. generator is the resistance of
- (*a*) field
- (*b*) load
- (*c*) brushes
- (*d*) armature

90. In the commutation process
- (*a*) current is reversed
- (*b*) voltage is reversed
- (*c*) both current and voltage are reversed
- (*d*) none of these

91. Difference between interpoles and compensation winding is that
- (*a*) interpoles additionally supply mmf for counter acting the reactance voltage induced in the coil under going commutalion
- (*b*) action of interpoles is localized
- (*c*) interpoles also helps in equalizing distribution of current in brushes
- (*d*) both (*a*) and (*b*)

92. Generator is called flat compounded if
- (*a*) rated voltage is less than no load voltage
- (*b*) series field AT produces same voltage at rated and no load
- (*c*) series field AT produces rated voltage greater than no load
- (*d*) series field AT produces rated voltage less than no load

93. Commutation process can be improved by
- (*a*) increasing the resistance of the brushes
- (*b*) reducing the number of turns in armature coil
- (*c*) neutralizing reactance voltage
- (*d*) all of these

94. When two d.c. series generators are running in parallel, equalizer bar is used
- (*a*) to increase the series flux
- (*b*) because both will pass equal currents to the load
- (*c*) to reduce combined effect of armature reaction of both
- (*d*) to increase speed and hence generated emf.

95. In d.c. generator, if field winding attains critical resistance then it will
- (*a*) not develop voltage at all
- (*b*) generate maximum power
- (*c*) generate maximum voltage
- (*d*) none of these

96. For paralleling two d.c. generators, their
- (*a*) polarities must be same
- (*b*) phase sequence must be same
- (*c*) polarities and voltage must be same
- (*d*) both (*b*) and (*c*)

97. Equalizer rings can be used by
- (*a*) lap wound armature
- (*b*) wave wound armature
- (*c*) both (*a*) and (*b*)
- (*d*) none of these

98. Generators are often run in parallel because of
- (*a*) greater reliabilty
- (*b*) greater efficiency
- (*c*) meeting more load demands
- (*d*) all of these

99. External characteristics of a d.c. generator can be obtained by
- (*a*) internal characteristic
- (*b*) no load saturation characteristic
- (*c*) both (a) and (b)
- (*d*) none of these

100. Commutator machines can be of the type of
- (*a*) d.c. machines
- (*b*) a.c. machines
- (*c*) universal machines
- (*d*) all of these

101. Which of the following is most suitable for parallel operation?
- (*a*) series generator
- (*b*) shunt generator
- (*c*) compound generator
- (*d*) any one of them

102. If two generator are running in parallel and field of one of the generator is weakened too much, then it will
- (*a*) take a smaller share of the total load
- (*b*) run as the motor in the same direction
- (*c*) take a large share of the total load
- (*d*) run in the oppoiste direction as motor

103. Critical resistance is resistance of the field winding of a generator
- (*a*) at which it develops maximum voltage
- (*b*) at which it supply maximum power
- (*c*) beyond which it can not develop any voltage
- (*d*) at which the speed of generator is infinity

104. With the increase of field winding of a d.c. generator, terminal voltage will
- (*a*) decrease
- (*b*) increase
- (*c*) remain same
- (*d*) none of these

105. A shunt generator do not build up any voltage at no load because
- (*a*) shunt coil may be connected in reverse direction
- (*b*) there is no residual magnetism in the poles
- (*c*) its shunt field resistance is more than critical resistance
- (*d*) any one of the above

106. Drop in the terminal voltage of a shunt generator under load conditions is due to
- (*a*) armature resistance drop
- (*b*) armature reaction
- (*c*) decrease in field current
- (*d*) all of them

107. Lap winding in a lap wound d.c. generator is provided because it
- (*a*) makes the current distribution at brushes equal to avoid sparks
- (*b*) helps the noiseless operation of the machine
- (*c*) provides a path for the circulation of unbalanced current
- (*d*) provides mechanical strength for the winding of the armature

108. Main reason of drop due to armature reaction in a d.c. generator is
- (*a*) armature flux due to armature current
- (*b*) load current
- (*c*) shunt and series field current
- (*d*) none of these

109. If there is no saturation of flux in the poles of a d.c. generator, then it will
- (*a*) not run
- (*b*) burn due to extraordinarily high potential building up in the armature
- (*c*) not build up any voltage
- (*d*) run under unstable operating conditions.

110. In an over compounded generator, field turns are adjusted such that no load voltage is
- (*a*) equal to the rated load voltage
- (*b*) greater than rated load voltage
- (*c*) less than rated load voltage
- (*d*) none of these

111. If a.c. voltage is applied on the field of d.c. generator, then output will be

(*a*) d.c. voltage

(*b*) a.c. voltage

(*c*) no output

(*d*) none of these

112. A series generator, any voltage may not build up because

(*a*) field winding is revervsed

(*b*) load is connected

(*c*) very high load is connected

(*d*) none of these

113. Which generators are in hotels and office building?

(*a*) under-compounded generators

(*b*) over-compounded generators

(*c*) flat-compounded generators

(*d*) none of these

114. Critical resistance of a d.c. generator can be increased by

(*a*) increasing its speed

(*b*) decreasing its armature resistance

(*c*) decreasing its speed

(*d*) none of these

115. Over-compounded generator is used for

(*a*) long distance transmission

(*b*) short distance transmission

(*c*) medium distance transmission

(*d*) none of these

ANSWERS

D.C. MACHINES

1. (*b*)	**2.** (*b*)	**3.** (*a*)	**4.** (*a*)	**5.** (*c*)	**6.** (*b*)	**7.** (*a*)	**8.** (*b*)	**9.** (*a*)	**10.** (*a*)
11. (*d*)	**12.** (*a*)	**13.** (*d*)	**14.** (*d*)	**15.** (*c*)	**16.** (*a*)	**17.** (*b*)	**18.** (*d*)	**19.** (*d*)	**20.** (*a*)
21. (*b*)	**22.** (*c*)	**23.** (*c*)	**24.** (*b*)	**25.** (*d*)	**26.** (*b*)	**27.** (*b*)	**28.** (*d*)	**29.** (*c*)	**30.** (*c*)
31. (*b*)	**32.** (*c*)	**33.** (*d*)	**34.** (*a*)	**35.** (*d*)	**36.** (*c*)	**37.** (*a*)	**38.** (*b*)	**39.** (*b*)	**40.** (*c*)
41. (*c*)	**42.** (*c*)	**43.** (*d*)	**44.** (*d*)	**45.** (*b*)	**46.** (*a*)	**47.** (*d*)	**48.** (*b*)	**49.** (*b*)	**50.** (*d*)
51. (*d*)	**52.** (*b*)	**53.** (*b*)	**54.** (*a*)	**55.** (*c*)	**56.** (*a*)	**57.** (*a*)	**58.** (*b*)	**59.** (*a*)	**60.** (*c*)
61. (*a*)	**62.** (*a*)	**63.** (*d*)	**64.** (*c*)	**65.** (*a*)	**66.** (*a*)	**67.** (*b*)	**68.** (*c*)	**69.** (*d*)	**70.** (*a*)
71. (*d*)	**72.** (*b*)	**73.** (*b*)	**74.** (*b*)	**75.** (*b*)	**76.** (*c*)	**77.** (*a*)	**78.** (*c*)	**79.** (*c*)	**80.** (*d*)
81. (*b*)	**82.** (*a*)	**83.** (*b*)	**84.** (*b*)	**85.** (*b*)	**86.** (*a*)	**87.** (*a*)	**88.** (*c*)	**89.** (*a*)	**90.** (*a*)
91. (*c*)	**92.** (*b*)	**93.** (*c*)	**94.** (*a*)	**95.** (*a*)	**96.** (*d*)	**97.** (*c*)	**98.** (*b*)	**99.** (*a*)	**100.** (*c*)
101. (*a*)	**102.** (*d*)	**103.** (*b*)	**104.** (*c*)	**105.** (*c*)	**106.** (*d*)	**107.** (*a*)	**108.** (*d*)	**109.** (*b*)	**110.** (*a*)
111. (*c*)	**112.** (*c*)	**113.** (*c*)	**114.** (*b*)	**115.** (*d*)	**116.** (*a*)	**117.** (*d*)	**118.** (*c*)	**119.** (*d*)	**120.** (*a*)
121. (*b*)	**122.** (*a*)	**123.** (*d*)	**124.** (*c*)	**125.** (*d*)	**126.** (*a*)	**127.** (*d*)	**128.** (*b*)	**129.** (*d*)	**130.** (*a*)
131. (*c*)	**132.** (*b*)	**133.** (*c*)	**134.** (*d*)	**135.** (*b*)	**136.** (*c*)	**137.** (*c*)	**138.** (*d*)		

<u>D.C. GENERATORS</u>

1. (b)	**2.** (c)	**3.** (a)	**4.** (b)	**5.** (b)	**6.** (d)	**7.** (c)	**8.** (b)	**9.** (c)	**10.** (a)
11. (d)	**12.** (b)	**13.** (d)	**14.** (b)	**15.** (a)	**16.** (b)	**17.** (d)	**18.** (b)	**19.** (d)	**20.** (b)
21. (c)	**22.** (b)	**23.** (c)	**24.** (d)	**25.** (d)	**26.** (a)	**27.** (c)	**28.** (b)	**29.** (a)	**30.** (c)
31. (d)	**32.** (d)	**33.** (c)	**34.** (a)	**35.** (a)	**36.** (c)	**37.** (a)	**38.** (a)	**39.** (a)	**40.** (c)
41. (a)	**42.** (b)	**43.** (c)	**44.** (d)	**45.** (b)	**46.** (c)	**47.** (d)	**48.** (c)	**49.** (b)	**50.** (b)
51. (c)	**52.** (d)	**53.** (d)	**54.** (c)	**55.** (d)	**56.** (d)	**57.** (d)	**58.** (d)	**59.** (d)	**60.** (d)
61. (b)	**62.** (b)	**63.** (a)	**64.** (c)	**65.** (a)	**66.** (d)	**67.** (a)	**68.** (d)	**69.** (b)	**70.** (a)
71. (a)	**72.** (b)	**73.** (b)	**74.** (a)	**75.** (a)	**76.** (b)	**77.** (b)	**78.** (d)	**79.** (c)	**80.** (d)
81. (d)	**82.** (d)	**83.** (a)	**84.** (b)	**85.** (d)	**86.** (b)	**87.** (b)	**88.** (b)	**89.** (a)	**90.** (a)
91. (d)	**92.** (b)	**93.** (d)	**94.** (b)	**95.** (a)	**96.** (d)	**97.** (a)	**98.** (d)	**99.** (c)	**100.** (d)
101. (b)	**102.** (b)	**103.** (c)	**104.** (b)	**105.** (d)	**106.** (d)	**107.** (a)	**108.** (a)	**109.** (c)	**110.** (c)
111. (b)	**112.** (b)	**113.** (c)	**114.** (a)	**115.** (a)					

■■

Transformers

Transformer is a static electrical apparatus which converts electrical energy from higher voltage to lower voltage or *vice versa* at the same supply frequency.

Types of transformers :

1. Core type
2. Shell type
3. Berry type

TRANSFORMERS AND DC MACHINES

Principle of Operation of a Transformer

A transformer basically consists of two separate windings, called the *primary winding and the secondary winding,* magnetically coupled with each other through low reluctance magnetic circuit. On connecting the primary winding to an a.c. source as shown below in figure an a.c. current I_1 flows through the primary winding producing an a.c. magnetic flux in the neighbourhood of the coil. A part of this magnetic flux links with the secondary winding producing an a.c. voltage E_2 across the secondary winding. Thus basically the voltage across the secondary winding is produced through the mechanism of mutual induction. If the output terminals of secondary are connected to a load impedance, currnt I_2 flows in the secondary winding and the load impedance and thus electrical energy is transferred entirely from primary to the secondary through the magnetic coupling. To provide high magnetic flux linkage between the two windings, a flow reluctance magnetic path is provided, typically using laminated steel core.

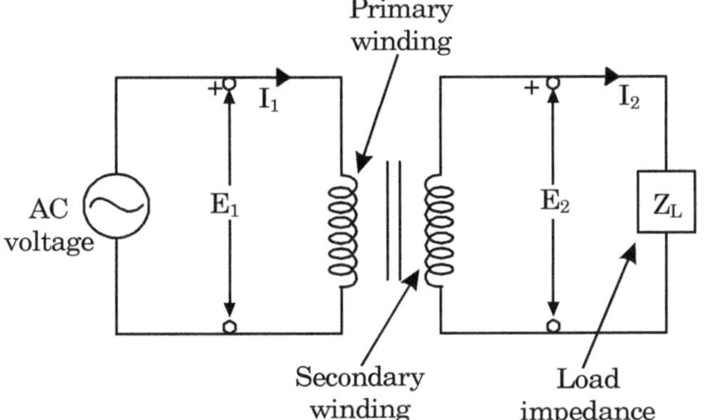

Basic circuit of a transformer

Voltage Transformation Ratio k. As a result on an ac voltage applied to the primary of the transformer, let E_1 volts (rms) be developed across the primary winding and let E_2 volts (rms) be developed across the secondary winding. Then the ratio E_2/E_1 is called the transformation ratio, usually denoted by k.

Thus voltage transformation ratio

$$k = \frac{\text{voltage induced across the secondary}}{\text{voltage induced across the primary}} = \frac{E_2}{E_1}$$

Thus magnitude of the voltage on the primary side gets multiplied by the factor k. This voltage transformer ratio k may be less than one, equal to one or more than 1. If $k < 1$, the transformer is called *step-down* transformer while if $k > 1$, the transformer is called *step-up* transformer.

Further it may be noted that only the magnitude of the voltage changes while the frequency and wave shape remain unchanged. Thus the main features of transformer are :

(*i*) It transfers electric energy from primary to the secondary side.

(*ii*) Voltage and current on the secondary side, in general, differ from those on the primary side.

(*iii*) There is no change in frequency.

(*iv*) Energy is transferred through electromagnetic induction.

Principle of transformers

Energy is transferred at the same frequency from primary winding to secondary winding by means of electromagnetic induction. The flux Φ links not only with the secondary winding but also with the primary winding, thus producing self-induced emf in primary winding which limits the primary current.

Transformer must not be connected to a dc source. If primary winding is connected to dc supply mains, flux produced will not vary but remain constant in magnitude and therefore no emf will be induced in secondary winding except at the moment of switching on. Also there will be no back back emf induced in the primary winding. Therefore a heavy current will be drawn from the supply which may result in the burning of the winding.

Transformer Losses. Losses occuring in the transformer are :

1. *Iron losses* (P_i) :

   These are independent of load which occur due to pulsation of flux in the core.

2. *Copper losses* (P_c) :

   These occur due to ohmic resistance of the transformer winding. The purpose of open-circuit test is to determine the iron loss and no-load current.

Open Circuit and Short Circuits Tests. In open-circuit test, secondary is open circuit, and normal voltage is applied to the primary winding of the transformer.

Short-circuit test is performed to determine the full load copper losses by short circuiting the secondary of the transformer.

Equivalent Resistance and Reactance. Equivalent resistance of the transformer as referred to primary R_{01} or as referred to secondary, R_{02} are :

$$R_{01} = r_1 + r_2/K^2$$

or $\qquad R_{02} = r_2 + K^2 r_1$

Equivalent reactance of transformer as referred to primary, X_{01} or as referred to secondary, X_{02} are :

$$X_{01} = x_1 + x_2/K^2$$

$$X_{02} = x_2 + K^2 x_1$$

where r_1, r_2, x_1, x_2 are the resistance and reactance of primary and secondary windings K being the transformation ratio.

Efficiency of Transformer. The parameter is given by :

$$\eta = \frac{V_2 I_2 \cos\phi}{V_2 I_2 \cos\phi + P_i + x^2 P_c}$$

where V_2 is the secondary terminal voltage, I_2 secondary load current, $\cos\phi$ is the power factor of load, and x is the fraction of the load.

Voltage Regulation. This is defined as

Percentage regulation

$$= \left(\frac{I_2 R_{02} \cos\phi \pm I_2 X_{02} \sin\phi}{V_{02}} \right) \times 100$$

where R_{02} and X_{02} are total resistance and reactance of transformer referred to the secondary.

Moreover, + sign to be used for inductive load, and - sign to be used for capacitive load.

Condition for Maximum Efficiency.

Iron losses includes both hysteresis loss and eddy current loss and is practically the same at all loads. Output current at which maximum efficiency occurs

is given by $= \text{Full load} \sqrt{\dfrac{\text{Iron Loss}}{\text{F.L. copper loss}}}$

All day efficiency.

$$\textit{All day efficiency} = \frac{\text{Output in kWh}}{\text{Input in kWh}} \ \text{(for 24 hours.)}$$

The distribution transformers are designed to keep core losses minimum and copper losses are relatively less.

Parallel Operation. *The conditions for successful parallel operation of the single phase transformers are :*

1. The primary and secondary windings should be suitable for supply voltage and frequency.

2. The transformers should be properly connected with regard to polarity.

3. The transformation ratio should be identical.

4. The percentage impedance should be equal.

Scott Connection. It is used to accomplish three-phase to three-phase and three-phase to two-phase transformation.

Stat-star connection is not suitable and economical for small high voltage transformation.

OBJECTIVE TYPE QUESTIONS

1. A transformer transforms
   (a) frequency
   (b) voltage
   (c) current
   (d) both voltage and current

2. A transformer does not change the following
   (a) voltage
   (b) frequency
   (c) waveform
   (d) both frequency and waveform

3. A transformer provides a path for magnetic flux of
   (a) high conductivity
   (b) high reluctance
   (c) low reluctance
   (d) low conductivity

4. An ordinary transformer works on
   (a) a.c
   (b) d.c
   (c) both a.c. and d.c.
   (d) pulsating d.c.

5. An ideal transformer is one which has
   (a) a common core for its primary and secondary windings
   (b) core of stainless steel and winding of pure copper wire
   (c) no losses and magnetic leakage
   (d) interleaved primary and secondary windings

6. The transformer core is generally made of
   (a) alumimium   (b) silicon steel
   (c) copper   (d) wood

7. Which of the following is minimized by laminating the core of a transformer ?
   (a) hysteresis loss
   (b) eddy current loss
   (c) heat loss
   (d) all of these

8. Thickness of laminations of trans-former core is usually of the order of
   (a) 0.35 mm to 0.5 mm
   (b) 3.5 mm to 5 mm
   (c) 35 mm to 50 mm
   (d) 5 mm to 10 mm

9. The main purpose of using core in a transformer is to
   (a) prevent eddy current losses
   (b) prevent hysteresis losses
   (c) decrease reluctance of the common magnetic circuit
   (d) decrease iron losses

10. Transformer works on the principle of
    (a) mutual induction
    (b) self induction
    (c) Faraday's law of electromagnetic induction
    (d) self and mutual induction both

11. If dc voltage is applied to the primary of a transformer it may
    (a) work
    (b) not work
    (c) burn the winding
    (d) give lower voltage on the secondary side

12. Which of the following will improve the mutual coupling between primary and secondary of a transformer ?
    (a) high reluctance magnetic core
    (b) transformer oil of high breakdown voltage
    (c) winding material of high resistivity
    (d) low reluctance magnetic core

13. Which type of core is used for a high frequency transformer
    (a) open iron core
    (b) air core
    (c) closed iron core
    (d) none of these

14. Transformer oil used in tranformer provides
    (a) insulation and cooling
    (b) cooling and lubrication
    (c) lubricaiton and insulation
    (d) insulation, cooling and lubrication

15. Enamel layer is coated over the lamination of a transformer core to
    (a) decrease the hum
    (b) attain adhesion between the lamination
    (c) insulate the laminations from each other
    (d) prevent corosion of laminations

16. The size of transformer core depends on
(*a*) frequency
(*b*) area of the core
(*c*) flux density of core material
(*d*) both (*a*) and (*c*)

17. In power tranformers, breather is used to
(*a*) extract moisture from the air
(*b*) take insulating oil from the con-servator
(*c*) provide cooling to the windings
(*d*) provide insulation to the windings

18. In a transformer, conservator con-sists of
(*a*) an air tight metal drum fixed at the top of the tank
(*b*) drum placed at the bottom of the tank
(*c*) overload protection circuit
(*d*) none of these

19. In a transformer, the resistance between its primary and secondary should be
(*a*) zero   (*b*) infinite
(*c*) about 1 MΩ (*d*) about 100 MΩ

20. For large power tranformer, best utilization of available core space can be made by using
(*a*) rectangular core section
(*b*) square core section
(*c*) stepped core section
(*d*) none of these

21. Five limb core construction of a transformer has advantage over three limb core construction that
(*a*) eddy current loss is less
(*b*) magnetic reluctance of the three phases can be balanced
(*c*) hysteresis loss is less
(*d*) permeability is higher

22. In a transformer, low voltage windings are placed nearer to the core in the case of concentric windings because it reduces
(*a*) hysteresis loss
(*b*) eddy current loss
(*c*) insulation requirement
(*d*) leakage fluxes

23. Transformer windings are tapped in the middle because
(*a*) it reduces insulation requirement
(*b*) it eliminates axial forces on the windings
(*c*) it eliminates radial forces on the windings
(*d*) none of these

24. The primary and secondary induced emfs E_1 and E_2 in two-winding transformer are always
(*a*) equal in magnitude
(*b*) antiphase with each other
(*c*) in phase with each other
(*d*) determined by load on transformer secondary

25. An step-up transformer increases
(*a*) voltage   (*b*) current
(*c*) frequency   (*d*) power

26. Eddy current losses in a transformer core may be reduced by
(*a*) reducing the thickness of lami-nations
(*b*) increasing the thickness of lami-nations
(*c*) increasing the air gap in the magnetic circuit
(*d*) reducing the air gap in the magnetic circuit

27. In a tranformer, the oil must be free from
(*a*) odour   (*b*) sulphur
(*c*) moisture   (*d*) both (*b*) and (*c*)

28. In a tranformer, the magnetic coupling between the primary and secondary circuits can be increased by
(*a*) increasing the number of turns
(*b*) using soft material for windings
(*c*) using magnetic core of low reluc-tance
(*d*) using tranformer oil of better quaitliy

29. If the flux density in the core of a tranformer is increased
(*a*) the frequency the secondary winding voltage increases
(*b*) waveshape of the secondary winding voltage gets distorted
(*c*) size of the transformer can be reduced
(*d*) eddy current losses increase

30. The power factor in a transformer
(*a*) is always unit
(*b*) is always leading
(*c*) is always lagging
(*d*) depends on the power factor of load

31. Which of the following tranformers will be largest is size ?
(*a*) 1 kVA, 50 Hz
(*b*) 1 kVA, 60 Hz
(*c*) 1 kVA, 100 Hz
(*d*) 1 kVA, 500 Hz

32. Which of the following materials is used to absorb moisture from air entering the transformer ?
 (a) sodium chloride (b) silica sand
 (c) felt pad (d) silical gel

33. Which of the following acts as a protection against high voltage surges due to lightening and switching ?
 (a) breather
 (b) conservator
 (c) horn gaps
 (d) thermal overload relays

34. A tap changer is used on a trans-former for
 (a) adjustments in primary voltage
 (b) adjustments in secondary voltage
 (c) adjustments in both primary and secondary voltages
 (d) adjustment in power factor

35. Overcurrents in a transformer affect
 (a) insulation life (b) temperature rise
 (c) mechanical stress (d) all of these

36. Highest rating tranformers are likely to find application in
 (a) distribution (b) generation
 (c) substation (d) transmission

37. Transformer ratings are usually expressed in terms of
 (a) volts (b) k Wh
 (c) kVA (d) kW

38. The noise in a tranformer due to vibration of laminations set by magnetic forces, is called
 (a) flicker noise (b) humming noise
 (c) transit-time noise (d) agitation noise

39. The maximum load that a power transformer can carry is limited by its
 (a) voltage ratio
 (b) copper loss
 (c) temperature noise
 (d) dielectric strength of oil

40. In a three-phase transformer, the phase difference between the pri-mary voltage and the induced secondary winding voltage is
 (a) 90° (b) 120°
 (c) 180° (d) 270°

41. The inductive reactance of a trans-former depends on
 (a) electromotive force
 (b) magnetomotive force
 (c) magnetic flux
 (d) leakage flux

42. When the secondary of the trans-former is loaded, the flux in the transformer constant will
 (a) remain same.
 (b) be directly proportional to secondary current
 (c) be directly proportional to the current drawn by primary winding
 (d) none of these

43. When the secondary of a transformer is loaded, the current in the primary side will
 (a) not be effected
 (b) increase
 (c) decrease
 (d) be the sum of no-load current and excess current drawn due to the secondary current

44. Electric power is transferred from one coil to the other coil in a transformer
 (a) electrically
 (b) electromagnetically
 (c) magnetically
 (d) physically

45. A transformer operates
 (a) always at unity power factor
 (b) has its own constant power factor
 (c) at a power factor always below 0.8
 (d) at power factor depending on the power factor of the load

46. In an ideal transformer on no-load, the primary applied voltage is balanced by
 (a) the secondary voltage
 (b) drop across resistances and reac-tances
 (c) secondary induced emf
 (d) primary induced emf

47. In a transformer, the no load current in terms of full load current is of the order of
 (a) 1 to 3%
 (b) 3 to 10%
 (c) 10 to 20%
 (d) 20 to 30%

48. In a transformer, the magnitude of the mutual flux is

(a) low at low loads and high at high loads

(b) high at low loads and low at high loads

(c) same at all loads

(d) varies at low loads and constant at high loads

49. Use of higher flux density in trans-former design

(a) increases the weight per kVA

(b) decreases the weight per kVA

(c) increases the weight per kW

(d) decreases the weight per kW

50. The efficiency of transformer compared with that of electric motors of the same rating is

(a) about the same   (b) much smaller

(c) slightly higher   (d) much higher

51. The no load current taken by a transformer lags the applied voltage approximately by

(a) $80°$ (b) $60°$

(c) $45°$ (d) $30°$

52. An ideal transformer is one which

(a) has no losses and magnetic leakage

(b) has core of stainelss steel

(c) has inter leaved primary and secondary windings

(d) has a common core for its primary and secondary windings

53. In a two winding transformer, the primary and the secondary induced emfs $E1$ and $E2$ are always

(a) in phase with each other

(b) antiphase with each other

(c) equal in magnitude

(d) of different frequency

54. Distribution transformers are designed to have maximum efficiency at about

(a) no load   (b) 50% of full load

(c) full load   (d) 75% of full load

55. Use of silicon steel for laminations in a transformer reduces

(a) eddy current losses

(b) hysteresis losses

(c) both eddy current and hysteresis losses

(d) noise generated in the transformer

56. Cross-over windings are used for

(a) high voltage winding of small rating transformer

(b) low voltage winding of small rating transformer

(c) high voltage winding rating of large transformer

(d) low voltage winding of large rating transformer

57. Advantage of putting tappings at the phase ends of a transformer is

(a) fine variation of voltage

(b) ease of operation

(c) reduction in number of bearings

(d) better regulation

58. The yoke sections of transformers using hot-rolled laminations is made about 15% larger than that of the core in order to

(a) reduce copper loss

(b) increase the size of transformer

(c) provide better cooling

(d) reduce iron loss in yoke and magnetising current

59. The primary and secondary windings of an ordinary transformer always have

(a) different number of turns

(b) copper wire of same diameter

(c) common magnetic circuit

(d) separate magnetic circuits

60. The leakage flux of a transformer is defined as

(a) the flux which is linked with both the primary and the secondary windings

(b) the flux which is linked either only with the primary or only with the secondary

(c) the flux whose path is exclusively through the air

(d) none of these

61. Helical coils are very well suited for

(a) HV winding of large rating trans-former

(b) HV winding of large rating trans-former

(c) LV winding of small rating trans-former

(d) LV winding of large rating trans-former

62. Compared with the secondary of a loaded step-up transformer, the primary has

(a) lower voltage and higher current

(b) higher voltage and lower current

(c) lower voltage and lower current

(d) higher voltage and higher current

63. Special silicon steel is used for the laminations of transformer, because it has
   (*a*) high resistivity and high hysteresis loss
   (*b*) high resistivity and low hysteresis loss
   (*c*) low resistivity and high hysteresis loss
   (*d*) low resistivity and low hysteresis loss

64. The commercial efficiency of a transformer while on open circuit is
   (*a*) zero   (*b*) 100%
   (*a*) 50 %   (*b*) none of these

65. The direction of the central phase winding of a three-phase shell type transformer is reversed with respect to the outer phases to
   (*a*) save considerable amount of core material
   (*b*) reduce leakage flux
   (*c*) reduce short circuit forces
   (*d*) minimize eddy current loss

66. In a transformer, spiral winding is suitable only for windings
   (*a*) carrying very low current
   (*b*) carrying very high current
   (*c*) rated for high voltage
   (*d*) rated for low voltage

67. In a transformer, continuous disc winding is suitable for
   (*a*) low voltage winding of small trans-formers
   (*b*) high voltage winding of small trans-formers
   (*c*) low voltage winding of large trans-formers
   (*d*) high voltage winding of large trans-formers

68. For transformation ratio k, the transformer secondary impedance has to be multiplied by the following factor to get its equivalent primary impedance
   (*a*) k   (*b*) 1/k
   (*c*) k^2 (*d*) $1/k^2$

69. The magnetic flux in a transformer follows a path of
   (*a*) high reluctance   (*b*) low reluctance
   (*c*) high conductivity   (*d*) low conductivity

70. Use of higher flux density in trans-former design
   (*a*) increases the weight/kVA
   (*b*) decreases the weight/kVA
   (*c*) reduces iron losses
   (*d*) improves insulation

71. In transformers, interlamination insulation is generally provided by
   (*a*) thick paper
   (*b*) thin mica sheet
   (*c*) thin coating varnish
   (*d*) none of these

72. The resistance of the low voltage winding of a transformer
   (*a*) is equal to the resistance of the HV winding
   (*b*) is greater than the resistance of the HV winding
   (*c*) is less than the resistane of the HV winding
   (*d*) may be either more or less han the resistance of the HV winding

73. Transfer of energy from primary to the secondary of a transformer results due to
   (*a*) the difference in the number of primary and secondary turns
   (*b*) changing currents in the two win-dings
   (*c*) magnetic flux linkage between the two windings
   (*d*) all of these

74. The leakage flux in a transformer depends on
   (*a*) the supply frequency
   (*b*) load current
   (*c*) mutual flux
   (*d*) none of these

75. In a transformer, at every instant, the direction of the secondary current is such as to oppose any change of flux. This is as per
   (*a*) Lenz's law
   (*b*) Faraday's law
   (*c*) Coulomb's law
   (*d*) Ampere's law

76. As the load in a transformer increa-ses, the mutual flux linkage in the core
   (*a*) increases
   (*b*) decreases
   (*c*) remains unchanged
   (*d*) first increases and becomes constant

77. The magnetic compting between the primary and the secondary of a transformer may be increased by
   (*a*) increasing the number of lamina-tions of core
   (*b*) changing the turns ratio
   (*c*) using the magnetic core of lower reluctance
   (*d*) none of these

78. A transformer is connected to a constant voltage supply. As the supply frequency increases, the magnetic flux in the core
   (*a*) decreases
   (*b*) increases toward saturation
   (*c*) becomes zero
   (*d*) becomes constant

79. Circular coil sections are generally used in transformer because they
   (*a*) have the toughest mechanical shape
   (*b*) are easy to wound
   (*c*) reduce copper losses
   (*d*) reduce iron losses

80. Good transformer oil should contain water less than
   (*a*) 4 ppm
   (*b*) 8 ppm
   (*c*) 12 ppm
   (*d*) 20 ppm

81. Stepped core limbs are used to
   (*a*) reduce iron material and iron losses
   (*b*) reduce copper material and copper losses
   (*c*) both (a) and (b)
   (*d*) increase mechanical strength of the core

82. Ferrite cores have less eddy current losses than iron losses because ferrites have
   (*a*) low permeability
   (*b*) high hysteresis
   (*c*) high resistance
   (*d*) all of these

83. The secondary of a transformer is never kept open circuited under actual operating conditions to
   (*a*) provide safety to human beings
   (*b*) protect the primary circuit
   (*c*) avoid saturation of core
   (*d*) avoid high voltage insulation

84. The end winding of a power transformer is given extra insulation to protect it against
   (*a*) oil leakage
   (*b*) excessive heating
   (*c*) travelling wave surges on distri-bution lines
   (*d*) none of these

85. The reactance of a transformer is determi-ned by its
   (*a*) leakage flux
   (*b*) common core flux
   (*c*) size of the core
   (*d*) permeability of the core material

86. For getting minimum weight of a transformer, the weight of iron should be
   (*a*) less than the weight of copper
   (*b*) greater than the weight of copper
   (*c*) equal to the weight of copper
   (*d*) none of these

87. A constant current transformer should not have
   (*a*) high value of reactance
   (*b*) a movable secondary winding
   (*c*) a high value of resistance
   (*d*) primary and secondary windings surroun-ding the core

88. The frequency of the impressed voltage of a transformer is increased keeping the magnitude fixed. Out of the two components of the exciting current
   (*a*) the magnetising current increases and the core loss component decreases
   (*b*) the magnetising component decrea-ses and the core loss component increases
   (*c*) both the magnetising and core loss components decrease
   (*d*) both the magnetising and core loss omponents increase

89. Eddy current loss in a transformer depends on
   (*a*) voltage alone
   (*b*) frequency alone
   (*c*) thickness of lamination
   (*d*) all of these

90. Routine efficiency of a transformer depends upon
   (*a*) load current alone
   (*b*) power factor of load alone
   (*c*) both (*a*) and (*b*)
   (*d*) supply frequency

91. Power transformers are usually designed to have maximum efficie-ncy at
   (*a*) a little more than full load
   (*b*) near full load
   (*c*) half load
   (*d*) quarter load

92. The main reason why open circuit test is performed on the low voltage winding of the transformer is that it

(a) draws sufficiently large no-load current for convenient reading

(b) requires least voltage to perform the test

(c) needs minimum power input

(d) has become customary

93. For short circuit and open circuit tests of a transformer, the instru-ments are connected on

(a) LV side and HV side respectively

(b) HV side and LV side respectively

(c) HV side only

(d) LV side only

94. Two transformers operating in pararllel share the load depending on their

(a) efficiency   (b) rating

(c) leakage reactance   (d) per unit impedance

95. Incorrect polarity in parallel operation of two transformers results in

(a) open circuit

(b) short circuit

(c) regeneration of power

(d) load sharing proportional to their kVA rating

96. In parallel operation of trans-formers, to reduce copper loss

(a) they should have equal turns ratio

(b) their phases should be the same

(c) they should have zero impedance

(d) none of these

97. Essential condition for parallel operation of two single phase trans-formers is that they should have same

(a) efficiency

(b) capacity

(c) voltage ratio

(d) polarity

98. In an autotransformer, power is transferred through

(a) conduction process alone

(b) induction process alone

(c) both conduction and induction processes

(d) mutual coupling

99. If a two-winding step down trans-former is converted into an auto-transformer by using additive polarity, then

(a) the kVA rating gets reduced

(b) the kVA rating gets increased considerably

(c) the kVA rating remain unchanged

(d) none of these

100. The main advantage of an auto-transformer over a two winding transformer is that

(a) is uses only one winding

(b) core losses are reduced

(c) it needs no cooling

(d) it has simple construction

<u>ANSWERS</u>

1. (d)	**2.** (d)	**3.** (c)	**4.** (a)	**5.** (c)	**6.** (b)	**7.** (b)	**8.** (a)	**9.** (c)	**10.** (d)
11. (c)	**12.** (d)	**13.** (b)	**14.** (a)	**15.** (c)	**16.** (d)	**17.** (a)	**18.** (a)	**19.** (b)	**20.** (c)
21. (b)	**22.** (c)	**23.** (b)	**24.** (c)	**25.** (a)	**26.** (a)	**27.** (d)	**28.** (c)	**29.** (c)	**30.** (d)
31. (d)	**32.** (d)	**33.** (c)	**34.** (b)	**35.** (d)	**36.** (b)	**37.** (c)	**38.** (b)	**39.** (a)	**40.** (c)
41. (d)	**42.** (a)	**43.** (d)	**44.** (c)	**45.** (d)	**46.** (c)	**47.** (a)	**48.** (c)	**49.** (b)	**50.** (d)
51. (a)	**52.** (a)	**53.** (a)	**54.** (b)	**55.** (b)	**56.** (a)	**57.** (c)	**58.** (d)	**59.** (c)	**60.** (b)
61. (d)	**62.** (a)	**63.** (b)	**64.** (a)	**65.** (a)	**66.** (b)	**67.** (d)	**68.** (c)	**69.** (b)	**70.** (b)
71. (c)	**72.** (c)	**73.** (c)	**74.** (b)	**75.** (a)	**76.** (c)	**77.** (c)	**78.** (b)	**79.** (a)	**80.** (b)
81. (b)	**82.** (c)	**83.** (c)	**84.** (c)	**85.** (b)	**86.** (c)	**87.** (c)	**88.** (c)	**89.** (d)	**90.** (c)
91. (c)	**92.** (a)	**93.** (b)	**94.** (d)	**95.** (b)	**96.** (a)	**97.** (d)	**98.** (c)	**99.** (b)	**100.** (a)

■■

Induction Motor. It is the most widely used a.c. motor because of its low cost, simple and extremely rugged construction, high efficiency, reasonably good power factor, and simple starting arrangement.

Principle of Operation. When a three-phase stator windings are fed by three-phase supply, a magnetic flux of constant magnitude but rotating at synchronous speed is set up. The flux passes through the air gap, and cuts the stationary rotor conductors. Due to relative speed between rotating magnetic flux and stationary conductors, an emf is induced in the conductors according to Faraday's law of electromagnetic induction and its direction is given by Fleming's right hand rule. Since the rotor conductors are in a closed circuit, rotor current is produced whose direction is such as to oppose the cause which is producing it. Rotor current is produced due to relative speed between rotating flux of stator and stationary rotor conductors. Hence to reduce the relative speed, the rotor starts running in the same direction as that of the flux and tries to catch up with the rotating flux.

Induction motor consists of two parts

1. Stationary part called stator
2. Revolving part called rotor.

It is mainly of two types :

1. Squirrel cage type
2. Wound rotor type

Phase supply produces a rotating magnetic field which rotate at synchronous speed, given by $N = \dfrac{120f}{P}$

An induction motor cannot run at synchronous speed. If it were possible, by some means for the rotor to attain synchronous speed, the rotor would then be standing still with respect to the rotating flux with the result that no emf would be induced in the rotor, no rotor current would flow and therefore there would be no torque developed.

Slip of an induction motor(s) :

$$s = \dfrac{\text{synchronous speed} - \text{rotor speed}}{\text{synchronous speed}}$$

Rotor current frequency,

$$f' = \text{slip} \times \text{supply frequency}$$

Starting torque is maximum when rotor resistance equals rotor reactance *i.e.,* $R_2 = X_2$.

Torque under running conditions is maximum at that value of slip s, which makes rotor reactance per phase equal to rotor resistance per phase.

The slip of an inductor motors can be measured by actual measurement of motor speed or, comparing rotor and stator supply frequencies with d.c. moving coil millivolt-meter, and stroboscopic method.

Rotor copper loss in induction motor = $s \times$ rotor input

Synchronous wattage. It is the power transferred across the air-gap to the rotor.

Torque is synchronous watt = rotor input.

No load current is 40%–50% of full load current.

Electrical equivalent of mechanical load on motor

$$= R_2 \, (1/s - 1).$$

Power output of an induction motor is maximum when equivalent load resistance is equal to the stand-still leakage impedance of the motor.

Double Squirrel Cage Motor. A double squirrel cage motor consists of two independent cages on the same rotor one inside the other. The outer cage consists of a high resistance metal whereas the inner cags has low resistance copper bars. It has high starting torque without sacrificing its electical efficiency under normal running conditions.

SPEED CONTROL OF INDUCTION MOTOR

It can be achieved by following methods :

(*i*) Changing the applied voltage

(*ii*) Changing the applied frequency

(*iii*) Changing the number of stator poles

(*iv*) Injecting an emf in the rotor circuit

(*v*) Cascading, and

(*vi*) Rotor rheostat control

OBJECTIVE TYPE QUESTIONS

1. In an induction motor, rotor slots are usually not quite parallel to the shaft but are given a slight skew
   - (*a*) to reduce the magnetic hum
   - (*b*) to reduce the locking tendency of the rotor
   - (*c*) both (*a*) and (*b*) above
   - (*d*) to increase the speed of the motor

2. In an induction motor, rotor runs at a speed
   - (*a*) equal to the speed of stator field
   - (*b*) lower than the speed of stator field
   - (*c*) higher than the speed of stator field
   - (*d*) having no relation with the speed of stator field

3. When an induction motor runs at rated load and speed, the iron losses are
   - (*a*) negligible
   - (*b*) very heavy
   - (*c*) independent of supply frequency
   - (*d*) independent of supply voltage

4. The emf induced in the rotor of an induction motor is proportional to
   - (*a*) voltage applied to stator
   - (*b*) relative velocity between flux and rotor conductors
   - (*c*) both (a) and (b) above
   - (*d*) slip

5. The starting torque of an indiction motor is maximum when
   - (*a*) rotor resistance equals rotor reactance
   - (*b*) rotor resistance is twice the rotor reactance
   - (*c*) rotor resistance is half the rotor reactance
   - (*d*) rotor resistance is R_2 times the rotor reactance

6. Wattmeter reading in no load test of induction motor gives
   - (*a*) copper losses in the stator
   - (*b*) friction and winding losses
   - (*c*) sum of (*a*) and (*b*) above
   - (*d*) total losses in the rotor on no load

7. The slip frequency of an induction motor is
   - (*a*) the frequency of rotor currents
   - (*b*) the frequency of stator currents
   - (*c*) difference of the frequencies of the stator and rotor currents
   - (*d*) sum of the frequencies of the stator and rotor currents

8. At zero in an induction motor
   - (*a*) the motor runs at synchronous speed
   - (*b*) motor runs as a generator
   - (*c*) motor does not run
   - (*d*) slip produced is zero

9. The field of an induction motor rotor rotates relative to the stator at
   - (*a*) rotor speed
   - (*b*) synchronous speed
   - (*c*) slip speed
   - (*d*) very low speed

10. Starters are used in induction motor because
    - (*a*) its starting torque is high
    - (*b*) it is run against heavy load
    - (*c*) it can not run in reverse direction
    - (*d*) its starting current is five times or more than its rated current

11. By synchronous wattage of an induction motor is meant
    - (*a*) stator input in watts
    - (*b*) rotor output in watts
    - (*c*) rotor input in watts
    - (*d*) shaft output in watts

12. The synchronous speed of an induction motor is defined as
    - (*a*) natural speed at which a magnetic field rotates
    - (*b*) the speed of a synchronous motor
    - (*c*) the speed of an induction motor at no load
    - (*d*) none of these

13. Three-phase induction motor is mainly suitable for which of the following application
    - (*a*) For running different machine tools where several speeds are required
    - (*b*) For running paper machine requiring exact speed control
    - (*c*) For running electric vehicles
    - (*d*) For running rolling mills needing exact speed control

14. The field winding of a three phase synchronous machine is excited by
 (a) single-phase ac supply
 (b) three-phase ac supply
 (c) dc supply
 (d) supply obtained from an inverter

15. When a polyphase induction motor is loaded
 (a) increases and its frequency decreases
 (b) increases and its frequency increases
 (c) decreases and its frequency increases
 (d) decreases and its frequency decreases

16. If in a 3-phase induction motor, two phases open accidently, the motor will
 (a) run at dangerously high speed
 (b) stop
 (c) continue to run depending on load
 (d) none of these

17. A three-phase synchronous machine is a
 (a) singly excited machine
 (b) doubly excited machine
 (c) machine in which three-phase supply is fed to both stator and rotor winding
 (d) none of these

18. Squirrel cage induction motor has
 (a) zero starting torque
 (b) very small starting torque
 (c) medium starting torque
 (d) very high starting torque

19. The purpose of blades in a squirrel cage induction motor is
 (a) to reduce the magnetic resistance of the roor
 (b) to cool the rotor
 (c) to reduce the electrical resistance of rotor cage
 (d) none of these

20. Which of the following is the advantage of double squirrel cage rotor as compared to the round bar cage rotor ?
 (a) larger slip
 (b) lower starting torque
 (c) higher power factor
 (d) higher efficiency

21. On open circuiting the rotor of a squirrel cage induction motor, the rotor
 (a) makes noise
 (b) does not run
 (c) does not run
 (d) runs at dangerously high speed

22. With increase of load, the speed of induction motor operating in the stable region
 (a) increases
 (b) decreases
 (c) remains constant
 (d) increases and then becomes constant

23. In the following motor, external resistance can be added to start the motor
 (a) slip ring induction motor
 (b) squirrel cage induction motor
 (c) salient pole synchronous motor
 (d) wound rotor synchronous motor

24. An induction motor is running at its rated torque and rated applied voltage of 440 volts. The effect of reducing the applied voltage to say 350 volts is
 (a) that the motor stops
 (b) current decreases slightly
 (c) speed reduces slightly
 (d) motor heats up with passage of time

25. The disadvantage of starting an induction motor with a star-delta starter is that
 (a) the starting torque is one-third of the torque in case of delta connection
 (b) during starting high losses result
 (c) the starting torque increases and the motor runs with jerks
 (d) none of these

26. Improvement of the power factor in an induction motor results in
 (a) decreased torque
 (b) increased torque
 (c) increased torque current
 (d) increased torque and decreased current due to increased impedance

27. Which of the following function is served by the resistance placed in parallel with one phase of three-phase induction motor ?
 (a) smooth starting
 (b) higher starting torque
 (c) higher maximum torque
 (d) highly reduced starting torque

28. The rotor output of an induction motor is $15\,kW$ and the slip is 4%. Then the rotor copper loss is
 (a) 600 watts
 (b) 300 watts
 (c) 700 watts
 (d) 1200 watts

29. The drawback of speed control of a slip ring induction motor with the help of resistances in the circuit is that

(a) the speed can be controlled only very broadly

(b) with reduction in speed, the torque decreases significantly

(c) it results in high losses

(d) it is applicable only to motors having power of more than 100 kW

30. In an induction motor, the rotor input is 600 W and slip is 4%. The rotor copper loss is

(a) 650 W

(b) 600 W

(c) 625 W

(d) 700 W

31. For smooth starting of three-phase squirrel cage induction motor, the starting method preferred is

(a) rotor resistance

(b) star-delta

(c) auto-transformer

(d) stator resistance

32. The power factor of star connected induction motor is 0.5. On being connected in delta, the power factor will ?

(a) become zero

(b) remain the same

(c) reduce

(d) increase

33. Any odd harmonic in the current of an induction motor will result in magnetic field which

(a) oscillates at harmonic frequency

(b) rotates in backward direction

(c) rotates in forward direction at the harmonic speed

(d) is stationary relative to the field of the fundamental

34. Cogging of motor implies that motor

(a) runs at very low speed

(b) runs at low speed and then stops

(c) refuses to start at no load

(d) refuses to start at load

35. In a double cage induction motor, the inner cage has

(a) low R and low X

(b) low R and high X

(c) high R and high X

(d) high R and low X

36. Number of different speeds that can be obtained from two induction motors in cascade is

(a) 2

(b) 3

(c) 4

(d) 6

37. Advantage of slip ring induction motor over squirrel cage induction motor is

(a) suitability of higher speeds

(b) higher efficiency

(c) higher power factor

(d) that it can be started using factor resistance

38. The starting torque of a cage rotor induction motor can be increased by using rotor having

(a) low inductance and low resistance

(b) low inductance and high resistance

(c) high inductance and high resistance

(d) high inductance and low resistance

39. Large air gap in an induction motor results in

(a) increased overload capacity

(b) better cooling

(c) reduced pulsation losses

(d) reduced noise

40. Simplest method of eliminating the harmonic induction torque is

(a) skewing

(b) chording

(c) integral slot winding

(d) none of these

41. The drive generally used for lathe machines are

(a) squirrel cage induction motors

(b) synchronous motors

(c) slip ring induction motors

(d) dc shunt motors

42. Motor commonly used for traction purpose is

(a) induction motor

(b) dc shunt motor

(c) dc series motor

(d) synchronous motor

43. Maximum power developed in a synchronous motor occurs at a coupling angle of

(a) 0°

(b) 60°

(c) 90°

(d) 120°

44. The back emf set up in the stator of synchro-nous motor depends on
(a) coupling angle
(b) rotor excitation
(c) speed of the rotor
(d) input to prime mover

45. Synchronous induction motors are mostly used for driving
(a) lathe machines
(b) cranes
(c) rotary compressors
(d) none of these

46. The noise and tooth pulsation losses may be reduced by using
(a) large number of open slots in stator
(b) large number of narrow slots in stator
(c) small number of open slots in stator
(d) small number of narrow slots in stator

47. When a 3-phase synchronous motor is switched on, there exists a rotating magnetic field. The magnitude of this field flux
(a) is constant at all loads
(b) varies with load
(c) varies with power factor
(d) none of these

48. Which of the following motors is most suitable for best speed control ?
(a) dc series motor
(b) dc shunt motor
(c) induction motor
(d) synchronous motor

49. If the frequency of input power to an induction motor increases, the rotor copper loss
(a) increases
(b) decreases
(c) remains the same
(d) none of these

50. The stator frame in an induction motor is used
(a) as a return path for the flux
(b) to hold the armature stampings/stator
(c) to protect the whole machine
(d) to provide ventilation to the armature

51. The speed of a three-phase cage-rotor induction motor depends on
(a) frequency of the supply only
(b) number of pole alone
(c) number of poles and frequency of supply
(d) input voltage

52. Dispersion coefficient σ is the ratio of
(a) magnetising current to supply voltage
(b) magnetising current to ideal short circuit current
(c) open circuit voltage to short circuit current for the same excitation
(d) none of these

53. The fractional slip of an induction motor is to ratio
(a) rotor Cu loss/rotor input
(b) stator Cu loss/stator input
(c) rotor Cu loss/rotor output
(d) rotor Cu loss/stator Cu loss

54. The complete circle diagram of a 3-phase induction motor can be drawn with the help of
(a) running-light test alone
(b) both running-light and blocked-rotor tests
(c) running-light and blocked-rotor and stator-resistance tests
(d) blocked rotor test alone.

55. A SCIM runs at constant speed only so long as
(a) torque developed by it remains constant
(b) its supply voltage remains constant
(c) its torque exactly equals the mechanical load
(d) stator flux remains constant

56. The synchronous speed of a linear induction motor does NOT depend on
(a) width of pole pitch
(b) number of poles
(c) supply frequency
(d) any of the above

57. If the stator voltage and frequency of an induction motor are reduced proportionately, its
(a) locked rotor current is reduced
(b) torque developed is increased
(c) magnetising current is decreased
(d) both (a) and (b)

58. Motor A has deeper and narrow slots, whereas motor B. It has shallow and wide slots. Induction motor A, as compared to motor B, has
(*a*) more starting torque
(*b*) more pull-out torque
(*c*) less starting torque
(*d*) more operating slip

59. Single phase induction motor can be made self starting by
(*a*) adding series combination of capacitor and auxiliary winding in parallel with the main winding
(*b*) adding an auxiliary winding in parallel with the main winding
(*c*) adding an auxiliary winding in series with a capacitor and the main winding
(*d*) none of these

60. All single phase motors have
(*a*) very small starting torque
(*b*) medium starting torque
(*c*) zero starting torque
(*d*) large starting torque

61. Single phase motors generally get overheated due to
(*a*) overloading   (*b*) short windings
(*c*) bearing troubles   (*d*) any of above

62. If a single phase motor runs slow, it may be due to
(*a*) overload   (*b*) low freuency
(*c*) low voltag   (*d*) any of these

63. Which of the following single phase motors is cheapest ?
(*a*) Capacitor start motor
(*b*) Capacitor run motor
(*c*) Reluctance motor
(*d*) All have almost the same cost

64. If a single phase motor runs hot, the probable cause may be
(*a*) overload   (*b*) low voltage
(*c*) high voltage   (*d*) amu pf the abpve

65. Which of the following single phase motors is relaively free from mechanical and magnetic vibration?
(*a*) Reluctance motor   (*b*) Hysteresis motor
(*c*) Universal motor   (*d*) Shaded pole motor

66. Which of the following single phase motors does not have constant speed characteristics ?
(*a*) Reluctance motor   (*b*) Hysteresis motor
(*c*) Universal motor   (*d*) All of the above

67. For the same rating which of the following motors has the highest starting torque ?
(*a*) Universal motor
(*b*) Split phase motor
(*c*) Synchronous motor
(*d*) all have identical starting torque

68. If a single phase motor fails to start, the probable cause may be
(*a*) open circuit in auxiliary winding
(*b*) open circuit in main winding
(*c*) blown fuses
(*d*) any of the above

69. The speed of the split phase induction motor can be reversed by reversing the leads of
(*a*) auxiliary winding
(*b*) main winding
(*c*) either (*a*) or (*b*)
(*d*) speed can not be reversed

70. A capacitor start single phase induction motor will usually have power factor of
(*a*) unity   (*b*) 0.6 leading
(*c*) 0.8 leading   (*d*) 0.6 lagging

ANSWERS

1. (*c*)	**2.** (*b*)	**3.** (*a*)	**4.** (*c*)	**5.** (*a*)	**6.** (*d*)	**7.** (*a*)	**8.** (*c*)	**9.** (*b*)	**10.** (*d*)
11. (*c*)	**12.** (*a*)	**13.** (*a*)	**14.** (*c*)	**15.** (*a*)	**16.** (*c*)	**17.** (*c*)	**18.** (*b*)	**19.** (*b*)	**20.** (*b*)
21. (*c*)	**22.** (*b*)	**23.** (*a*)	**24.** (*d*)	**25.** (*a*)	**26.** (*d*)	**27.** (*a*)	**28.** (*a*)	**29.** (*c*)	**30.** (*c*)
31. (*c*)	**32.** (*c*)	**33.** (*b*)	**34.** (*c*)	**35.** (*b*)	**36.** (*c*)	**37.** (*d*)	**38.** (*c*)	**39.** (*c*)	**40.** (*b*)
41. (*a*)	**42.** (*c*)	**43.** (*c*)	**44.** (*b*)	**45.** (*c*)	**46.** (*b*)	**47.** (*a*)	**48.** (*b*)	**49.** (*a*)	**50.** (*a*)
51. (*c*)	**52.** (*b*)	**53.** (*a*)	**54.** (*c*)	**55.** (*c*)	**56.** (*a*)	**57.** (*d*)	**58.** (*c*)	**59.** (*a*)	**60.** (*c*)
61. (*d*)	**62.** (*d*)	**63.** (*a*)	**64.** (*d*)	**65.** (*b*)	**66.** (*c*)	**67.** (*a*)	**68.** (*d*)	**69.** (*c*)	**70.** (*d*)

■■

5

CHAPTER

Alternators and Synchronous Motors

An alternator consists of a stator and a rotor. The stator provides the armature windings whereas rotor provides the rotating magnetic field.

Basic Principle.

When rotor is rotated by the prime-mover, the stator winding or conductors are cut by the magnetic flux of the rotor magnetic poles. Hence an emf is induced in the stator conductors. The emf generated in the stator conductors is taken out from three leads connected to the stator winding as shown in the figure.

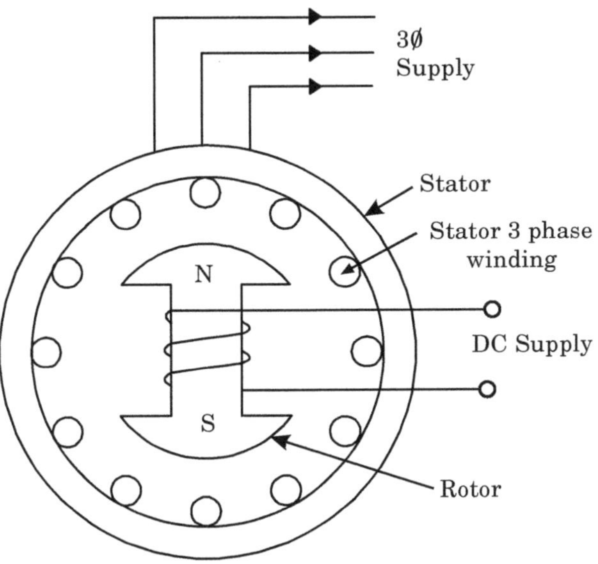

Types of Pole.

The rotors are of two types :

1. **Salient pole type :** It is used for low and medium speed alternators.

2. **Smooth cylindrical type :** It is used for turbo-alternator.

Frequency of alternating current produced is

$$f = \frac{PN}{120} \text{Hz,}$$

P and N being the no. of poles and speed.

EMF equation of an alternator

$$E = 4.44 \, K_c \, K_d \, \Phi \, fT \text{ volts/phase}$$

where K_c coil span factor = $\cos(\alpha/2)$, (α is angle by which the coil span falls short),

$$K_d = \text{distribution factor} = \frac{\sin m\beta/2}{m\sin\beta/2},$$

(*m* is number of slots/pole/phase)

$$\beta = \left(\frac{180°}{\text{No. of slots/pole}}\right)$$

Voltage Regulation. Terminal voltage V is less than open-circuit voltage E_0 because of

(*i*) armature drop, IR_a

(*ii*) synchronous reactance drop IX_s

(*iii*) armature reaction drop IX_a.

$$\% \text{ Voltage regulation} = \frac{E_0 - V}{V} \times 100$$

Voltage regulation can be found by Synchronous Impedance Method, M.M.F. Method, and Zero Power-Factor method.

SYNCHRONOUS MOTORS

Synchronization

For proper synchronization of alternators, the following conditions must be satisfied :

1. terminal voltage of the incoming alternator must be the same as bus-bar voltage.

2. speed of the incoming machine must be such that its frequency equals bus-bar frequency.

3. phase of the alternator voltage must be identical with the phase of the bus-bar voltage.

Synchronizing current, $I_{sy} = \dfrac{E_r}{Z_s}$

Synchronizing power, $P_{sy} = \alpha E I_{sy}$ watts/phase

Synchronizing torque, $T_{sy} = \dfrac{3 \times 60 \times P_{sy}}{2\pi N_s}$ N m

Synchronous Motor. It is electrically identical with an alternator.

Characteristics of synchronous motors :

(*a*) It runs at synchronous speed, $N_s = 120f/P$

(*b*) It is not inherently self-starting.

(*c*) It is capable of being operated under a wide range of power factors both lagging as well as leading.

Magnitude of armature current varies with excitation. When over-excited, motor runs with leading p.f., and with lagging p.f. when under-excited.

Torque developed by the motor depends on the coupling angle.

In synchronous motor, minimum current corresponds to unity power factor.

Methods of Starting Synchronous Motors.

Since the synchronous motors has no self-starting torque, therefore it is necessary that an external means is to be employed to start the motor.

Various methods are :

1. **D.C. source.** The synchronous motor is coupled to a d.c. compound motor, whose speed is adjusted by a speed regulator. The synchronous motor is then excited and synchronized with the a.c. supply. At the moment of synchronizing the synchronous motor is switched on to a.c. mains and d.c. motor is disconnected from the d.c. supply mains or its field is strengthened until it begins to function as a generator. Otherwise synchronous motor will act as an a.c. motor with d.c. motor as its load.

2. **By means of a.c. Motor.** Synchronous motor with an exciter is coupled with a small induction motor. Before switching the a.c. supply to the synchronous motor it must be synchronized to the bus-bar. The induction motor used for starting should have lesser number of poles than synchronous motor so that it may be capable of bringing the synchronous motor to the synchronous speed. After normal operation has been established, the induction motor is sometimes uncoupled from the synchronous motor.

3. **Self-starting.** The synchronous motor can be made self-starting by providing a special winding on the rotor poles known as *damper winding or squirrel cage winding*. It consists of short-circuited-copper bars embedded in the face of the field pole. A.C. supply given to the stator produces a rotating magnetic field which causes the rotor to rotate. Therefore in the beginning the synchronous motor with damper winding starts as squirrel cage induction motor.

When the motor approaches its synchronous speed, the rotor winding is connected to the exciter winding so that the rotor is magnetically looked by the rotating field of the stator and thus the motor runs as synchronous motor.

HUNTING

When a synchronous motor is connected to a varying load, a condition known as hunting is produced which may also occur if the supply frequency is pulsating (*e.g.* when connected to reciprocating engines). When a synchronous motor is on load, its rotor falls back in phase by a coupling angle δ. As the load is increased progressively, this angle also increases so as to produce more torque, to follow with the increased load. If there is sudden decrease in the load, the motor is immediately pulled up or advanced to a new value corresponding to a new load. But in this process, the rotor overshoots, hence it is again pulled back. In this way the rotor starts oscillating about its new position of equilibrium corresponding to new load. If the time period of these oscillation happens to be equal to natural time period of the machine, the mechanical resonance is set up. The amplitude of these oscillations is built up to a large value and may eventually become so great that the machine is thrown out of synchronism. To stop the build up of these oscillations, circuit dampers are employed which consist of short-copper bars embedded in the faces of the field poles of the motor. The oscillation of the rotor sets up eddy currents in the dampers which flow in such a way so as to suppress the oscillations.

Application of synchronous motors :

1. It is used in power houses and substations in parallel with bus-bars to improve the power-factor.

2. In factories having large number of induction motors or other apparatus operating with lagging power factor, these motors are used in order to improve the power factor.

3. It is used as booster to control the voltage at the end of transmission line by varying its excitation.

4. It is used in rubber, textile and cement mills, and other big industries for power application.

5. It is used to derive continuously operating and constant speed equipment such as centrifugal pumps, blowers, and motor generators.

OBJECTIVE TYPE QUESTIONS

1. Alternator works on the principle of
   (a) mutual induction
   (b) Faraday's law of electromagnetic induction
   (c) self mutual induction
   (d) self and mutual induction

2. The rotor of alternator has
   (a) no slip rings
   (b) two slip rings
   (c) three slip rings
   (d) four slip rings

3. The generator which gives dc supply to the rotor of an alternator is called
   (a) convertor   (b) exciter
   (c) inverter   (d) rectifier

4. In alternators, salient pole type rotors are generally used with prime movers of
   (a) high speed
   (b) low speed
   (c) medium speed
   (d) any speed

5. In alternators, cylindrical pole type rotors are generally used with prime movers of
   (a) high speed
   (b) low speed
   (c) medium speed
   (d) both low and high speeds

6. The frequency of voltage generated in an alternator depends on
   (a) number of poles
   (b) speed of alternator
   (c) both (a) and (b)
   (d) type of winding

7. Salient pole type rotors are
   (a) larger in diameter and smaller in axial length
   (b) larger in diameter and larger in axial length
   (c) smaller in diameter and larger in axial length
   (d) smaller in diameter and smaller in axial length

8. The emf generated in alternator depends on
   (a) frequency
   (b) flux per pole
   (c) coil span factor
   (d) all of these

9. The number of electrical degrees passed through in one revolution of a four pole synchronous alternator is
   (a) 360°
   (b) 720°
   (c) 1440°
   (d) 2880°

10. As the speed of an alternator increases, the frequency
   (a) increases
   (b) decreases
   (c) remains constant
   (d) may increase or decrease depending on the power factor

11. An alternator is said to be overexcited when it is operating at
   (a) unity power factor
   (b) leading power factor
   (c) lagging power factor
   (d) either lagging or leading power factor

12. The frequency per pole in an alternator is equal to
   (a) number of poles
   (b) number of armature conductors
   (c) number of pair of poles
   (d) none of these

13. The exciter for a generator is a
   (a) series motor
   (b) shunt motor
   (c) compound motor
   (d) shunt generator

14. The rotor of a salient pole alternator has 12 poles. The number of cycles of emf per revolution would be
   (a) 12   (b) 6
   (c) 3   (d) 4

15. The advantage of salient poles in an alternator is
   (a) reduced noise
   (b) reduced windage loss
   (c) adaptability to low and medium speed operations
   (d) reduced bearing loads and noise

16. In an alternator, when the load increases due to armature reaction, the terminal voltage
   (*a*) drops
   (*b*) rises
   (*c*) remains unchanged
   (*d*) may drop or rise

17. The exciting field coil of an alternator is generally excited by
   (*a*) a separate dc generator driven by some source
   (*b*) a separate ac generator driven by some source
   (*c*) a dc generator coupled directly to the armature shaft
   (*d*) a battery

18. The ratio of armature leakage reactance to synchronous reactance of large size modern alternator is about
   (*a*) 0.05   (*b*) 0.2
   (*c*) 0.4   (*d*) 0.6

19. High speed alternators usually have
   (*a*) salient pole rotors
   (*b*) cylindrical rotors
   (*c*) both salient pole and cylindrical rotors
   (*d*) none of these

20. Cylindrical rotor alternators have
   (*a*) large length to diameter ratio
   (*b*) small length to diameter ratio
   (*c*) vertical configuration
   (*d*) none of these

21. To ensure effective cooling, cylindrical rotor alternators use
   (*a*) radial ducts only
   (*b*) axial ducts only
   (*c*) both radial and axial ducts
   (*d*) forced air cooling

22. The main advantage of using fractional pitch winding in an alternator is to reduce
   (*a*) amount of copper in the winding
   (*b*) size of the machine
   (*c*) harmonics in the generated emf
   (*d*) cost of the machine

23. The pitch factor in rotating electrical machines is defined as the ratio of the resultant emf of a
   (*a*) full pitched coil to that of a chorded coil
   (*b*) full pitch to the phase emf
   (*c*) chorded coil to the phase emf
   (*d*) chorded coil to that of a full pitched coil

24. In a rotating electrical machine, the chording angle for eliminating fifth harmonic should be
   (*a*) 30°   (*b*) 33°
   (*c*) 36°   (*d*) 38°

25. The material used for the manufacture of large turbo-alternator is
   (*a*) hot rolled grain oriented steel
   (*b*) cold rolled grain oriented steel
   (*c*) cast steel
   (*d*) wrought iron

26. Use of damped winding in alternators results in
   (*a*) elimination of harmonic effects
   (*b*) a low resistance path for the currents due to unbalancing of voltage
   (*c*) oscillations when two alternators operate in parallel
   (*d*) all of these

27. In a synchronous machine, if the field flux axis ahead of the armature field axis in the direction of rotation, the machine is working as
   (*a*) asynchronous motor
   (*b*) asynchronous generator
   (*c*) synchronous motor
   (*d*) synchronous generator

28. In an alternator, the armature reaction is completely magnetising when the load power factors is
   (*a*) unity   (*b*) 0.07
   (*c*) zero lagging   (*d*) zero leading

29. Which of the following is not an integral part of a synchronous generator system ?
   (*a*) Prime mover
   (*b*) Excitation system
   (*c*) Distribution transformer
   (*d*) Protection system

30. Cross magnetisation in an alternator field results in output which is
   (*a*) true sinusoidal
   (*b*) nonsinusoidal
   (*c*) harmonic free
   (*d*) none of these

31. In an alternator, in order to reduce the harmonics in the generated emf
   (*a*) slots are skewed
   (*b*) salient pole tips are changed
   (*c*) winding is made well distributed
   (*d*) all of these

32. Permissible variation in supply frequency of alternators is
(a) ±1%
(b) ±2%
(c) ±4%
(d) ±6%

33. Unbalanced 3-phase stator currents in an alternator cause
(a) heating of rotor
(b) vibrations
(c) double frequency currents in the rotor
(d) all of these

34. In large synchronous generators, protection provided against external faults is
(a) biased differenctial protection
(b) sensitive earth fault protection
(c) inter-turn fault protection
(d) all of these

35. The following part plays important role in overspeed protection of an alternator
(a) overcurrent relay
(b) alarm
(c) differential protection
(d) governor

36. In alternators, the distribution factor is defined as the ratio of emfs of
(a) distributed winding to concentrated winding
(b) full pitch winding to distributed winding
(c) distributed winding to full pitch winding
(d) concentrated winding to distributed winding

37. For the same power rating, an alternator operating at lower voltage will be
(a) less noisy
(b) costlier
(c) larger in size
(d) more efficient

38. The maximum current that can be supplied by an alternator depends on
(a) speed of the exciter
(b) number of poles
(c) exciter current
(d) strength of the magnetic field

39. In an alternator, use of short pitch coil of 160° will indicate the absence of following harmonic
(a) third
(b) fifth
(c) seventh
(d) ninth

40. Overheating of windings of an alternator
(a) reduces generated voltage
(b) reduces power factor
(c) reduces life of the machine
(d) causes no significant evil effect

41. The necessary condition for parallel operation of two alternators is
(a) terminal voltage should be the same
(b) frequency should be the same
(c) phase sequence should be the same
(d) all of these

42. When two alternators are running in parrallel, if the prime mover of one of the alternators is disconnected, then alternator will
(a) stop running
(b) run as a synchronous motor
(c) run as a generator
(d) none of these

43. Two alternators are running in parallel. If the driving force of both the alternators is changed, there will be changed in
(a) frequency
(b) back emf
(c) generated voltage
(d) all of these

44. In a synchronous machine with damped winding, the damping torque at negative slip developed by damped winding acts to
(a) increase the speed
(b) decrease the speed
(c) either increase or decrease the speed
(d) change the frequency

45. The rotor of a high speed tubro-alternator is made up of solid steel forging to get
(a) high mechanical stress
(b) economy
(c) reduction of eddy current loss
(d) reduction of bearing friction

46. In a 3-phase alternator, the unsaturated synchronous reactance of 3Ω per phase. Then saturated synchronous reactance is
(a) 3Ω
(b) $>3\Omega$
(c) $<3\Omega$
(d) $>> 3\Omega$

47. The rated voltage of alternaors used in power satations is usually
(a) 11 kV
(b) 33 kV
(c) 66 kV
(d) 132 kV

48. Salient pole machines have
(a) large number of poles
(b) small number of poles
(c) small diameters
(d) long cores

49. The stator of modern alternators are wound for
(a) 60° phase groups
(b) 120 ° phase groups
(c) 180° phase groups
(d) 240° phase groups

50. The armature reaction of an alternator influences
(a) windage losses
(b) operating speed
(c) generated voltage per phase
(d) waveform of generated voltage

51. When an alternator is supplying unity power factor load, the armature reaction will produce
(a) magnetisation of the main field
(b) demagnetisation of the main field
(c) distortion of the main field
(d) none of these

52. Two alternators are running in parallel. The excitation of one of the alternators is increased. The result will be that
(a) machine with excess excitation will burn
(b) both machines will start vibrating
(c) power output will decrease
(d) wattless component will change

53. Alternators are generally designed to generate
(a) fixed frequencies
(b) variable frequencies
(c) fixed currents
(d) fixed power factors

54. In thermal stations, the number of poles used in alternators are usually
(a) 48   (b) 12
(c) 24   (d) none

55. In a synchronous alternator, the frequency f in Hz is given by
(a) $f = \dfrac{PN}{120}$ (b) $f = \dfrac{PN}{60}$
(c) $f = \dfrac{P}{60N}$ (d) $f = \dfrac{N}{60P}$
where N *is the speed in rpm and* P *is the number of poles.*

56. In a synchronous alternator, armature reaction is solely determined by
(a) power factor of the load
(b) amount of current drawn from the alternator
(c) speed of the prime mover driving the alternator
(d) none of these

57. For zero power factor leading, the effect of armature reaction in an alternator on the main flux is
(a) magnetising
(b) demagnetising
(c) cross-magnetising
(d) none of these

58. The emf generated in an alternator due to nth harmonic is
(a) n times the fundamental emf
(b) equal to the fundamental emf
(c) less than the fundamental emf
(d) zero

59. The armature reaction of an alternator will be cross-magnetising if the power factor of the load is
(a) zero leading
(b) less than unity
(c) unity
(d) more than unity

60. The effect of cross-magnetizing field in an alternator may be reduced by
(a) shifting the brush positions
(b) using interpoles
(c) using a magnetizing pole
(d) none of these

61. The following method is best suited for finding the voltage regulation of an alternator
(a) synchronous impedance method
(b) Poltier triangle method
(c) MMF method
(d) none of these

62. Power factor of an alternator driven by constant prime mover input can be changed by changing its
(a) speed   (b) load
(c) field excitation   (d) phase sequence

63. In an a.c. machine, the armature winding is kept stationary while the field winding is kept rotating for the following reason
  (a) armature handles very large currents and high voltages
  (b) armature friction involving deep slots to accommodate large coils is easy if armature is kept stationary
  (c) ease of cooling the stator than rotor
  (d) none of these

64. For given output, steam turbo-alternators are smaller in size than water turbine alternators for the following reason
  (a) steam turbo-alternators have long speeds
  (b) steam turbo-alternators run at higher speeds
  (c) steam turbo-alternators are built with smaller capacities
  (d) none of these

65. In a large alternator, the moving part is
  (a) the poles   (b) armature
  (c) brushes   (d) none of these

66. To reverse the phase sequence of voltage generated in an alternator, we should
  (a) reverse the connection of its field winding
  (b) interchange any two of its phase terminals
  (c) both (a) and (b)
  (d) none of these

67. The length l of the rotor of a turbo-alternator and its diameter D are related as below
  (a) $l = D/2$ (b) $l = D$
  (c) $l = 2D$ (d) $l >> D$

68. If the terminal voltage of an alternator is required to decrease with increase of load, the pf of the load should be
  (a) zero lagging   (b) zero leading
  (c) unity   (d) more than unity

69. Short pitch coils are used in alternators
  (a) to reduce the size of the machine
  (b) to reduce the stray losses
  (c) to reduce harmonic output
  (d) to reduce accurate phase shift of 120° between each phase

70. The most accurate method of measuring the hot spot temperature in field winding is
  (a) thermocouple method
  (b) thermometer method
  (c) by measuring the increase in winding resistances
  (d) none of these

71. In case of two alternators running in parallel and perfectly synchronized, the synchronizing power is
  (a) zero
  (b) positive
  (c) negative
  (d) ideally infinite

72. On keeping the input to the prime mover of an alternator constant and increasing the excitation
  (a) kVA becomes leading
  (b) kVA becomes lagging
  (c) kW will change
  (d) pf of the load remains unaltered

73. If an alternator is operating at a leading power factor, its voltage regulation is
  (a) more than one
  (b) equal to zero
  (c) negative
  (d) none of these

74. Hunting in synchronous machines can be reduced by using
  (a) damped bars
  (b) flywheel
  (c) machines having suitable synchronization power
  (d) all of these

75. In parallel operation of alternators, the synchronizing power is maximum, if armatures have
  (a) reactances equal to resistance
  (b) reactances less than resistances
  (c) reactances greater than resistances
  (d) none of these

76. For same power rating, the higher voltage alternator is
  (a) larger in size
  (b) smaller in size
  (c) cheaper
  (d) costlier

77. To run two alternators in parallel, the black Amp test is performed to ensure proper
  (a) voltage matching
  (b) frequency matching
  (c) phase difference matching
  (d) phase sequence matching

78. For successful parallel operation of two alternaors, it is necessary that

(a) they are synchronized using synchoscope and dark and bright lamp method of synchronization

(b) their phase sequence, voltage, frequency and polarity be the same

(c) both (a) and (b)

(d) none of these

79. When a single alternator connected to infinite busbar supplies a local load, the change in excitation of the machine results in change of

(a) power factor

(b) power output

(c) input power

(d) terminal voltage

80. In parallel operation of two alternator, the synchronizing torque comes into operation where there is

(a) phase difference between the two voltages

(b) frequency difference between two voltages

(c) voltage difference between the two voltages

(d) either (a), (b) or (c)

81. In alternator, during hunting when the speed becomes supersynchronous, the damped bars develop

(a) reluctance torque

(b) pseudo-stationary torque

(c) eddy current torque

(d) induction generator torque

82. The slip rings employed in a three-phase alternator in hydrostation are insulated for

(a) full armature voltage

(b) extra high tension voltage

(c) low voltage

(d) very high voltage

83. An alternator is capable of delivering power at a particular frequency. The frequency can be increased by

(a) increasing the current supplied to the field elecromagnets

(b) reversing the armature rotation

(c) increasing armature speed

(d) reversing the field polarity

84. Distributing the armature winding of alternator in more than one number of slot per pole per phase results in

(a) economy of material used in winding

(b) reduction of irregularities produced in waveform

(c) less weight of the entire armature

(d) increase of generated emf per phase

85. Regulation of an alternator is likely to be negative in case of

(a) high speed alternators

(b) low speed alternators

(c) lagging power factor of the load

(d) leading power factor of the load

86. Maximum power in a synchronous machine is obtained when the load angle is

(a) $0°$

(b) $85°$

(c) $120°$

(d) $135°$

87. One of the advantages of distributing the winding in alternator is to

(a) reduce noise

(b) same on copper

(c) improve voltage waveform

(d) reduce harmonics

88. In case of a uniformly distributed winding in an alternator, the value of distribution factor is

(a) 0.995

(b) 0.90

(c) 0.80

(d) 0.70

89. Two alternators are connected in parallel. Their kVA and kW load shares can be changed by changing respectively their

(a) driving torque and excitation

(b) excitation and driving torque

(c) excitation only

(d) driving torques only

90. The voltage of field system for an alternator is usually

(a) less than 200 V

(b) between 200 V and 500 V

(c) 500 V

(d) above 500 V

91. The following are the experimental data required for Poltier method for finding the voltage regulation of an alternator

    (*a*) no load curve, short circuit test values

    (*b*) no load curve, zero power factor curve

    (*c*) zero power factor curve, short circuit test curve

    (*d*) none of these

92. Salient-pole rotors are not used for high speed turbo alternators because of

    (*a*) large eddy loss

    (*b*) high centrifugal force and windage loss

    (*c*) excessive bearing friction

    (*d*) harmful mechanical oscillations

93. The short circuit characteristic of an alternator is

    (*a*) always linear

    (*b*) always nonlinear

    (*c*) sometimes linear and sometimes nonlinear

    (*d*) none of these

94. In an alternator, if the armature current is leading the generated voltage by 90°, the effect of armature reaction will be

    (*a*) demagnetising

    (*b*) magnetising

    (*c*) partly magnetising and partly cross-magnetising

    (*d*) none of these

95. In order to reduce the harmonics in the emf generated in an alternator

    (*a*) slots are skewed

    (*b*) silent pole tips are chamfered

    (*c*) winding is well distributed

    (*d*) all of these

96. The hunting in synchronous machines can be guarded against by

    (*a*) using a flywheel

    (*b*) designing the synchronous machine with suitable synchronizing power

    (*c*) damped bars

    (*d*) all of these

97. Of the following conditions, the one which does not have to be met by alternators working in parallel is

    (*a*) terminal voltage of each machine must be the same

    (*b*) the machines must have the same phase rotation

    (*c*) the machines must operate at the same frequency

    (*d*) the machines must have equal ratings

98. The power factors of an alternator is determined by its

    (*a*) speed

    (*b*) loud

    (*c*) excitation

    (*d*) prime mover

99. With a load p.f. of unity, the effect of armature reaction on the main-field flux of an alternator is

    (*a*) distortional

    (*b*) magnetising

    (*c*) demagnetising

    (*d*) nominal

100. An alternator and a synchronous motor are connected to an infinite bus. Both are working at unity p.f. and reactive power handled by them is

    (*a*) both deliver it to the bus

    (*b*) both absorb it from the bus

    (*c*) alternator is delivering it and motor is absorbing it

    (*d*) neither of these machines is delivering nor absorbing it.

101. Large synchronous machines are constructed with armature winding on the stator because stationary armature winding

    (*a*) can be insulated satisfactorily for higher voltages

    (*b*) can be cooled more efficiently

    (*c*) all of these

    (*d*) both (*a*) and (*b*)

102. Main disadvantage of using short-pitch winding in alternators is that it

    (*a*) reduces harmonics in the generated voltage

    (*b*) reduces the total voltage around the armature coils

    (*c*) produces a symmetry in the three phase windings

    (*d*) increases Cu of end connections

103. If two machines are running in synchronism and the voltage of one machine is suddenly increased
  (a) the machines will burn
  (b) both machines will stop
  (c) synchronising torque will be produced to restore further synchronism
  (d) none of these

104. Maximum current that can be supplied by an alternator depends on
  (a) speed of the exciter
  (b) number of poles
  (c) exciter current
  (d) strength of the magnetic field.

105. Advantage of using short pitched windings in an alternator is that it
  (a) suppresses the harmonics in generated emf
  (b) reduces the total voltage around the armature coils
  (c) saves copper use in windings
  (d) improves cooling by better circulation of air.

106. When an alternator is running on no load, the power supplied by the prime mover is mainly consumed
  (a) to meet iron losses
  (b) to meet copper losses
  (c) to meet all no load losses
  (d) to produce induced emf in armature winding.

107. Two alternators are running in parallel. If the field on one of the alternator is adjusted, it will
  (a) reduce its speed
  (b) change its load
  (c) change its power
  (d) change its frequency.

108. The advantage of a short pitch winding is
  (a) low noise
  (b) increased inductance
  (c) suppression of harmonics
  (d) reduced eddy currents.

109. The regulation of an alternator is
  (a) the reduction in terminal voltage when alternator is loaded
  (b) the variation of terminal voltage under the conditions of maximum and minimum excitation
  (c) the increase in terminal voltage when load is thrown off
  (d) the change in terminal voltage from lagging power factor to leading power factor.

110. In synchronous generator operating at zero pf lagging, the effect of armature reaction is
  (a) magnetizing
  (b) demagnetizing
  (c) cross-magnetizing
  (d) both magnetizing and cross-magnetizing.

111. Main advantage of distributing the winding in slots is to
  (a) add mechanical strength to the winding
  (b) reduce the amount of copper required
  (c) reduce the harmonics in the generated e.m.f.
  (d) reduce the size of the machine.

112. One turn consists of
  (a) two coilsides   (b) two conductors
  (c) four conductors (d) four coilsides

ANSWERS

1. (b)	**2.** (b)	**3.** (b)	**4.** (b)	**5.** (a)	**6.** (c)	**7.** (a)	**8.** (d)	**9.** (a)	**10.** (a)
11. (b)	**12.** (c)	**13.** (d)	**14.** (b)	**15.** (c)	**16.** (d)	**17.** (c)	**18.** (b)	**19.** (b)	**20.** (a)
21. (c)	**22.** (c)	**23.** (d)	**24.** (c)	**25.** (d)	**26.** (d)	**27.** (d)	**28.** (d)	**29.** (c)	**30.** (b)
31. (d)	**32.** (b)	**33.** (d)	**34.** (d)	**35.** (d)	**36.** (c)	**37.** (c)	**38.** (d)	**39.** (d)	**40.** (c)
41. (d)	**42.** (c)	**43.** (a)	**44.** (b)	**45.** (a)	**46.** (c)	**47.** (a)	**48.** (a)	**49.** (a)	**50.** (c)
51. (c)	**52.** (d)	**53.** (a)	**54.** (d)	**55.** (a)	**56.** (a)	**57.** (a)	**58.** (c)	**59.** (c)	**60.** (a)
61. (b)	**62.** (c)	**63.** (d)	**64.** (b)	**65.** (a)	**66.** (c)	**67.** (d)	**68.** (b)	**69.** (c)	**70.** (a)
71. (c)	**72.** (b)	**73.** (c)	**74.** (d)	**75.** (d)	**76.** (b)	**77.** (b)	**78.** (c)	**79.** (a)	**80.** (d)
81. (d)	**82.** (c)	**83.** (c)	**84.** (b)	**85.** (d)	**86.** (b)	**87.** (c)	**88.** (a)	**89.** (b)	**90.** (a)
91. (b)	**92.** (b)	**93.** (a)	**94.** (b)	**95.** (d)	**96.** (d)	**97.** (d)	**98.** (b)	**99.** (a)	**100.** (d)
101. (d)	**102.** (b)	**103.** (c)	**104.** (d)	**105.** (b)	**106.** (c)	**107.** (b)	**108.** (c)	**109.** (c)	**110.** (b)
111. (c)	**112.** (b)								

6

CHAPTER

Power Generation

HYDRO–ELECTRIC POWER PLANTS

These power plants utilises potential energy of the water at a high level for the generation of electrical energy.

Requirements.

(*i*) Ample quantity of water at sufficient head

(*ii*) Suitable site

Amount of power that can be developed depends on

(*i*) quantity of water available,

(*ii*) rate at which it is available,

(*iii*) head

Electrical power developed,

$$P = w\,Q\,H\eta \times 9.81 \times 10^{-3}\ \text{kW}$$

where W = specific weight of water in kg/m^3,

Q = rate of flow of water in m^3/s,

H = height of fall or head in m, and

h = generation efficiency.

In a hydro–electic power station, water head is created by constructing a dam across a river or lake. The pressure head of water or kinetic energy of water is utilised to drive the water turbines coupled to alternators and, therefore generation of electrical power.

Advantages.

(*i*) These plants are neat and clean, robust, highly reliable, cheapest in operation and maintenance and have got longer life.

(*ii*) These plants do not need any fuel.

(*iii*) Can be run up and synchronised in few minutes.

(*iv*) These have no stand by losses.

Disadvantages.

(*i*) These needs long area, enormously high construction cost, long time for erection and long transmission lines.

(*ii*) Reservoir of such a plants submerges huge areas

(*iii*) Long dry season may affect the power supply.

Selection of Site.

Selected site should have

(*i*) large catchment area

(*ii*) high average rain fall

(*iii*) favourable place for constructing the storage or reservoir.

(*iv*) land should be cheap in cost and rocky in order to withstand the weight of large building and heavy machinery.

(*v*) possibility of providing adequate transportation facilities so that the necessary equipment and machinery could be easily transported.

CLASSIFICATION OF HYDRO-ELECTRIC POWER PLANTS

(1) Classification according to the extent of water flow regulation available.

(*i*) *Run off river power flow :*

These plants without pondage do not store water and uses the water as it comes. Such plants can be built at a considerably low cost but the head available and the amount of power generated are usually very low. During the high flow periods such plants can be employed to supply a substantial portion of base load.

(*ii*) *Run-off river power plants with pondage :*

These plants with pondage have increased usefulness because of pondage which usually refers to the collection of water behind a dam at the plant and increases the firm capacity for a short-period, say a week or more depending on the size of pondage. Such power plants are comparatively more reliable and its generating capacity is less dependent on available rate of flow of water.

Depending on the flow of stream, these power plants can serve as

(*a*) Base load plans-during high flow periods.

(*b*) Peak load plants-during low flow periods.

(*iii*) *Reservoir power plants :*

These are with reservoirs of sufficiently large size to permit carry-over storage from the wet season to the dry season, and thus to supply firm flwo substantially more than the minimum natural flow. Such plants can be used as base load plants or peak load plants as per requirement. Most of the hydro-electric power plants everywhere in the world are of this type.

(2) Classification according to availability of water head.

(i) *Low head (below 60m) :*

Low head power plant usually consists of a dam across a river. A side way stream diverges from the river at the dam and over this strem the power house is constructed. Later this channel joins the river further down stream. Such a plant uses vertical shaft Francis, propeller or Kaplan turbine. Structure of such a plant is extensive and expensive. Generators used in such plants are of low speed and large diameter.

(ii) *Medium head (above 60m and below 300m) :*

Medium head power plant uses horizontal shaft Francis, propeller or Kaplan turbines. In such a plant water is carried from main reservoir to foreby through open channel and then to turbines through the penstock. the forebay itself serves as the surge tank in this case.

(iii) *High head power plants (above 300m) :*

High head power plant uses Pelton wheels or jet impulse turbines as a prime-movers. In such a plant, the water from the reservoir is carrried through tunnel upto the surge tank and from surge tank to the power house through the penstock. The generators used in such plants are of high speed and small diameter. Penstocks used are of large lengths and comparatively smaller cross-section.

(3) Classification according to the load supplied.

(i) *Base load plants :*

These cater the base load of the system. Such plants have high load factors and continue to run for longer durations. Such plants are usually of large capacity.

(ii) *Peak load plants :*

These are used only when the power demand exceeds the limits of other power plants in the inter-connected system. Diesel engine plant, gas turbine plant or even steam power plants is used as a peak load plant.

(iii) *Pumped storage power plants:*

These uses reversible turbines which operate as turbines for power generation during peak load hours and as pumps for pumping water during peak-off hours.

WATER TURBINES

In hydro-electric power plants, water turbines are used. The water turbines are

(i) simple in constrution

(ii) highly efficient in operation (about 90% on full load)

(iii) easily controllable

(iv) pick up the load in a very short time

They are built in various size to 10,00,000 hp with speeds varying from 80 rpm to 1,275 rpm depending on their size. Hydraulic turbines may be vertical of horizontal.

The water turbines used as prime movers in hydro-electric power stations.

CLASSIFICATION OF WATER TURBINES

(1) According to the type of flow of water.

(i) *Axial flow turbines :* These have flow of water along the shaft axis such as propeller and Kaplan turbines.

(ii) *Inward radial flow turbines:* These have flow of water along the radius such as Francis turbine.

(iii) *Tangential flow turbines :* These have flow of water along the tangential directions such as Pelton wheel turbine.

(iv) *Mixed flow (radial inlet and axial outlet) turbines :* e.g. Francis turbine.

(2) According to the action of water on moving blades.

(i) *Impulse turbines :* When the entire pressure of water is converted into kinetic energy in a nozzle and the jet thus formed drives the wheel, the turbine is of impulse type,

(ii) *Reaction turbines :* When the water pressure combined with its velocity work on the runner the turbine is known as reaction type turbine.

(3) According to the name of the originator.

(i) *Pelton wheel :* Pelton wheel is an impulse turbine and is used for high head poer plants and their speed is about 1275 rpm.

(ii) *Kaplan turbines :* These are used for medium head power plants and for variable load. Their speed range is 320 to 1000 rpm.

(iii) *Francis reaction turbines:* In these vertical shaft arrangement has proved better and is therefore universally adopted. In case of large sized impulse turbines, horizontal shaft arrangement is mostly adopted.

STEAM POWER PLANTS

In steam power plants, the heat of combustion of fossil fuels (coa, oil or gas) is utilized by the boilers to raise steam at high pressure and temperature. The steam so produced is used in driving the steam turbines or sometimes steam engines coupled to generators and thus in generating electrical energy.

Essential features of power plants.

Boilers, turbines coupled to electrical generators, condensers and large number of auxiliaries. The thermal efficiency of steam power plants is quite low (about 30%) and overall efficiency is about 29%. In steam power plants more than 50 percent of total heat of combustion is lost as heat rejected to the condenser.

Steam power plant basically operates on the Rankine cycle. Coal is burnt in a boiler, which converts water into steam. The stam is expanded in a turbine, which produces mechanical power driving the alternator coupled to the turbine. The steam after expansion in prime mover (turbine) is ususally condensed in a condenser to be fed into the boiler again.

Arrangement is divided into four main circuits.

(*i*) Fuel and ash circuit

(*ii*) Air and fuel gas circuit

(*iii*) Feed water and steam circuit

(*iv*) Cooling water circuit.

Advantages.

(*i*) Fuel used is cheaper

(*ii*) Less space is required

(*iii*) Low initial cost

(*iv*) Less production cost

(*v*) Ability of responding to rapidly changing loads without difficiult

(*vi*) Capability of working under 25% of over load continuously.

Disadvantages.

(*i*) High maintenance and operating costs.

(*ii*) Pollution of atmosphere.

(*iii*) Requirement of water in huge quantity,

(*iv*) Handling of coal and disposal of ash-quite difficult,

(*v*) Long time requirement for erection and put into action.

Selection of Site

Factors considered for site selection of steam power plants are

(*i*)   Nearnerss to load centre

(*ii*)   Supply of water

(*iii*) Availability of coal

(*iv*) Availability of land at a reasonable price

(*v*)   Type of availability of land

(*vi*) Transportation facilities

(*vii*) Availability of labours

(*viii*) Distance from populated area.

FUELS

Fuels may be classified as

(*i*) Solid

(*ii*) Liquid

(*iii*) Gaseous

Fuels may also be classified as

(*i*) Natural fuels

(*ii*) Prepared fuels

Fuels commonly used for combustion in the thermal power plants are

(*i*) Coal

(*ii*) Oil

(*iii*) Gas.

Gaseous fuel is rarely economical except when the power plant is located near natural gas field or gas manufacturing industries. Oil is used only where it is plentiful and cheap. Coal is the most commonly used fuel in thermal power plants.

Plant Efficiency

Efficiency of thermal power plants is quite low. The overall plant efficiency is not more than 40% but for majority of plants it is between 25 and 30%.

NUCLEAR POWER PLANTS

These plants are not well suited for varying loads since the reactor does not respond to the load fluctuation efficiently. They are usually operated at a load factor not below 80%

Advantages.

(*i*) Low fuel requirement resulting in low fuel cost and no problem of transportation and storage,

(*ii*) Less area requirement

(*iii*) Most economical in large capacity

(*iv*) Conservation of coal, oil etc

(*v*) Extremely flexible output control.

Disadvantages.

(*i*) Very high initial capital cost

(*ii*) Greater technical know how requirements in erection and commissioning

(*iii*) Possibility of occurrence of a dangerous amount of radio-active pollution

(*iv*) High mainteance cost owing to lack of standardisation

(*v*) High maintenance

(*vi*) Problem of disposal of the products, which are radio-active.

Selection of Site

Factors considered for site selection of nuclear power plants

(*i*) Nearness to load centre

(*ii*) Availability of water supply

(*iii*) Distance from populated area

(*iv*) Transportation facilities during erection period

(*v*) Type of land

(*vi*) Availability of space for disposal of waste.

Atomic Fuels

(*i*) Uranium (U$-_{235}$)

(*ii*) Thorium (Th$_{232}$)

(*iii*) Plutonium (Pu$_{239}$)

NUCLEAR REACTOR

It is that part of nuclear power plant where nuclear fuel is subjected to nuclear fission and the energy released in the process is utilised to heat the coolant which may in turn generate steam to be used in gas turbine.

A nuclear reactor consists of

(*i*) *Reactor core :* These contains a number of fuel rods made of fissile material

(*ii*) Moderator material in the reactor core is provided to moderate, or reduce the neutron speeds to a value that increases the possibility of fission occurring.

(*iii*) *Reflector :* These completely surrounds the reactor core within the thermal shielding arrangement and bounces back most of the neutrons that escape from the fuel core. This conserves the nuclear fuel, as the low speed neutrons thus returned are useful in continuing the chain reaction.

(*iv*) *Thermal shielding :* This is provided to prevent the reactor wall from getting heated,. Coolant flows over the shielding to take away the heat.

(*v*) *Control rods :* Meant for regulating the fissioning in the reactor by absorbing the excess neutrons and. These are made of boron and are inserted into the reactor core from the top of the reactor vessel.

(*vi*) *Reactor vessel :* It is a tank encloses the reactor core, reflector and the thermal shielding and provides the entrance and exit for the coolant and also the passage for its flow through and around the reactor core.

(*vii*) *Coolant.* It is a medium through which heat generated in the reactor is transferred to the heat exhanger for further utilisation in power generation.

Classification of Nuclear Reactors

(1) According to the applications.

(*i*) Research and development reactors (used for testing new reactor designs and research)

(*ii*) Production reactors (used for converting fertile materials into fissile materials)

(*iii*) Power reactors (used for generation of electrical energy)

(2) According to the type of fission.

(*i*) Fast

(*ii*) Slow

(*iii*) Intermediate reactors.

(3) According to the type of fuel used.

(*i*) Natural uranium

(*ii*) Enriched uranium

(*iii*) Plutonium

(4) According to the state of fuels used.

(*i*) Solid

(*ii*) Liquid

(5) According to the fuel cycel.

(*i*) Burner

(*ii*) Converter

(*iii*) Breeder

(6) According to the arrangement of fissile and fertile material.

(*i*) One region (fissile and fertile material mixed)

(*ii*) Two region (fissile and fertiale material separate) reactors.

(7) According to the arrangement of fuel and the moderator.

(*i*) Homogeneous

(*ii*) Heterogeneous

(8) According to the moderator materials used.

(*i*) Heavy water

(*ii*) Graphite

(*iii*) Ordinary water

(*iv*) Beryllium or organic reactors

(9) According to the cooling system employed.

(*i*) Direct

(*ii*) Indirect reactors.

(10) According to the coolants used.

(*i*) Gas

(*ii*) Water

(*iii*) Heavy water

(*iv*) Liquid metal reactors

TYPES OF POWER REACTORS

(1) Pressurized Water Reactor (PWR).

Such a reactor is a thermal reactor and uses zirconium clad enriched uranium fuel.

Advantages

(i) Compactness

(ii) Possibility of breeding plutonium

(iii) Isolation of radioactive material from the main steam system

(iv) Cheap light water can be used as coolant-cum-moderator

(v) High power-density

Disadvantages

(i) Use of high pressure water system

(ii) Formation of low tememperature (250°C) steam

(iii) Use of expensive cladding material for corrosion prevention

(iv) High losses from heat exchanger

(v) High power consumption of auxiliaries

(vi) Poor thermal efficienty (20%).

(2) Boiling Water Reactor (BWR).

This is the simplest type of water reactor.

Advantages

(i) Small size pressure vessel

(ii) High steam pressure

(iii) Simple construction

(iv) Elimination of heat exchanger circuit resulting in reduction of cost and gain in thermal efficiency

(3) Gas Cooled Reactor.

This type of reactor employs a gas (CO_2 or helium) in place of water as the coolant and graphite as the moderator.

Advantages.

(i) Less severe corrosion problems

(ii) Possibility of use of natural uranium as fuel

(iii) Greater safety in comparison with water cooled reactors

Disdvantages.

Large energy consumption by gas blowers which may consume as much as 20% of the energy generated.

DIESEL-ELECTRIC POWER PLANTS

Diesel electric power plant is a power plant in which a diesel engine is used as the prime-mover for the generation of electric energy.

Advantages.

(i) Layout, design and construction of foundation and building is simple and cheap

(ii) Procurement, installation and commissioning quick

(iii) Flexibility in location

(iv) Simple design and installation

(v) Less space requirement because of minimum auxiliaries

(vi) No stand by losses

(vii) Limited cooling water requirement

(viii) High operation efficiency irrespective of load

(ix) Less fire hazard

(x) Can be started and put on load quickly

(xi) Can respond to varying loads without any difficulty

(xii) Need less space for fuel storage

(xiii) Free from ash handling problem

(xiv) Overall capital cost including installation per unit of installed capacity is lesser

(xv) Simple in operation

Disadvantages.

(i) Limited diesel unit capacity

(ii) Serious problem of noise from the exhaust

(iii) High maintenance and lubrication cost

(iv) High fuel cost

(v) Cannot supply over loads continuously.

Selection of site

Factors considered for site selection of diesel power plants are

(i) Availability of water supply

(ii) Availability of fuel

(iii) Availability of transportation facilities

(iv) Distance from populated area

(v) Availability of land

(vi) High bearing capacity to withstand the load of the plant

(vii) Vibrations transmitted to the foundation from compressors and diesel engines.

Elements of Diesel Electric Power Plants

(i) Diesel engine

(ii) Engine air intake (including air filters, ducts and supercharger (integral with the engine)

(iii) Engine fuel system (including fuel storage tanks, fuel transfer pumps) (*iv*) Engine exhaust system (including silencers and connecting ducts.)

(*v*) Engine cooling system (including cooling pumps, cooling towers or spray ponds)

(*vi*) Engine lubricating oil system (including lurbricating oil pumps, oil tanks, filters ,coolers, purifiers and connecting pipe work.)

(*vii*) Engine starting equipment (including batter, compressed air supply.)

GAS TURBINE ELECTRIC POWER PLANTS

Gas turbine electric power plant is a power plant in which a gas turbine is used as the prime-mover for the generation of electrical energy.

Advantages.

(*i*) Simplicity of design and installation

(*ii*) High realiability

(*iii*) Simple lubrication system

(*iv*) Clean exhaust requiring no stack

(*v*) Compactness

(*vi*) Low initial cost

(*vii*) Requiring small building space and light foundations requiring little cooling water.

(*viii*) Delivery and installation time for such power plants is much less

(*ix*) Can be started quickly

(*x*) Can be put to share full load within a few minutes

(*xi*) Efficiency can be improved considerably by using heat economy devices.

(*xii*) Gas turbines may be operated by remote control and need little or no personnel while operating and while shutdown maintance costs is low.

Disadvantages.

(*i*) Inability of using coal or heavy residual petroleum as fuel

(*ii*) Low net output low overall efficiency

(*iii*) Noisy operation

(*iv*) High specific fuel consumption

(*v*) Limited unit capacity

Selection of Site

Factors considered for the site selection of gas turbine power plants are follows.

(*i*) Distance from load centre

(*ii*) Availability of land at reasonable rate

(*iii*) Availability of fuel at reasonable rate

(*iv*) Availability of transportation facilities

(*v*) Distance from populted area

(*vi*) Type of land

Fuels For Gas Turbines

A vartiety of fuels (solid, liquid and gaseous) are available for use in gas turbines. The petroleum fuels such as kerosene, gas oil diesel oil, residual oil, are quite suitable for use in gas turbines. Natural gas which is mainly methane, has a very high calorific value and is generally used for auxiliary power generation in oil fields.

OPEN AND CLOSED GAS CYCLE TURBINE POWER PLANT.

Open cycle gas turbine power plant.

In these, the fuel is mixed with air in the combustion chamber and the combustion gases are expanded in the gas turbine, which causes erosion and corrosion of turbine blades and, therefore, it becomes essential to use fuel of superior quality in the combustion chamber. This draw-back is overcome in case closed cycle power plant is adopted, in which fuel is not mixed with the working medium (air or any other gas such as helium, argon, hydrogen and neon).

Closed cycle gas turbine power plant.

In these plants, the medium is heated externally and is continuously circulated through the compressors, heat exchangers, intercoolers, reheaters and gas coolers. Load variation is affected by controlling the absolute pressure and the mass flow of the circulating air.

Combination gas turbine power plants.

The gas turbine power plants are mainly used for supplying peak loads in other types of power plants e.g. in steam and hydro-electric power plants. The heat content of gas turbine exhaust is quite substantial. A combination gas turbine-steam turbine cycle aims at improving the overall plant efficiency by using the heat of exhaust gases from the gas turbine as a heat source for a steam plant cycle.

Arrangements of combination cycles generally employed

(*i*) Use of exhaust gases of gas turbine power plant for heating of feed water

(*ii*) Use of exhaust gases from turbine as combustion air in steam boiler

(*iii*) Use of gases from a supercharged boiler for expansion in gas turbine

Advantages

(*i*) Saving in exhaust heat of the gas turbine resulting in increase of its heat rate

(*ii*) Reduction in stack emissions

(*iii*) Reduction in space requirement

(*iv*) Reduction in requirements of condensing water by 60% as compared to fossil fuel plant of given capacity

(*v*) Reduction in starting time

Uses.

(*i*) For supplying peak loads in other types of power plants (steam and hydro plants) because of their higher fuel costs and low initial costs

(*ii*) For driving auxiliaries in other power plants

(*iii*) As standby power plants in hydro-power plants

(*iv*) To operate as combination plants with conventional steam boilers and as base-load plants where fuel oil or natural gases are cheap and easily available, water supply is scarce

(*v*) Load factor is very low, say 15-18 %.

NON-CONVENTIONAL METHODS OF POWER GENERATION

(*i*)   Magneto-hydrodynamic (MHD) power generation

(*ii*)   Solar cells

(*iii*)   Fuel cells

(*iv*)   Thermo-electric generator

(*v*)   Thermionic convertor

(*vi*)   Solar power generation, wind power generation

(*vii*)   Geo-thermal energy generation

(*viii*) Tidal power generation

(*i*) **Magneto-Hydro-Dynamic (MHD) power generation.**

The basic principle of MHD generation is the same as that of a conventional electrical generator, i.e motion of a conductor through a magnetic field induces an emf in it. In MHD generation, electrical energy is directly generated from hot combustion gases produced by the combustion of the fuel without moving parts. MHD generator is heat engine operating on a turbine cycle and transforming the internal energy of gas directly into electrical energy.

Advantages.

(*i*)   High conversion efficiency (about 50%)

(*ii*)   High capital costs

(*iii*) More realiable having no moving part

(*iv*) More efficient heat utilisation reduces the amount of heat discharged to environments and so the amount of cooling water required is reduced.

(*ii*) **Thermionic convertor.**

In such a device, electrons act as the working fluid in place of a vapour or gas.

These electrons are driven by heat energy across a potential difference to produce electrical energy.

(*iii*) **Fuel cells.**

A fuel cell is a device in which chemical energy is directly converted into electrical energy. In fuel cells, chemical energy of the reactants is converted into electrical energy as an isothermal process. Thus heat is not involved in the conversion process and a high conversion efficiency is possible.

BASE LOAD AND PEAK LOAD

The unvarying load, which occurs almost the whole day on the power plant is called the base load whereas the various peak demands of the load over and above the base load of the power plant is called the peak loads.

Power plants to be employed as base power plants should have

(*i*)   low operating cost

(*ii*)   capability of working continuously for the long periods

(*iii*) requirement of few operating personnel and their repairs should be economical and speedy.

The power plants to be employed as peak power plants should have the capability of quick start, synchronisation and taking up of system load and quick response to load variation.

The hydro-power plants should be employed for base load operation as far as possible because of their higher capital cost. However during the periods of draught, the hydro-plants may be used as peak load plants. A steam power plant gives minimum cost of generation per unit when used as base load plant. However, in order to save fuel it may be used as peak load plant. Nuclear power plants are suitable only for base load operation at high load factors exceeding 0.8. Gas turbine power plants are suitable for supplying peak loads and diesel power plants play a very little role in bulk power generation because of their uneconomical operating costs.

INTERCONNECTION OF POWER STATIONS

Several generating stations connected to each other form an interconnected system.

Advantages.

(*i*)   Reduced reserve plant capacity in the system as a whole, improved load factor (*ii*) Diversity factor and operation efficiency

(*iii*) Increased reliability of supply and effective capacity of the whole system

(*iv*) Reduced capital cost per kW

(*v*) Economical operation of power plants.

COSTS OF POWER GENERATION

Total annual cost incurred in the power generation is given by

$$\text{E} = a + b\ kw + c\ kwh$$

where a, b, and c are constants.

Fixed and semi-fixed cost being independent of the amount of energy generated is also called "standing cost."

In deciding any scheme for any given service, the choice must be such that the total operating cost (sum of annual fixed cost, semi-fixed cost and operating cost) be minimum.

Classification of costs.

(1) *Fixed cost.*

This cost is independent of maximum demand and energy output. It is due to

(*i*)   annual cost of central organisation

(*ii*)   interest on the capital cost of land (especially if some land is held for furture development)

(*iii*) salaries of high officials

(2) *Semi-fixed cost.*

This cost depends upon the maximum demand but is independent of energy output. The semi-fixed cost is due to

(*i*)   annual interest and depreciation on the capital cost of the generating plant

(*ii*)   transmission and distribution network

(*iii*) building and other civil engineering works

(*iv*) all types of taxes and insurance charges

(*v*)   salaries of management and clerical staff.

(3) *Running or operating cost.*

This cost depends upon

(*i*)   number of hours the plants is in operation or

(*ii*)   number of units of electrical energy generated

The running or operating cost is due to

(*i*)   annual cost of fuel

(*ii*)   lubricating oil

(*iii*) water

(*iv*) maintenance and repair cost of equipment

(*v*)   wages and salaries of operational and maintenance staff and salaries of supervisory staff engaged on the running of the plant.

ECONOMICS OF GENERATION

The generation of electrical energy economically depends on the type, location and the rating of generating stations. The generating stations may be steam, hydro, diesel or other type. The power stations should be as near as possible to the centre of the loads so that the transmission cost and losses are minimum. The other consideration for the design of the power station are reliability, minimum capital and operating costs.

Considerations deciding the type and rating of generating plant:

(i)   **Load curves.**

The load on the power station varies from time to time. The daily variations in load on the power station from time to time-hourly or half hourly can be plotted on a graph taking load on y-axis and time on x-axis. The curve so obtained is known as *daily load curve*. From the daily load curves of a particular month, the monthly load curve can be plotted by calculating the average value of power at a particular time of the day. Simiarly if we consider such monthly load curves of a particular year, and from the average value of power at a particular time of the day, the annual load curve can be obtained.

Informations obtained by the load curves

(*a*) Variation of the load during different hours of the day

(*b*) Area under the curve represents the total number of units generated in a day.

(*c*) Peak of the curve represents the maximum demand on the station on a particular day.

(*d*) Area under the load curve divided by the number of hours represents the average load on the power station.

(*e*) Ratio of the area under the load curve to the total area of the rectangle in which it is contained gives the load factor.

(ii)   **Load duration curve.**

This type of curve indicates the variation of load, but with the loads arranged in descending order of magnitude i.e. the greatest load on the left, lesser loads towards the right and the least load at the extreme right. This curve gives the number of hours for which a particular load lasts during the day. The area under this curve like load curve or chronological curve gives the total number of units generated for the period considered. From this curve the load factor of the station can also be determined. From these curves, the distribution of load between various generating units can also be predicted.

(iii) *Mass curve.*

This curve is plotted with units (kWh) as ordinate and time as abscissa. Thus a mass curve gives the total energy consumed by the load upto a particular time a day.

(iv) *Connected load.*

The sum of continuous ratings of all the electrical equipment connected to the supply is known as connected load.

(v) *Maximum demand.*

It is not necessary that all the connected load be switched to a system at a time. The greatest of all "short time interval averaged" (15 minutes or $\frac{1}{2}$ hour or 1 hour) during a given period   a day, a month or a year), on the power station is called the maximum demand. It is sometimes also called as system peak. It is the maximum demand which determines the size and cost of the installation.

(vi) *Demand factor.*

The ratio of actual maximum demand on the system to the total rated load connected to the system is called the demand factor. It is always less than unity.

(vii) *Average load or demand.*

The average load or demand on the power station is the average of loads occurring at the various events.

(viii) *Load factor.*

The ratio of average load to the maximum demand during a certain period of time such as a day or a month or a year is called the load factor. Since average load is always less than the maximum demand, load factor is therefore, always less than unity.

(ix) *Diversity factor.*

The maximum demands of all the consumers supplied from an installation do not occur usually at the same time. Maximum demand on the installation is, thus always less than the sum of individual maximum demands of all consumers connected to it.

The ratio of sum of the individual maximum demands of all the consumers supplied by it to the maximum demand of the power station is called the *diversity factor*. It is always greater than unity.

(x) *Capacity factor or Plant factor.*

Every plant has to have a reserve capacity so as to take care of the future expansion and increase in load and therefore total installed capacity of the plant is usually greater than that actually required (maximum demand). Capacity (or plant) factor is defined as the ratio of the average load to the rated capacity of the power plant.

(xi) *Utilisation factor.*

It is a measure or the utility of the power plant capacity and is the ratio of maximum demand to the rated capacity of the power plant. It is always less than unity.

(xii) *Plant operating factor or plant use factor.*

It is defined as the ratio of actual energy generated during a given period (say a year) to the product of capacity of the plant and the number of hours the plant has been actually in operation during the period.

(xiii) *Installed capacity.*

The total of station capacities available to supply the system load is called the installed capacity.

(xiv) *Firm power.*

It is the power intended to be always available (even under emergency conditions).

(xv) *Cold reserve.*

It is that portion of the installed reserve kept in operable conditions and available for service, but not normally ready for immediate loading.

(xvi) *Hot reserve.*

It usually refers to boiler excess capacity, which is kept hot and with steam pressure, ready for use.

(xvii) *Operating reserve.*

It refers to capacity in service in excess of peak load.

(xviii) *Spinning reserve.*

It is the generating capacity connected to the bus and ready to take load.

Significance of Load factor and Diversity factor.

Higher the values of load factor and diversity factors, lower will be the over all cost per unit generated.

The capital cost of the power station depends upon the capacity of the power station. Lower the maximum demand of the power station, lower is the capacity required and therefore lower is the capital cost of the plant. With a given number of consumers higher the diversity factor of their loads, smaller will be the capacity of the plant required and consequently the fixed charges due to capital investment will be much reduced.

Similarly higher load factor means more average load or more number of units generated for a given maximum demand and therefore overall cost per unit of electrical energy generated is reduced due to distribution of standing charges which are proportional to maximum demand and independent of number of units generated.

Thus the suppliers should always try to improve the load factor as well as diversity factor by inducing the consumers to use the electrical energy during off peak hours and they may be charged at lower rates for such schemes.

TARIFF

Tariff means the schedule of rates framed for supply of electrical energy to the various categories of consumers.

All types of tariffs must cover the recovery of costs of

(*i*)   capital investment in generating, transmitting and distributing equipment

(*ii*)   operation, supplies and maintenance of equipment and

(*iii*) metering equipment, billing, collection and miscellaneous serivces and

(*iv*) a satisfactory return on the total capital investment.

COMMON TYPES OF TARIFFS

(*i*) *Flat demand tariff.*

This is one of the earliest forms of tariffs used for charging the consumers for electrical energy consumption. This tariff is expressed as

$$\text{energy charges, } y = \text{Rs. } ax$$

where a = rate per lamp or kW of connected load and

x = number of lamps or load connected in kw.

In this types of tariff, the metering equipmetn, meter reading, billing, and accounting costs are eliminated.

(*ii*) *Simple tariff.*

This is the simplest type of tariff according to which the cost of energy is charged on the basis of units consumed and can be expressed in the form

$$y = \text{Rs } ax$$

where a = charges in rupees per unit, and

x = total electrical energy consumed in units or kwh.

(*iii*) *Flat rate tariff.*

This types of tariff differs from the former one in the sense that the different types of consumers are charged at different rates, i.e. flat rate for light and fan loads is slightly higher than that for power load. The rate for each category of consumers is arrived at by taking into account its load factor and diversity factor.

(*iv*) *Step rate tariff.*

The step rate tariff is a group of flat rate tariffs of decreasing unit charges for higher range of consumption.

(*v*) *Block rate tariff.*

In this type of tariff a given block of energy is charged at higher rate and succeeding blocks of energy are charged at progressively reduced rates.

(*vi*) *Hopkinson demand rate or two part tariff.*

The total energy charge to be made to the consumer is split into two components

(*a*)   Fixed charge

(*b*)   Running charge. This type of tariff is expressed as

$$y = \text{Rs } a \text{ kw} + \text{Rs } b \text{ kwh}$$

where Rs a = charge per kw of maximum demand assessed

Rs b = charge per kwh of energy consumed.

This tariff is mostly applicable to medium industrial consumers.

(*vii*) *Maximum demand tariff.*

This tariff is similar to that of two part tariff except that in this case maximum demand is actually measured by a maximum demand indicator instead of merely assessing it on the basis of rateable value.

(*viii*)*KVA maximum demand tariff.*

It is a modified form of two part tariff. In this case maximum demand is measured in KVa instead of in kW. This type of tariff encourages the consumers to operate their machines/ equipment at improved power factor because low power factor will cause more demand charges.

(*ix*) *Doherty rate or three part tariff.*

In this tariff total energy charge is split into three elements

(*a*) fixed charg

(*b*) semi-fixed charge and

(*c*) variable charge.

Such a tariff is expressed as,

$$y = \text{Rs } a + b\text{kw} + c \text{ kwh}$$

where a = a constant charge

    b = unit charge in Rs per kw of maximum demand in kw during billing period

    c = unit charge for energy in Rs per kwh of energy consumed.

This type of tariff is usually applicable to bulk supplies.

(x) *Off peak tariff.*

The load on the power station usually has pronounced peak loads in the morning and early evening and a very low load during the night (from 10 P.M to 6 A.M). Thus during the nigh and other off-peak period which may occur, a large proportion of the generating and distribution equipment will be lying idle. In case the consumers are encouraged to use electricity during off peak hours by giving a special discount, the energy can be supplied without incurring an additional capital cost and should therefore prove very profitable. This type of tariff is very advantageous for certain processes such as water heating by thermal storage, pumping, refrigeration etc.

POWER FACTOR IMPROVEMENT

The low power factor leads to high capital cost for the alternators, switchgears, transformers, transmission lines, distributors and cables etc.

Cause of Low Power Factor.

All ac motors (except over excited synchronous motors and certain types of commutator motors), arc lamps and discharge lamps, industrial heating furnaces operate at low lagging power fact ro. The power factor at which ac motors operate falls with the decrease in load and increase in supply voltage and because of improper maintenance and repairs of motors.

Advantages of Power Factor Improvement.

(i)   Reduction in load current

(ii) Increase in voltage level across the load

(iii) Reduction in energy loss in the system (generators, transformers, transmission lines and distributors) due to reduction in load current

(iv) Reduction in KVA loading of the generators and the transformers which may relieve an over loaded system or release capacity for additional growth of load

(v) Reduction in KVA demand charge for large consumers.

Methods of Power Factor Improvement.

(1) *By use of static capacitors.*

Power factor can be improved by connecting the capacitors in parallel with the equipment operating at lagging power factor such as induction motors, fluorescent tubes.

Advantages.

(i) small losses (less than $\frac{1}{2}\%$)

(ii) higher efficiency (say 99.6%)

(iii)low initial cost;

(iv)little maintenance

(v) easy installation

Power factor can also be improved by connecting static capacitors in series with the line. Capacitors connected in series with the line neutralize the line reactance. The capacitors, when connected in series with line, are called the series capacitors, and when connected in parallel with the equipment, are called the shunt capacitors.

(2) *By use of synchronous or high power factor machines.*

Synchronous machines are excited by dc, and the power factor may be controlled by controlling the field excitation.

(3) *By use of synchronous condensers.* An over-excited synchronous motor running on no load is called the synchronous condenser or synchronous phase advancer and behaves like a capacitor, the capacitive reactance of which depends upon the motor excitation. Power factor can be improved by using synchronous condensers like shunt capacitors connected across the supply.

OBJECTIVE TYPE QUESTIONS

1. Coolant used in fast breeder reactor is

(*a*) sodium

(*b*) heavy water

(*c*) air

(*d*) cadmium

2. Percentage of U^{235} in naturally available uranium is about

(*a*) 0.01   (*b*) 0.7

(*c*) 0.001   (*d*) 10

3. Coolant used in nuclear reactors should have

(*a*) high melting and boiling point

(*b*) high melting and low boiling point

(*c*) low melting and boiling point

(*d*) low melting and high boiling point

4. In fast breeder reactors

(*a*) heavy water is used as moderator

(*b*) no moderator is used

(*c*) graphite is used as moderator

(*d*) cadmium is used as moderator

5. Moderator in a nuclear reactor

(*a*) stops the chain reaction

(*b*) absorbs neutrons

(*c*) reduces the speed of fast moving neutrons

(*d*) acts as a cooling agent

6. Function of using reflector in nuclear reactor is to

(*a*) economize the reactor

(*b*) send back the escaping neutrons

(*c*) both (a) and (b)

(*d*) none of these

7. Overall efficiency of a thermal plant is

(*a*) ratio of heat equivalent of energy transferred to shaft to heat equivalent of electrical output

(*b*) heat equivalent of electrical output to heat of combustion

(*c*) heat equivalent of energy transferred to shaft to heat to combustion

(*d*) none of these

8. Feedwater in the economizer is in the form of

(*a*) steam at high pressure

(*b*) water at low temperature

(*c*) water at high temperature

(*d*) super saturated water

9. Which of the following plant has maximum efficiency?

(*a*) Tidal power station

(*b*) Hydro power station

(*c*) Thermal power station

(*d*) Nuclear power station

10. Condenser used in steam power plant is to

(*a*) reduce the back pressure at the turbine exhaust

(*b*) increase the back pressure at the turbine exhaust

(*c*) to make the back pressure zero

(*d*) none of these

11. Overall efficiency of thermal plant is reduced due to low value of

(*a*) generator efficiency

(*b*) boiler efficiency

(*c*) efficiency of steam turbine and condenser

(*d*) none of these

12. Turbo alternators are used in thermal plants is

(*a*) stationary field type

(*b*) cylindrical rotor type

(*c*) salient pole type

(*d*) none of these

13. Gross head of a hydroelectric power plant is

(*a*) height of water level in river where tail race is located

(*b*) height of water level in reservoir behind the dam

(*c*) difference of two

(*d*) water level in penstock

14. Frequency of the generated voltage is maintained constant by adjusting

(*a*) speed of prime mover

(*b*) excitation

(*c*) load

(*d*) number of poles

15. Fluctuations of speed in the diesel plant can be smoothened by fly wheel with

(*a*) high moment of inertia

(*b*) low moment of inertia

(*c*) both (a) and (b)

(*d*) none of these

16. Peak load plants supply power at
    (a) low capital cost and low running cost
    (b) high capital cost and high running cost
    (c) low capital cost and high running cost
    (d) low capital cost and low running cost

17. Base load plants supply power at
    (a) low capital cost and low running cost
    (b) low capital cost and high running cost
    (c) high capital cost and high running cost
    (d) high capital cost and low running cost

18. Hydro electric generators are
    (a) stationary field type
    (b) cylindrical rotor type
    (c) double cage rotor type
    (d) salient pole type

19. Pilot exciter is needed if
    (a) induction motor is used
    (b) main exciter is self excited
    (c) main exciter is separately excited
    (d) main exciter is not working

20. For separately exciter, complication of additional rotating machine is
    (a) not there   (b) less
    (c) more   (d) none of these

21. For centralised excitation system, number of exciters used are
    (a) more than generatng units
    (b) less than generating units
    (c) equal to generating units
    (d) uncertain

22. For greater power system stability, speed of the exciter response should always
    (a) increase   (b) decrease
    (c) remain same   (d) zero

23. Centralised excitable system is
    (a) more reliable than unit system
    (b) less reliable than unit system
    (c) same as unit system
    (d) none of these

24. Response of separately excited exciter is
    (a) equal to that of self excited generator
    (b) slower than that of self excited generator
    (c) faster than that of self excited generator
    (d) none of these

25. Division of reactive and active powers in two generators operating in parallel depend upon
    (a) voltage load curve
    (b) speed load curve
    (c) speed load and voltage load curves respectively
    (d) voltage load and speed load curves respectively

26. Connected load is sum of
    (a) maximum load consumed per year
    (b) maximum load consumed any particular time
    (c) continuous ratings of load-consuming apparatus connected
    (d) none of these

27. Cold reserve is that reserve which is
    (a) available for use but is not in service
    (b) available for service but is not in use
    (c) always available
    (d) connected to the bus and ready to take load

28. Spinning reserve is that generating capacity, which is
    (a) connected to the bus bar and is ready to take load
    (b) always available
    (c) available for service but not in use
    (d) available for use but not in service

29. Amortization of a plant is
    (a) more than the plant life
    (b) less than the plant life
    (c) equal to the plant life
    (d) none of these

30. Diversity factor reduces
    (a) simultaneous maximum demand on station for same individual demands
    (b) capital cost for the station
    (c) overall rate for generation of electricity
    (d) all of these

31. Station maximum demand is mostly dependent upon
    (a) line losses
    (b) domestic consumers
    (c) industrial consumers
    (d) all of these

32. Load factor is defined as
    (a) Maximum demand/average demand
    (b) Average demand/Maximum demand
    (c) Maximum demand/Peak load
    (d) Maximum demand/Minimum load

33. In flat rate tariffs, rate is fixed by taking into account their
   (a) diversity factor   (b) load factor
   (c) plant use factor   (d) a and b

34. Consumers pay less fixed charges in
   (a) two part tariff
   (b) flat rate tariff
   (c) block rate tariff
   (d) maximum demand tariff

35. Generators kept for spinning reserve are
   (a) not in operation
   (b) kept running on light loads
   (c) kept running on heavy loads
   (d) none of these

36. Maximum demand for a bulk consumer is measured in
   (a) KV   (b) KVA
   (c) KVAR   (d) KW

37. Operating plant factor is
   (a) ratio of average load to maximum load
   (b) ratio of maximum load to peak load
   (c) ratio of average load to the plant capacity
   (d) average load on the machine

38. If load factor is varied; in two part tariff
   (a) running cost is affected
   (b) fixed cost is affected
   (c) both (a) and (b)
   (d) depreciation is affected

39. By interconnection of stations, the cost is
   (a) increased   (b) reduced
   (c) same as before   (d) uncertain

40. Frequency of the system
   (a) should be constant
   (b) need not be constant
   (c) can be tolerated upto $\pm 10\%$
   (d) should be unity

41. Energy accumulations are balanced by deliveries of power
   (a) during off-peak periods
   (b) on weak ends
   (c) during the corresponding period of accumulation
   (d) none of these

42. Synchronous impendance of an alternator is defined as the ratio of open circuit voltage to the short circuit current for same
   (a) speed   (b) excitation
   (c) both (a) and (b)   (d) none of these

43. Speed drop of governor means
   (a) reduction in speed as load changes from no load to full load
   (b) increase in speed as load changes from no load to full load
   (c) degree of speed change needed to cause a change in the power output of turbine
   (d) none of these

44. While determining the regulation of an alternator by actual test, constant parameters are
   (a) speed and current
   (b) voltage and current
   (c) speed and excitation
   (d) short circuit current and excitation

45. Incremental rate is defined as
   (a) rate of change of given input
   (b) ratio of change in input to change in output
   (c) ratio of rate of change of output to input
   (d) ratio of rate of change of input to rate of change of output

46. For maximum power transfer to take place between two interconnected stations, angle between voltages of the two should be
   (a) $0°$ (b) $45°$
   (c) $60°$ (d) $90°$

47. Economical loading based on incremental rate gives
   (a) turbine efficiency
   (b) overall efficiency
   (c) brake thermal efficiency
   (d) best thermal efficiency

48. Different methods of prices charging is called
   (a) tariff
   (b) KVAR method
   (c) KW method
   (d) KVA method

49. For stable operation of interconnected stations, the element used is
   (a) resistor   (b) capacitor
   (c) reactor   (d) none of these

50. Quadrature boost employed in the interconnected system is used to transfer
(a) real power
(b) reactive power
(c) apparant power
(d) all of these

51. Power loss is important for the design of
(a) generator
(b) motor
(c) feeder
(d) transmission line

52. Voltage regulation is important for the design of
(a) generator
(b) motor
(c) feeder
(d) transmission line

53. Capital cost of the thermal plant depend on
(a) fuel cost
(b) size of the plant
(c) both (a) and (b)
(d) labour charges

54. For an alternator delivering a balanced load at unity power factor, phase angle between line voltage and line current is
(a) $0°$
(b) $180°$
(c) $30°$
(d) $90°$

55. Coincidence factor is always obtained as increase of the
(a) load factor
(b) plant use factor
(c) plant capacity factor
(d) deversity factor

56. Which of the following has highest capital cost?
(a) Thermal plant
(b) Hydro plant
(c) Diesel plant
(d) Nuclear plant

57. For conventional power plants, running cost is minimum for
(a) thermal plant
(b) nuclear plant
(c) hydro plant
(d) diesel plant

58. Disadvantage of flat rate tariff is that it is difficult to
(a) arrive at a load factor and diversity factor to decide the tariff
(b) estimate the cost of generation
(c) control the desired power factor
(d) all of these

59. Difference between load factor and capacity factor is the indication of
(a) hot reserve
(b) cold reserve
(c) reserve capacity
(d) spinning reserve

60. In the two part tariff, running charges increases as
(a) maximum energy consumed increases
(b) maximum energy consumed decreases
(c) average energy consumed decreases
(d) average energy consumed increases

61. When power factor of the load increases, losses in the transmission and distribution lines
(a) increases
(b) decreases
(c) remains same
(d) uncertain

62. Advantages of d.c. over a.c. is
(a) no skin effect
(b) charging currents are eliminated
(c) line regulation is improved
(d) all of these

63. Alternative source of energy should be utilised such that
(a) production cost is minimised
(b) efficient plant should be loaded to maximum
(c) generation is maximum
(d) fuel used is maximum

64. To improve the overall efficiency of thermal plant
(a) boiler pressure is decreased
(b) load on the units is decreased
(c) initial pressure and temperature and exhaust pressure and temperature are at maximum
(d) additional fuel is used

65. Transfer of power between two power systems take place with power flowing from the system with the
(a) leading power factor
(b) lagging power factor
(c) higher voltage level
(d) none of these

66. Load division between two parallel operating alternators are affected by
(a) more lagging power angle
(b) change in generated voltage
(c) change in input to prime mover
(d) increasing the system frequency

67. If fuel input increases, the load on thermal unit
(a) decreases
(b) increases
(c) remain same
(d) bears no relation

68. If load on the isolated generator is decreased without decreasing the power input to the prime mover speed of the generator
(a) remain unaltered
(b) decrease
(c) increase
(d) uncertain

69. Advantage of computer control of generating unit is that
(a) all the units will be equally loaded
(b) feedback is easy
(c) VAR output of units is decreased
(d) loading of the units are adjusted at equal incremental fuel costs

70. Phase shift between sending and receiving ends is determined by
(a) operating voltage
(b) reactance of the lines
(c) cross-section of conductor
(d) none of these

71. If field current is increased by 25% above rated value and load is kept constant on an alternator,
(a) it may go out of synchronism
(b) speed will cross the rated speed
(c) it will burn
(d) it will stop instantaneously

72. In interconnection of hydro and thermal plant, hydro-generation is increased by
(a) increasing load on the plant
(b) decreasing load on the plant
(c) keeping load on the plant constant
(d) none of these

73. Accumulated time error in power system can be corrected by
(a) increasing generation
(b) decreasing generation
(c) coordinating with other interconnected systems
(d) none of these

74. Speed control by governors of electric generating units normally have a/an
(a) increase of speed with increasing load
(b) decrease of speed with increasing load
(c) decrease of speed with decreasing load
(d) flat load characteristic

75. Time error for system operating at less than 50 Hz is
(a) slow
(b) fast
(c) zero
(d) none of these

76. In interconnected systems, each system
(a) should operate with flat frequency response
(b) can provide its own reserve capacity
(c) should depend on other for reserve capacity
(d) should be feeded with frequency changes

77. Equal area criterion is used to find
(a) solution of swing equation
(b) critical reclosure time
(c) change in frequency errors
(d) change in velocity errors

78. Equal area criterion is applicable for only
(a) single machine and infinite bus
(b) two machines and infinite bus
(c) three machines and infinite bus
(d) four machines and infinite bus

79. Steady state stability mean
(a) a constant power is flowing
(b) frequency is exactly 50 Hz
(c) there is synchronism between machines and external tie lines
(d) all of these

80. If torque angle increases infinitely, the system will show
(a) stability
(b) instability
(c) steady state stability
(d) none of these

81. Transient stability depends on
(a) fault clearing time
(b) strength of transmitting network
(c) short circuit ratio of generating unit
(d) all of these

82. Transiently stable power system
(a) may be dynamically unstable
(b) is always dynamically unstable
(c) will oscillate beyond the first swing
(d) none of these

83. Steady state stability limit refers to maximum flow of power through a point
(a) with stability loss when the power is increased gradually
(b) without stability loss when the power is increased gradually
(c) both (a) and (b)
(d) none of these

84. Factors affecting the power system reliability is
(a) nominal transmission voltage levels
(b) available reserve capacity margin
(c) increased ambient air temperature
(d) flow of power from open tie

85. Disadvantage of low power factor is
(a) Cost of station and distribution equipment is more for a given load
(b) Low power factor makes voltage regulation poor
(c) Bigger sized conductors are required for same energy transmission at low power factor
(d) All of these

86. Cause of low power factor is
(a) transformer drawing more magnetising current
(b) extensive use of induction motors
(c) use of arc lamps
(d) all of these

87. Low power factor be avoided by
(a) using synchronous motors instead of induction motors
(b) using high speed induction motors to low speed machines
(c) not operating induction motors at less than rated output
(d) all of these

88. Power factor is improved by the use of
(a) static capacitors
(b) synchronous compensators or phase modifiers
(c) phase advancer
(d) all of these

89. Best location for power factor improvement apparatus is
(a) where the apparatus responsible for low power factor is installed
(b) at the receiving end
(c) both (a) and (b)
(d) none of these

90. As the frequency of the supply increases, capacity of the static condenser required for phase advancement
(a) decreases   (b) increases
(c) remains same   (d) uncertain

91. Stepless control of power factor is achieved by using
(a) static condenser
(b) series capacitor
(c) synchronous condenser
(d) none of these

92. In KWH and KV Arh tariff, the KV Arh rate is
(a) higher than KWH rate
(b) lower than KWH rate
(c) equal to KWH rate
(d) none of these

93. Static condensers to be connected to improve the power factor should be in
(a) delta
(b) star
(c) parallel with the supply
(d) series with the supply

94. Maximum power transferred through the interconnected is called
(a) maximum capacity
(b) percentage regulation
(c) synchronous capacity
(d) none of these

95. The overall efficiency of thermal plant is low due to low efficiency of
(a) boiler
(b) alternator
(c) steam turbine and condenser
(d) non-salient pole rotor

96. Heat balance in a boiler furnace is improved by sending air to the furnace
(a) at low temperature
(b) at high temperature
(c) mixed with CO_2
(d) both (b) and (c) above

97. Induced draught fan in steam power plant is used to create draught
(a) in the boiler
(b) in the chimney
(c) at the inlet of air preheater
(d) in the alternator

98. Speed fluctuation in diesel electric plant occurs in engine employing which of the following number of strokes ?

   (*a*) 2   (*b*) 4

   (*c*) 6   (*d*) 8

99. Fluctuating speed of dielectric electric plants may be reduced by the use of flywheel having moment of inertia which is

   (*a*) zero   (*b*) low

   (*c*) medium   (*d*) high

100. Main features of a typical hydro-electric station are

   (*a*) dam, reservoir, catchment area

   (*b*) tunnels, surge tanks, pipelines and tailrace

   (*c*) hydraulic turbines and coupled alternators

   (*d*) all of these

101. Prime movers for water turbines are

   (*a*) reaction turbines for low and medium heads

   (*b*) impulse turbines for medium and high heads

   (*c*) both (*a*) and (*b*) above

   (*d*) Pelton turbines for low heads

102. As compared to steam-station, hydro-electric stations have

   (*a*) more cost of installation

   (*b*) less maintenance and fuel cost

   (*c*) both (*a*) and (*b*) above

   (*d*) low depreciation charges

103. The rotor used in alternators of hydro-electric station is

   (*a*) cylindrical rotor

   (*b*) salient pole rotor

   (*c*) nonsalient pole rotor

   (*d*) round rotor with ac excitation

104. The cross-sectional area of the penstock will be smaller if the velocity of water is to be

   (*a*) high

   (*b*) low

   (*c*) under pressure

   (*d*) both (*b*) and (*c*) above

105. Water hammer is developed in

   (*a*) penstock   (*b*) dam

   (*c*) surge tank   (*d*) turbine

106. Effect of water hammer is reduced by using

   (*a*) surge tank   (*b*) an anvil

   (*c*) spillway   (*d*) overhead tank

107. Spillways are used to

   (*a*) discharge excess water in the reservoir

   (*b*) reduce loss of head due to friction in penstock

   (*c*) get more head for hydel plant

   (*d*) both (*b*) and (*c*) above

108. A positive pressure is developed in the penstock when the alternator load is suddenly

   (*a*) increased   (*b*) decreased

   (*c*) removed   (*d*) short-circuited

109. Surge tank is located

   (*a*) close to the power house

   (*b*) at an elevated place

   (*c*) both (*a*) and (*b*) above

   (*d*) at a lower place

110. Vacuum is created in penstock when the turbine gates are suddenly

   (*a*) opened

   (*b*) closed

   (*c*) loaded

   (*d*) both (*b*) and (*c*) above

111. The curve between discharge in m³/s and time is called

   (*a*) discharge duration curve

   (*b*) hydrograph

   (*c*) load curve

   (*d*) flow histogram

112. Energy produced by fission reaction uranium having mass of atom m and velocity of light c is

   (*a*) mc (*b*) $\frac{1}{2}m^2c$

   (*c*) mc^2 (*d*) $\frac{1}{2}mc^2$

113. Percentage of U-235 in natural uranium is

   (*a*) 0.235   (*b*) 235

   (*c*) 2.35   (*d*) 0.7

114. In a nuclear power station, moderator is used to

   (*a*) absorb neutrons

   (*b*) reduce the speed of neutrons

   (*c*) accelerate the speed of neutrons

   (*d*) stop the chain reaction

115. Commonly used atomic fuels are

   (*a*) Uranium, U-235

   (*b*) Plutonium, Pu-239

   (*c*) Thorium, Th-232

   (*d*) all of these

116. The heat produced by 1 kg of atomic fuel is equal to that produced by coal of weight
 (a) 1 ton
 (b) 100 tons
 (c) 1000 tons
 (d) 4237 tons

117. Coolents used in reactors are
 (a) air, hydrogen, helium
 (b) water, graphite
 (c) liquid metals, lead bismuth alloys
 (d) all of these

118. Reactor used in nuclear reactor serves to
 (a) reflect back the escaping neutrons
 (b) improve its economy
 (c) both (a) and (b) above
 (d) none of these

119. Cooling system used in boiler water reactor is
 (a) direct cooling
 (b) single circuit
 (c) double circuit
 (d) reflector type radiator

120. Single circuit coolant system is preferred in
 (a) fast breeder reactor
 (b) boiler water reactor
 (c) pressurized water reactor
 (d) none of these

121. Coolant used is fast breeder reactor is
 (a) heavy water
 (b) graphite
 (c) sodium
 (d) none of these

122. Moderator used in fast breeder reacor is
 (a) heavy water
 (b) graphite
 (c) both (a) and (b) above
 (d) none of these

123. In fast breeder reactors, neutron shielding is provided by
 (a) graphite
 (b) copper
 (c) tinalloy
 (d) boron

124. Location of nuclear plant is
 (a) dependent upon the geographical factors
 (b) independent of the geographical factors
 (c) requires large quantity of water
 (d) both (b) and (c) above

125. Steam produced by geothermal field is
 (a) dry
 (b) wet
 (c) both (a) and (b) above
 (d) none of these

126. Water steam mixture in geothermal field is separated by the use of
 (a) filters
 (b) evaporators
 (c) bypass valve
 (d) centrifugal action

127. Geothermal steam contains
 (a) CO_2
 (b) H_2S
 (c) NH_3
 (d) all of these

128. Constructional material used in geothermal plant is
 (a) steel
 (b) brass
 (c) stainless steel
 (d) any of these

129. The source of geoenergy is
 (a) radioactivity within crystal rocks
 (b) boiling of water in the ground due to oil burning
 (c) use of jet type of condenser
 (d) both (a) and (b) above

130. Photo-voltaic cell produces electric energy from
 (a) electromagnetic energy
 (b) electrostatic energy
 (c) geothermal energy
 (d) both (a) and (b) above

131. Collectros used for collecting solar energy are
 (a) paraboloid
 (b) solar radiators
 (c) flat plate and focussing solar collectors
 (d) none of these

132. Photo-chemical electric generation is possible if the reverse reaction involves
 (a) reduction
 (b) oxidation
 (c) either (a) or (b) above
 (d) none of these

133. Cell having hydrogen and lithium electrodes produce electricity at an operating temperature of
 (a) –150°C
 (b) 0°C
 (c) + 150°C
 (d) 350°C

134. In MHD generation, emf induced is
(a) motionally induced emf
(b) static emf
(c) Hall emf
(d) both (a) and (c) above

135. The essential parts of MHD generators are
(a) gas   (b) field poles
(c) duct   (d) all of these

136. The current developed in MHD generator is
(a) ac
(b) dc
(c) pulsating
(d) either (a) or (b) above

137. The conduction used in MHD generator is
(a) copper   (b) aluminum
(c) liquid   (d) gas

138. The rating of MHD generator per unit volume is proportional to
(a) square of magnetic flux density
(b) square of the flow velocity of the fluid
(c) the electrical conductivity of the fluid
(d) all of these

139. Wind energy
(a) is clean, almost free and domestically produced
(b) has higher cost comparatively
(c) develops power proportional to the power of the wind
(d) all of these

140. The magnitude of power constant in wind mill depends on
(a) shape of rotor blades
(b) wind velocity
(c) orientation of rotor blades
(d) both (a) and (b) above

141. The principal type of failure in wind power generation is in
(a) aerodynamic system
(b) electrical system
(c) mechanical system
(d) both (b) and (c) above

142. The EHV system is one operating beyond
(a) 11 kV
(b) 132 kV
(c) 200 kV
(d) 400 kV

143. The advantage of dc systems over ac systems is
(a) improved line regulation
(b) no skin effect
(c) no charging currents
(d) all of these

144. Pilot exciter is used when main exciter is
(a) self excited
(b) separately excited
(c) induction motor driven
(d) none of these

145. Static voltage regulators use
(a) saturable reactor
(b) integrated circuit
(c) microprocessors
(d) any of these

146. Current reactors are used
(a) to improve voltage regulation
(b) to reduce the fault level
(c) to improve efficiency
(d) to improve power factor

147. Regulating transformers are used in power system to control
(a) load flow   (b) power factor
(c) voltage   (d) all of these

148. Series reactors usually have
(a) low resistance   (b) high resistance
(c) low impedance   (d) high impedance

149. As per Indian Standard, the permissible range of power supply frequency is
(a) 49.5 to 50.5 Hz
(b) 49 to 51 Hz
(c) 48 to 52 Hz
(d) 47.5 to 52.5 Hz

150. Which of the following generating station has minimum running cost ?
(a) thermal power station
(b) hydro-electric power station
(c) nuclear power station
(d) none of these

151. Which of the following method of generating electric power from sea water is more advantageous ?
(a) ocean currents   (b) tidal power
(c) wave power   (d) none of these

152. Which of the following hydraulic turbine is used for water heads exceeding 400 metres ?
   (*a*) kaplan turbine   (*b*) Francis turbine
   (*c*) Pelton wheel   (*d*) none of these

153. Nuclear reactors generally employ
   (*a*) fission
   (*b*) fusion
   (*c*) both fission and fusion
   (*d*) none of these

154. Heavy water implies
   (*a*) H_2O (*b*) W_2O
   (*c*) B_2O (*d*) D_2O

155. Running cost of a power plant is based on the cost of
   (*a*) energy or fuel
   (*b*) consumable items
   (*c*) maintenance and operation
   (*d*) all of these

156. In straight line method of depreciation, the money to be reserved for depreciation is
   (*a*) directly proportional to time
   (*b*) inversely proportional to time
   (*c*) directly proportional to square of time
   (*d*) inversely proportional to square of time

157. In straight line method of depreciation, the money deposited carries
   (*a*) fixed interest
   (*b*) compound interest
   (*c*) no interest
   (*d*) a straight line interest

158. In diminishing value method of depreciation
   (*a*) a fixed rate is set aside each year
   (*b*) depreciation charges are heavy in early years and maintenance charges are low
   (*c*) in later years, maintenance charges are heavy and depreciation charges are low
   (*d*) all of these

159. In reducing balance method of depreciation, the calculation of depreciaiton in any year is a fixed proportion of the cost at the
   (*a*) beginning of that particular year
   (*b*) beginning of the project
   (*c*) average of that particular year
   (*d*) maximum of that particular year

160. In sinking fund method of depreciation
   (*a*) a fixed amount is deposited annually
   (*b*) the rate of interest is compounded yearly
   (*c*) it requires smaller amount as compared to straight line method
   (*d*) all of these

161. The book value of plant is
   (*a*) cost of plant
   (*b*) accrued depreciation
   (*c*) difference of (*a*) and (*b*) above
   (*d*) sum of (*a*) and (*b*) above

162. The main objective of tariff is to distribute equatabily the cost of
   (*a*) installation and fuel
   (*b*) power transmission and distribution
   (*c*) supplying energy among the various classification of users
   (*d*) energy production among all its consumers

163. All types of tariffs must recover the cost of
   (*a*) capital investment in generating equipment
   (*b*) operation, supplies and maintenance of equipment
   (*c*) metering equipment, billing, collection costs, profit and wages
   (*d*) all of these

164. Factors involved in fixing tariffs are
   (*a*) secured return from each consumer
   (*b*) simplicity, cheapness and easy explainability
   (*c*) incentive to consumers and charge according to use
   (*d*) all of these

165. Depreciation rate is less in the case of
   (*a*) diesel engine plant
   (*b*) nuclear plant
   (*c*) hydro-electric plant
   (*d*) steam power plant

166. Economical loading based on the incremental rate gives
   (*a*) maximum conversion efficiency
   (*b*) good energy conversion efficiency
   (*c*) best system efficiency
   (*d*) economical demand factor

167. Causes of low power factor are
   (a) induction motors and arc lamp loads
   (b) generating equipment during low loads
   (c) industrial heating furnaces and arc furnaces
   (d) both (a) and (c) above

168. Drawbacks of low power factor are
   (a) high ratings of generating, transmitting and distributing equipment
   (b) large voltage drop and poor voltage regulation
   (c) large copper losses and high capital costs
   (d) all of these

169. Power factor of a power system can be improved by
   (a) using phase advances, static capacitors, capacitance boosters
   (b) unexcited synchronous motors on load
   (c) over excited synchronous motors on no load
   (d) both (a) and (b) above

170. Diversity factor of a power system is the
   (a) ratio of sum of consumer's maximum demands to maximum load on the station
   (b) ratio of average demand to maximum demand
   (c) reciprocal of (a) above
   (d) reciprocal of (b) above

ANSWERS

1. (a)	**2.** (b)	**3.** (d)	**4.** (b)	**5.** (c)	**6.** (c)	**7.** (b)	**8.** (c)	**9.** (d)	**10.** (a)
11. (c)	**12.** (b)	**13.** (c)	**14.** (a)	**15.** (a)	**16.** (c)	**17.** (d)	**18.** (d)	**19.** (c)	**20.** (c)
21. (b)	**22.** (a)	**23.** (b)	**24.** (c)	**25.** (d)	**26.** (c)	**27.** (b)	**28.** (a)	**29.** (b)	**30.** (d)
31. (c)	**32.** (b)	**33.** (d)	**34.** (d)	**35.** (b)	**36.** (b)	**37.** (d)	**38.** (a)	**39.** (b)	**40.** (a)
41. (c)	**42.** (c)	**43.** (a)	**44.** (c)	**45.** (b)	**46.** (d)	**47.** (d)	**48.** (a)	**49.** (c)	**50.** (a)
51. (d)	**52.** (c)	**53.** (b)	**54.** (c)	**55.** (d)	**56.** (d)	**57.** (c)	**58.** (a)	**59.** (c)	**60.** (d)
61. (b)	**62.** (d)	**63.** (a)	**64.** (c)	**65.** (a)	**66.** (c)	**67.** (b)	**68.** (c)	**69.** (d)	**70.** (b)
71. (a)	**72.** (a)	**73.** (c)	**74.** (b)	**75.** (a)	**76.** (b)	**77.** (b)	**78.** (a)	**79.** (c)	**80.** (b)
81. (d)	**82.** (a)	**83.** (a)	**84.** (b)	**85.** (d)	**86.** (d)	**87.** (d)	**88.** (d)	**89.** (c)	**90.** (b)
91. (c)	**92.** (b)	**93.** (c)	**94.** (c)	**95.** (c)	**96.** (b)	**97.** (b)	**98.** (b)	**99.** (d)	**100.** (d)
101. (c)	**102.** (c)	**103.** (b)	**104.** (a)	**105.** (c)	**106.** (a)	**107.** (a)	**108.** (b)	**109.** (c)	**110.** (a)
111. (b)	**112.** (b)	**113.** (d)	**114.** (b)	**115.** (d)	**116.** (d)	**117.** (d)	**118.** (a)	**119.** (a)	**120.** (c)
121. (c)	**122.** (d)	**123.** (d)	**124.** (d)	**125.** (c)	**126.** (d)	**127.** (d)	**128.** (c)	**129.** (a)	**130.** (a)
131. (c)	**132.** (c)	**133.** (d)	**134.** (d)	**135.** (d)	**136.** (b)	**137.** (d)	**138.** (d)	**139.** (d)	**140.** (b)
141. (a)	**142.** (d)	**143.** (d)	**144.** (b)	**145.** (d)	**146.** (b)	**147.** (a)	**148.** (a)	**149.** (d)	**150.** (b)
151. (b)	**152.** (c)	**153.** (a)	**154.** (d)	**155.** (d)	**156.** (b)	**157.** (c)	**158.** (d)	**159.** (a)	**160.** (d)
161. (c)	**162.** (c)	**163.** (d)	**164.** (d)	**165.** (c)	**166.** (c)	**167.** (d)	**168.** (d)	**169.** (d)	**170.** (a)

Transmission and Distribution

DISTRIBUTION SYSTEM

The part of power system which distributes electrical power for local use is called distribution system.

Distribution system is the electrical system, between the sub-station fed by the transmission system and the consumers meters. *It generally consists of*

(*i*) **Feeders.** A feeder is a conductor which connects the sub-station (or localised generating station) to the area where power is to be distributed. Generally, no tappings are taken from the feeder so that current in it remains the same throughout. The main consideration in the design of the feeder is the current carrying capacity.

(*ii*) **Distributor.** A distributor is a conductor from which tappings are taken for supply to the consumers. The current through a distributor is not constant because tappings are taken at various places along its length. While designing a distributor, voltage drop along its length is the main consideration since the statutory limit of voltage variations is ± 6% of rated value at the consumer's terminals.

(*iii*) **Service mains.** A service mains is generally a small cable which connects the distributor to the consumer's terminals.

Classification of distribution system

1. Nature of Current. According to nature of current, distribution system may be classified as

(*i*) d.c. distribution system

(*ii*) a.c. distribution system

Now-a-days, a.c. system is universally adopted for distribution of electric power as it is simpler and more economical than direct current method.

2. Type of Construction. According to type of construction, distribution system may be classified as

(*i*) **Overhead system :** It generally employed for distribution as it is 5 to 10 times cheaper than the equivalent underground system.

(*ii*) **Underground system :** It is used at places where overhead construction is impracticable or prohibited by the local laws.

3. Scheme of Connection. According to scheme of connection, the distribution system may be classified as

(*i*) radial system,

(*ii*) ring main system,

(*iii*) inter-connected system.

A.C. TRANSMISSION AND DISTRIBUTION

Alternating current is used in preference to direct current due to fact that alternating voltage can be conveniently changed in magnitude by means of a transformer. High transmission and distribution voltages have greatly reduced the current in the conductors and the resulting line losses.

Types of a.c. distribution system

(*i*) **Primary distribution system.** It is that part of a.c. distribution system which operates in voltage somewhat higher than general utilisation and handles large blocks of electrical energy than the average low-voltage consumer uses. The most commonly used primary distribution voltages are 11 kV, 6·6 kV and 3·3 kV. Due to economic considerations, primary distribution is carried out by 3-phase, 4-wire system.

(*ii*) **Secondary distribution system.** It is that part of a.c. distribution system which includes the range of voltages at which the ultimate consumer utilises the electrical energy delivered to him. The secondary distribution employees 400/230 V, 3-phase, 4-wire system.

SYSTEMS OF A.C. DISTRIBUTION

A.C. power transmission is always at high voltage and mostly by 3-phase system. The use of single-phase system is limited to single-phase electric railways. Single-phase power transmission is used only for short distances and for relatively low voltages. 3-phase power transmission requires less copper than either single-phase or 2-phase power transmission.

The distribution system begins either at the sub-stations where power is delivered by overhead transmission lines and stepped down by transformers or in some cases at the generating station itself. Where a large area is involved, primary and secondary distributions may be used.

Systems available for the distribution of a.c. power.
1.   Single-phase, 2-wire system.
2.   Single-phase, 3-wire system.
3.   Two-phase, 3-wire system.
4.   Two-phase, 4-wire system.
5.   Three-phase, 3-wire system.

Single-phase, 2-wire system.

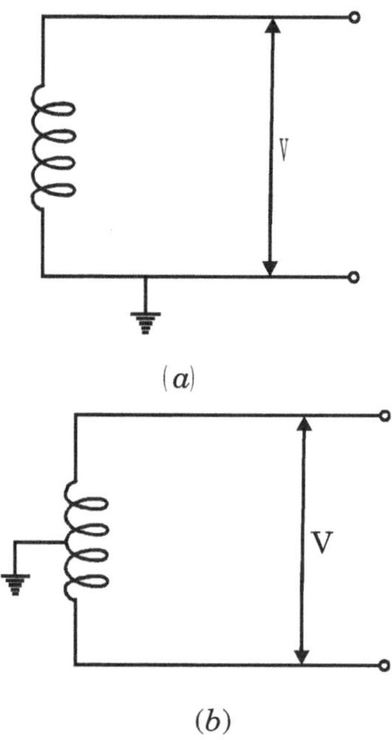

(a)

(b)

Single phase, 3-wire system. The 1-phase, 3-wire system is identical in principle with the 3-wire d.c. system. As shown below in figure, the third wire or neutral is connected to the centre of the transformers secondary and earthed for protecting personnel from electric shock should the transformer insulation break down or the secondary main contact high voltage wire.

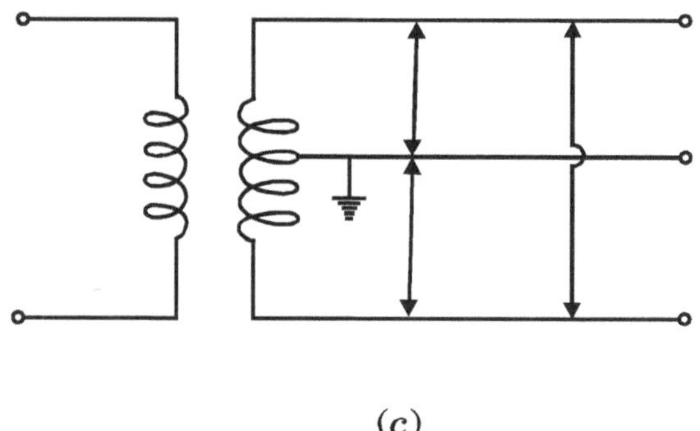

(c)

CONDUCTOR MATERIALS FOR OVERHEAD SYSTEMS

Assumptions :
1.   Amount of power transmitted by each system is the same.
2.   Distance of transmission is the same in each case.

3.   Transmission efficiency is the same *i.e.*, the losses are the same in each case.
4.   Loads are balanced in the case of 3-wire system.
5.   Cross-section of the neutral wire is half that of any outer.
6.   Maximum voltage to earth is the same in all cases.

Requirements of a good system
1.   The voltage at the consumer's premises must be maintained within ± 4 or ± 6% of the declared voltage, the actual value depending on the type of load.
2.   The loss of power in the system itself should be a small percentage (About 10%) of the power transmitted.
3.   The transmission cost should not be unduly excessive.
4.   The maximum current passing through the conductor should be limited to such a value as not to overheat the conductor or injure its insulation.
5.   The insulation resistance of the whole system should be very high so that there is no undue leakage or danger to human life.

Reasons for producing power in the form of alternating current rather than direct current.
1.   It is possible, to construct large high-speed a.c. generators of capacities up to 500 MW. Such generators are economical both in the matter of cost power kWh of electric energy produced as well as in operation. Unfortunately d.c. generators cannot be built of ratings higher than 5 MW because of commutation trouble. Moreover, since they must operate at low speeds, it necessitates large and heavy machines.
2.   A.C. voltage can be efficiently and conveniently raised or lowered for economic transmission and distribution of electric power respectively.

Generation and transmission is almost exclusively three-phase. The secondary transmission is also 3-phase whereas the distribution to the ultimate customer may be 3-phase or single phase depending upon the requirements of the customers.

Primary or high voltage transmission is carried out at 132 kV. The transmission voltage is, to a very large extent, determined by economic consideration. High voltage transmission requires conductors of smaller cross-section which results in economy of copper or aluminium. But at the same time cost of insulating the line and other expenses are increased. *Economical voltage of transmission is that for which the saving in copper or aluminium is not offset by the increased.*

(*i*)   cost of insulating the line

(*ii*) size of transmission-line structures

(*iii*) size of generating stations and sub-stations.

3-phase, 3-wire overhead high-voltage transmission line next terminates in step-down transformers in a sub-station known as Receiving Station which usually lies at the outskirts of a city because it is not safe to bring high-voltage overhead transmission lines into thickly-populated areas. Here, the voltage is stepped down to 33 kV. It may be noted here that for ensuring continuity of service transmission is always by duplicate lines.

From Receiving Sation, power is next transmitted at 33 kV by underground cables (and occasionally by overhead lines) to various sub-stations located at various strategic points in the city. This is known as secondary or low-voltage transmission.

At the sub-station (SS) voltage is reduced from 33 kV to 3.3 kV 3-wire for primary distribution. Consumers whose demands exceeds 50 kVA are usually supplied from SS by special 3.3 kV feeders.

Secondary distribution is done at 400/230 V for which purpose voltage is reduced from 3.3 kV to 400 V at the distribution sub-station. Feeders radiating from distribution sub-station supply power to distribution networks in their respective areas. If distribution network happens to be at a great distance from sub-station, then they are supplied from the secondaries of distribution transformers which are either pole-mounted at else housed in kiosks at suitable points of the distribution networks. The most common system for secondary distribution is 400/230-V, 3-phase 4-wire system. The single-phase residential lighting load is connected between any one line and the neutral whereas 3-phase, 400-V motor load is connected across 3-phase lines directly.

HVDC TRANSMISSION

In a combined AC and DC system, generated ac voltage is converted into dc voltage at the sending end, then the dc voltage is inverted back to AC voltage at the receiving end for distribution purpose.

CLASSIFICATION.

HVDC can be classified into two scheme.

1. Mono polar link.

A mono polar link has a single conductor, usually of negative polarity and uses earth or sea for return path of current. Some timer metallic return is also used.

Bipolar link has two conductor one positive and the other negative with respect to earth. The mid-points of converters at each terminal station are earthed via electrode lines and earth electrode.

2. Bipolar link.

A bipolar system is advantageous in the sense that when one pole goes out of operation, the system may be changed to monopolar mode with ground returns.

Advantages of HVDC transmission over AC transmission.

(*i*)   In dc, number of conductors are lesser and therefore reduced conductor and insulator cost.

(*ii*)   Lesser phase to phase clearance and lesser phase to ground clearance.

(*iii*) Lighter and cheaper towers.

(*iv*)   Lesser right of way requirements.

(*v*)   Lesser corona loss and reduced television and radio interference.

(*vi*)   Power losses is reduced.

(*vii*) There is flexibility of operation, bipolar and unipolar operation.

(*viii*) No stability problem with dc line.

(*xii*) Power flow can be controlled more rapidly and accurately.

GROUND RETURN LINES

H.V.D.C. transmission lines use ground or sea water as the return conductor either continuously (monopolar) or for short time of emergency (bipolar). These return paths are called *ground return* even if sea water is used as a return path. For the same length of transmission resistance offered by the ground in case of d.c. is much less as compared to a.c. transmission because d.c. spreads over a very large cross sectional area in both depth and width as compared to a.c. or transient currents. In fact the earth resistance in case of d.c. is independent of the length (for long lines) and equals sum of the electrode resistances. Since resistance in case of d.c. is low as compared to a.c. there is low power loss in comparison with a metallic line conductor of economical size and equal length if ground electrodes are properly designed.

Advantages

(*i*)   A line with ground return (monopolar) is more economical than a bipolar line because ground return saves most of the cost of one metallic conductor and the losses in it.

(*ii*) A d.c. line can be built in two stages if initial load requirement demands. Initially it will operate as a monopolar line with ground as return and later on in the second stage it can be built as a bipolar line. Thus a considerable part of the total investment can be deferred until the second stage.

(*iii*) Reliability of the system *i.e.*, in the event of an outage of one conductor of the bipolar line, it can be operated temporarily at almost half of its rated power by the use of the healthy line and the ground. For this reason the reliability of a bipolar line is equal to that of a double circuit 3-phase line although it has only two conductors instead of six for 3-phase line.

Disadvantages

(*i*) The ground currents cause electrolytic corrosion of buried or immersed metallic structures.

(*ii*) It is difficult to design ground electrodes for low resistance and low cost of installation and maintenance.

(*iii*) Ground currents cause dangerous step and touch voltages.

(*iv*) The ground currents interfere with the operation of other services such as a.c. power transmission, ships' compasses and reilway signals.

CIRCUIT BREAKING

It is easy to interrupt a.c. currents because of their natural zeros. Since d.c. is a steady unidirectional current it does not have a natural zero and therefore it is difficult to interrupt large d.c. currents at high voltages.

The d.c. transmission projects till this date are two terminal projects and it is not difficult to interrupt the fault currents. The faults on the d.c. line or in the converters are cleared by using control grids of the converter valves to stop the direct current temporarily. The lack of d.c. breakers has inhibited the networking of d.c lines. The transient faults can be cleared using grid control, but permanent faults can be cleared using a combination of grid control, fault locators and isolating switches. Reasonable proposals have been made for clearing faults on such lines by running the whole system to zero using grid control, opening switches to isolate the faulty section and then reising the voltage back to normal. The time taken for this sequence of operation is approximately equal to the rapid reclosure of a.c. circuit breakers.

The requirement for d.c. circuit breaking is not to break the actual short circuit currents but to interrupt load currents in circuits at high potential with respect to ground because the short circuit currents can be limited to normal load currents using the gird control. If such switches could be developed, lines could be switched into or out of an unfaulted network without running the voltage down. Some such switches have been suggested wherein an artificial zero of current is created through the contacts of the switch by the oscillatory discharge of a capacitor. The crest value of the oscillatory currents should be greater than the direct current to be interrupted.

D.C. TRANSMISSION

Advantages

1. d.c. power vary much more with the voltages than in the case of a.c. transmission, where the power is proportional to the product of line end voltages.

2. **Line circuit.** The line construction is simpler as compared to a.c. transmission. A single conductor line with ground as return can be compared with a 3-phase single circuit line. Hence the line is relatively cheaper and has the same reliability as that of a 3-phase single circuit line because 3-phase lines cannot operate, except for a short time when there is a single line to ground fault or a L-L fault as this creates unbalancing in the voltages and hence interfere with the communication lines and other sensitive apparatus on the system. Bipolar d.c. lines has same reliability index as a two-circuit 3-phase line having six line conductors.

3. **Power per conductor.** For transmitting power both on a.c. and d.c circuits, assume that two lines have same number of conductors and insulators. Assuming that the current is limited by temperature rise, direct current equals rms alternating current. Since crest voltage in both cases is same for the insulators, the direct voltage is $\sqrt{2}$ times the rms alternating voltage.

4. **Power per circuit.** The d.c. line is cheaper and simpler as it requires two conductors instead of three and hence $\dfrac{2}{3}$ as many insulators, and the towers are cheaper and narrower and hence a narrow right of way could be used.

5. **No charging current.** In case of a.c. charging current flows in the cable conductor; a severe decrease in the value of load current transmittable occurs if thermal rating is not to be exceeded; in the higher voltage range lengths of the order of 32 km create a need for drastic derating. A further current loading reduction is caused by the appreciable magnitude of dielectric losses at high voltages. Since in case of d.c. charging current is totally absent, length of transmission is not limited and the cable need not be derated.

6. **No skin effect.** a.c resistance of a conductor is somewhat higher than its d.c. resistance because in case of a.c. current is not uniformly distributed over the section of the conductor. The current density is higher on the outer section of the

conductor as compared to the inner section. This is called *skin effect*. As a result of this, conductor section is not utilized fully. This effect is absent in case of d.c.

7. **No compensation required.** Long distance a.c. power transmission is feasible only with the use of series and shunt compensation, applied at intervals along the line. For such lines shunt compensation (shunt reactors) is required to absorb the line charging kVAs during light load conditions and series compensation (use of series capacitors) forstability reasons. Since d.c. line operate at unity power factor and charging currents are absent no compensation is required.

8. **Less corona loss and radio interference.** In case of d.c., the corona losses are less as compared to a.c. Corona loss and radio interference are directly related and hence radio interference in case of d.c. is less as compared to a.c. Also corona and radio interference slightly decrease by foul weather conditions (snow, rain or fog) in cas of d.c. whereas they increase appreciably in case of a.c. supply.

9. **Higher operating voltages possible.** The modern high voltage transmission lines are designed based on the expected switching surges rather than the lightning voltages because former are more severe as compared to the latter. The level of switching surges due to d.c. is lower as compared to a.c. and hence, same size of conductors and string insulators can be used for higher voltages in case of d.c. as compared to a.c. In cables, where limiting factor is usually the normaly working voltage the insulation will withstand a direct voltage higher than that of alternating voltage, which is already 1.4 times the rms value of the alternating voltage.

10. **No stability problem.** Longer the length of the line, higher is the value of X and hence lower will be the capability of the system to transmit power from one end to the other. With this the steady state stability limit of the system is reduced. The transient state stability limit is normally lower than the steady state; therefore with longer lines used for transmission the transient stability also becomes very low. A d.c. transmission line does not have any stability proble in itself because d.c. operation is an asynchronous operation of the machines. In fact two separate a.c. systems interconnected only by a d.c. link do not operate in synchronism even if their nominal frequencies are equal and they can operate at different nominal frequencies *e.g.*, one operating at 60 Hz and the other at 50 Hz.

11. **Low short circuit currents.** The interconnection of a.c. system through an a.c. system increases the fault level to the extent that sometimes existing switchgear has to be replaced. However, interconnection of a.c. system with d.c. links does not increase the level so much and is limited automatically by the grid control to twice its rated current. As a result of this fault, d.c. links do not draw large currents from the a.c. system.

Disadvantages

1. **Expensive converters.** The converters required at both ends of the line have proved to be reliable but they are much more expensive than the conventional a.c. equipments. The converters have very little overload capacity and they absorb reactive power which must be supplied locally. The converters produce lot of harmonics both on d.c. and a.c. sides which may cause interference with the audio-frequency communication lines. Filters are required on the a.c. side of each converter for diminishing the magnitude of hamonics in the a.c. networks. These also increase the cost of the converters.

2. **Voltage transformation.** The power transmitted can be used at lower voltage only. Voltage transformation is not easier in case of d.c. and hence it has to be done on the a.c. side of the system.

3. Circuit breaking for multi-terminal lines is difficult.

CABLES

The a.c. transmission through cables is limited in distance due to the charging current.

The charging kVA of 3-phase single circuit cables per km are 1250 kVA at 132 kV; 3125 kVA at 220 kV; 9375 kVA at 400 kV

Enormous amount of charging kVA are required; therefore, if a.c. transmission by cables is required, charging current has to be absorbed at intermediate stations if distances exceed the following:

64 km at 132 kV; 40 km at 220 kV; 24 km at 400 kV

Since in case of d.c. charging current is absent, there is no distance limitation on transmission by underground or undersea cables.

LINE INSULATORS AND SUPPORT

In the design of insulator following considerations are made.

(*i*) The insulator should have high permittivity so that it can withstand high electrical stress i.e. dielectric strength of the insulator should be high.

(*ii*) Insulator should have high mechanical strength to bear the conductor load.

(*iii*) High resistance to temperature changes to reduce damage from power flashover.

(*iv*) Leakage current to earth should be minimum to reduce the corona loss and radio interference.

(*v*) Insulator material should not be porous.

Insulation Failure.

It may take place by two processes:

(*i*) **By puncture.** If puncture takes place then the insulator will be permanently damaged. Hence flashover should take place before puncture. In puncture arc passes through the body of insulator.

(*ii*) **By flash-over.** In flash over. arc discharge between conductor and earth through air surrounding the insulator.

For satisfactory operation flashover should take place before puncture. Ratio of puncture voltage to flashover is called *factor of safety* and is kept high. For satisfactory operation, the rain sheds should have the shape like those of equipotential surfaces and the insulator body should be constructed along the line of electrostatic field around the pin.

INSULATOR MATERIALS

Insulators (EHV lines) are made from toughened glass or high quality wet process procelain.

Proclain insulator are glazed over all exposed surface.

Toughened glass insulators have their surface layers in state of high compression due to which their resistance to with-stand mechanical and thermal stress is greater.

Advantages of Toughened glass over porcelain insulators

(*i*) Toughened glass insulators have greater puncture strength.

(*ii*) Possess greater mechanical strength.

(*iii*) High thermal shock resistance hence flash over is limited.

CORONA AND RADIO INTERFERENCE

For EHV lines when electric field in the air due to high voltage in the lines reaches upto (3×10^6 V/m or 3000 kV/m), then air in the immediate vicinity of conductors no more remains a dielectric but it is ionised and become conducting.

Electric break-down.

It results in following phenomenas.

(*i*) A giant glow around conductors.

(*ii*) There is an accoustical noise.

(*iii*) There is a tendency in the conductor to vibrate.

(*iv*) Ozone and oxides of nitrogens are produced.

(*v*) There is a loss of power.

(*vi*) There is radio interference.

If voltage gradient is increased further, then size of brightness of luminous envelope increases and finally a spark or arc is established between conductor because of complete breakdown of the insulating property of air between them.

Factors affecting corana.

(*i*) Conductor surface gradient.

(*ii*) Condition of conductor surface.

(*iii*) Atmospheric conditions.

(*iv*) Frequency and waveform of supply voltage.

(*v*) Air density factor.

Disruptive critical voltage.

Minimum voltage at which breakdown of the insulating property of air occurs and corona starts is called *disruptive critical voltage*.

Visual critical voltage.

Visual flow of corona occurs at a voltage higher than the disruptive critical voltage. The voltage at which the visual corona begins is called *visual critical voltage*.

Bundled conductors.

Bundled conductors are used mainly to minimize corona. The bundled acts as far as the electric field is concerned like a conductor of diameter much larger than that of the component conductors. This reduces the voltage gradient. In other words, a higher voltage can be used for permissible levels of radio interference. The GMR of a bundle is high and therefore the conductive reactance of the line is low. The bundle conductors have higher capacitance and therefore lower surge impedance as compared to single conductor of equivalent diameter. The lower value of inductive reactance helps in reducing the cost of series capacitor which are used to increase the transient stability limit of very long lines. Due to higher capacitance of bundled conductor; generated reactive power capacity is also reduced.

OBJECTIVE TYPE QUESTIONS

1. The topmost conductor in hv transmission line is
   (a) R-phase conductor (b) Y-phase conducto
   (c) B-phase conductor (d) earth conductor

2. Insulators used on EHT transmission lines are made of
   (a) PVC   (b) porcelain
   (c) glass   (d) stealite

3. HV transmission line uses
   (a) pin type insulators
   (b) suspension insulators
   (c) both(a) and (b)
   (d) none of these

4. The insulators used on 220 kv transmission lines are of
   (a) suspension type   (b) pin type
   (c) shackle type   (d) none of these

5. Corona occurs between two transmission conductors when they
   (a) have high potential difference
   (b) are closely spaced
   (c) carry d c power
   (d) both (a) and (b)

6. Which of the following affects the corona least ?
   (a) Mean free length
   (b) Atmospheric temperature
   (c) Number of ions
   (d) Size and charge per ion

7. The effect of corona is
   (a) increased inductance
   (b) increased reactance
   (c) increased power loss
   (d) all of these

8. Corona is affected by
   (a) size of conductor
   (b) shape and surface condition of the conductor
   (c) operating voltage
   (d) all of these

9. The only advantage of corona is that is
   (a) produces a pleasing luminous glow
   (b) makes line current sinusoidal
   (c) works as a safety valve for surges
   (d) ozone gas is produced

10. Corona has the disadvantage(s) of
    (a) power loss
    (b) interference with neighbouring communication circuits
    (c) introducing the harmonics, predominately third harmonics, into the transmission lines
    (d) all of these

11. The dielectric strength of air under normal conditions is around
    (a) 30 kv/cm.   (b) 100 kv/cm.
    (c) 150 kv/cm.   (d) 200 kv/cm

12. Power loss due to corona is directly proportional to
    (a) spacing between conductors.
    (b) radius of conductor
    (c) supply frequency
    (d) none of these

13. Critical voltage limit of a transmission line is increased by
    (a) increasing the radius of the conductors
    (b) increasing the spacing between conductors
    (c) reducing the spacing between conductors
    (d) reducing the radius of the conductors

14. Transmission line constants are
    (a) resistance   (b) inductance
    (c) capacitance   (d) all of these

15. The inductance of line is minimum when
    (a) G M D is high
    (b) G M R is high
    (c) both G M D and G M R are high
    (d) G M D is low but G M R is high

16. The inductance of single phase two wire power transmission line per km gets doubled when the
    (a) distance between the wires is doubled
    (b) distance between the wires is doubled
    (c) distance between the wires is increased as square of the original distance
    (d) radius of the wore is doubled

17. Capacitance of a transmission line
    (a) increases
    (b) decreases
    (c) remains same with increase in its length
    (d) none of these

18. Capacitance in equivalent circuit of a transmission line is due to
  (*a*) current in the line
  (*b*) difference in potential of line
  (*c*) leakage of current
  (*d*) presence of magnetic flux

19. In a transmission line the distributed constants are
  (*a*) resistance and shunt conductance only
  (*b*) resistance and inductance only
  (*c*) resistance, inductance and capacitance only
  (*d*) resistance, inductance, capacitance and shunt conductance.

20. Skin effect in transmission line is due to
  (*a*) supply frequency
  (*b*) self inductance of conductor
  (*c*) high sensitivity of material in the centre
  (*d*) both (*a*) and (*b*)

21. The conductor carries more current on the surface in comparison to its core. This phenomenon is called the
  (*a*) skin effect
  (*b*) corona
  (*c*) Ferranti effect
  (*d*) Lenz's effect

22. Increase in frequency of transmission line causes
  (*a*) no change in line resistance
  (*b*) increase in line resistance
  (*c*) decrease in line resistance
  (*d*) decrease in line series reactance

23. Skin effect
  (*a*) increases the effective resistance and effective internal reactance
  (*b*) reduces the effective resistance and effective internal reactance
  (*c*) increases the effective resistance but reduces the effective internal reactance
  (*d*) reduces the effective resistance but increases the effective internal reactance.

24. The skin effect of a conductor reduces with the increase in
  (*a*) supply frequency
  (*b*) resistivity of the conductor material
  (*c*) x-section of conductor
  (*d*) permeability of conductor material

25. Skin effect in conductor is proportional to
  (*a*) (diameter of conductor).$^{1/2}$
  (*b*) diameter of conductor.
  (*c*) (diameter of conductor).^{2}
  (*d*) (diameter of conductor).^{4}

26. The presence of earth in case of overhead lines
  (*a*) increases the capacitance
  (*b*) increases the inductance
  (*c*) decreases the capacitance
  (*d*) decreases the inductance

27. If the effect of earth is taken into account, then the capacitance of line to ground
  (*a*) decreases   (*b*) increases
  (*c*) remains unaltered (*d*) becomes infinite

28. The presence of earth in case of overhead lines
  (*a*) increases the capacitance
  (*b*) increases the inductance
  (*c*) decreases the capacitance and increases the inductance
  (*d*) does not effect any of the line constants

29. Transposition of transmission line is done to reduce the
  (*a*) line losses
  (*b*) capacitive effect
  (*c*) disturbances to nearby communication circuits
  (*d*) effect of surge voltages induced on the line

30. Transposition of transmission line is done to
  (*a*) reduce line loss
  (*b*) reduce skin effect
  (*c*) balance line voltage drop
  (*d*) reduce corona

31. High voltage transmission lines are transposed because then
  (*a*) corona losses can be minimized
  (*b*) computation of inductance becomes easier
  (*c*) voltage drop in the lines can be minimized
  (*d*) phase voltage imbalances can be minimized

32. Compared with solid conductor of the same radius, corona appears on a stranded conductor at a lower voltage, because stranding
  (*a*) assists ionisation
  (*b*) makes the current flow spirally about the axis of the conductor
  (*c*) produces oblique sections to a plane perpendicular to the axis of the conductor
  (*d*) produces surfaces of smaller radius.

33. Proximity effect
  (*a*) is more pronounced for large conductors, high frequencies and close proximity
  (*b*) increases the resistance of the conductors and reduces the self reactance
  (*c*) is substantially eliminated with stranded conductors
  (*d*) all of these

34. Following effects are associated with transmission lines
  1. Skin effect
  2. Corona effect
  3. Proximity effect
  The effective resistance of conductor is increased by
  (*a*) 1 only
  (*b*) 2 and 3 only
  (*c*) 1 and 3 only
  (*d*) 1, 2 and 3

35. The transmission lines are said to be long if the length of the line exceeds
  (*a*) 50 km.
  (*b*) 150 km.
  (*c*) 250 km.
  (*d*) 500 km.

36. Shunt capacitance is neglected in case of
  (*a*) short transmission lines
  (*b*) medium transmission lines
  (*c*) long transmission lines
  (*d*) medium and long transmission lines

37. The effect of capacitance can be neglected when the length of overhead transmission line does not exceed
  (*a*) 20 km.
  (*b*) 60 km.
  (*c*) 120 km.
  (*d*) 300 km.

38. 120 km ling transmission line is considered as a
  (*a*) short line
  (*b*) medium line
  (*c*) long line
  (*d*) either (*a*) or (*b*)

39. A 25 km 33 kv transmission line is considered to be
  (*a*) short transmission line
  (*b*) medium transmission line
  (*c*) long transmission line
  (*d*) high power line

40. A 160 km, 110 kv transmission line falls under the category of
  (*a*) short transmission line
  (*b*) medium transmission line
  (*c*) long transmission line
  (*d*) ultra high voltage line

41. Which of the following is neglected while analysing a short transmission line?
  (*a*) Shunt admittances.
  (*b*) Power losses.
  (*c*) Series impedance.
  (*d*) None of these.

42. For 11 kV transmission line the inductance per km will be about
  (*a*) 1 H.
  (*b*) 0.1 H.
  (*c*) 1 mH.
  (*d*) 0.1 mH.

43. For 11 kV transmission line the cpacitance per km will be about
  (*a*) 0.01 F.
  (*b*) 0.1 F.
  (*c*) 0.1μF.
  (*d*) 0.1μF.

44. Percentage regulation of transmission line is given by the expression
  (*a*) $\dfrac{V_R - V_S}{V_R} \times 100$
  (*b*) $\dfrac{V_R - V_S}{V_S} \times 100$
  (*c*) $\dfrac{V_S - V_R}{V_R} \times 100$
  (*d*) $\dfrac{V_S - V_R}{V_S} \times 100$

45. Which of the following regulations is considered best ?
  (*a*) $\dfrac{21}{2}$ %
  (*b*) 15%
  (*c*) 25%
  (*d*) 40%

46. For a short line if the receiving end voltage is equal to sending end voltage under loaded conditions
  (*a*) the sending end power factor is unity
  (*b*) the receiving end power factor is unity
  (*c*) the sending end power factor is leading
  (*d*) the receiving end power factor is leading

47. Transmission efficiency of a transmission line increases with the
  (*a*) decrease in power factor and voltage
  (*b*) increase in power factor and voltage
  (*c*) increase in power factor but decrease in voltage
  (*d*) increase in voltage but decrease in power factor

48. Constant power locus of a transmission line at a particular sending end and receiving end voltage is
  (*a*) a straight line
  (*b*) a circle
  (*c*) a parabola
  (*d*) an ellipse

49. Constant voltage transmission have the advantage(s) of
    - (a) increase of short-circuit current of the system
    - (b) large reserve of lines in case of line trouble
    - (c) improvement of power factor at the times fo moderate and heavy loads
    - (d) all of these

50. A synchronous phase modifier as compared to synchronous motor of the same rating has
    - (a) larger shaft diameter and higher speed
    - (b) smaller shaft diameter and higher speed
    - (c) larger shaft diameter and smaller speed
    - (d) smaller shaft diameter and smaller speed

51. Phase modifier is normally installed in case of
    - (a) short transmission lines
    - (b) medium length lines
    - (c) long lines
    - (d) for any length of lines

52. Series acpacitors on transmission lines are of little use when the required reactive voltamperes are
    - (a) small
    - (b) large
    - (c) fluctuating
    - (d) any of the these

53. The function of guard ring transmission lines is
    - (a) to reduce the transmission losses
    - (b) to reduce the earth capacitance of the lowest unit
    - (c) to increase the earth capacitance of the lowest unit
    - (d) none of these

54. Use of bundle conductors causes the critical voltage for corona formation
    - (a) to decrease
    - (b) to increase
    - (c) to remain unlatered
    - (d) does not existent

55. For maximum efficiency in transmission of bulk ac power, the power factor of the load should be
    - (a) unity
    - (b) slightly less than unity lagging
    - (c) slightly less than unity leading
    - (d) considerably less than unity

56. The surge impedance of a long power transmission line is of the order of
    - (a) 50 Ω
    - (b) 75 Ω
    - (c) 400 Ω
    - (d) 800 Ω

57. As the height of the transmission tower is increased, the line capacitance and line inductance respectively
    - (a) decreases, decreases
    - (b) increases, decreases
    - (c) decreases, remains unlatered
    - (d) increases, increases

58. The corona discharge on transmission lines may be avoided by
    - (a) increasing effective conductor radius
    - (b) increasing the operating voltage
    - (c) decreasing the spacing between the conductors
    - (d) none of these

59. Voltage gradient on a transmission line conductor is highest
    - (a) at the surface of the conductor
    - (b) at the centre of the conductor
    - (c) at the distance equal to one radius from the surface
    - (d) none of these

60. Booster transformer is located at
    - (a) sending end of transmission line
    - (b) receiving end of transmission line
    - (c) intermediate point on a transmission line
    - (d) none of these

61. The transmission line between tower assumes the shape of a
    - (a) parabola
    - (b) hyperbola
    - (c) catanary
    - (d) arc of a circle

62. Voltage control in a power transmission line is achieved by
    - (a) booster transformer
    - (b) tap-changing transformer
    - (c) injection of reactive power
    - (d) all of these

63. In a power transmission line, the sag depends on
    - (a) conductor material alone
    - (b) tension in conductors alone
    - (c) span of transmission line
    - (d) all of these

64. If the span of a transmission line is increased by 10%, the sag of line increases by about
  (a) 7%   (b) 14%
  (c) 21%   (d) 28%

65. String efficiency is defined as
  (a) V_{Fn}/V_{F1}
  (b) $n\,V_{F1}/V_{Fn}$
  (c) $VF_n/(n\,V_{F1})$
  (d) V_{F1}/V_{Fn}
  where V_{F1} is the flash over voltage of one unit V_{Fn} is the flash over voltage of string of n-units.

66. The string efficiency of an insulator can be increased by
  (a) reducing the number of strings in the insulator
  (b) increasing the number of strings in the insulator
  (c) correct grading of insulators of various capacities
  (d) none of these

67. The topmost wire in a distribution line is
  (a) neutral wire   (b) earth wire
  (c) phase wire   (d) any of these

68. Sheaths are used in power cables to
  (a) provide adequate insulation
  (b) increase the strength of the cable
  (c) prevent moisture from entering the cable
  (d) none of these

69. For high voltage applications, the insulators used are of
  (a) suspension type
  (b) pin type
  (c) strain type
  (d) none of these

70. On a transmission line, whenever the conductors are dead ended or there is change in the direction of transmission line, the insulators used are
  (a) strain type
  (b) suspension type
  (c) pin type
  (d) none of these

71. Pin insulators are normally used for voltages upto
  (a) 30 kV   (b) 50 kV
  (c) 70 kV   (d) 100 kV

72. Conductors used in high voltage transmission lines are stranded to
  (a) make it easy to handle
  (b) reduce the cost
  (c) increase its conductivity
  (d) increase its tensile strength

73. Due to skin effect at high frequencies, the effective value of conductor resistance
  (a) decreases
  (b) increases
  (c) remains unaltered
  (d) may increase or decrease

74. Surge conductance in power transmission lines is due to leakage over
  (a) insulators   (b) conductors
  (c) poles   (d) jumpers

75. Charging current in a transmission line
  (a) increases the line losses
  (b) decreases the line losses
  (c) does not effect the line losses
  (d) none of these

76. Ground wire is used in transmission system
  (a) to avoid overloading
  (b) to give good insulation
  (c) to connect a circuit conductor or other device to an earth plate
  (d) none of these

77. The current by alternate charging and discharging of transmission line due to ac voltage is called
  (a) oscillating voltage
  (b) charging current
  (c) line current
  (d) discharging current

78. Transposition of conductors in transmission line system is done when
  (a) the conductors are not spaced equilaterally
  (b) the conductors are spaced equilaterally
  (c) a telephone line runs parallel to power line
  (d) none of these

79. The surge impedance of a transmission line differs from its characteristic impedance in that the surge impedance considers line
  (a) inductance to be zero
  (b) capacitance to be zero
  (c) resistance to be infinite
  (d) both (a) and (b)

80. Relative to fair wheather, in humid weather corona occurs at
(a) lower voltage
(b) higher voltage
(c) almost the same voltage
(d) none of these

81. In a power transmission line, grounding is generally done at
(a) the supply end
(b) the receiving end
(c) middle of the line
(d) none of these

82. Earthing of power transmission line is necessary to provide protection against
(a) overload
(b) voltage fluctuation
(c) electric shock
(d) temperature rise of conductors

83. As the height of a transmission tower is altered, the parameter which changes is
(a) inductance
(b) capacitance
(c) conductance
(d) none of these

84. In conductor of power transmission line, the voltage gradient is maximum at its
(a) centre
(b) surface
(c) circle with half the radius
(d) somewhere between (b) and (c) above

85. EHV cables are filled with thin oil under pressure to
(a) prevent formation of voids
(b) prevent entry of moisture
(c) to strengthen the cable conductor
(d) to provide insulation

86. Cables in power transmission line are provided with intersheaths to
(a) minimize stress
(b) minimize high voltage
(c) provide uniform stress distribution
(d) minimize charging current

87. Impedance and capacitance of a transmission line depend upon
(a) current in the line alone
(b) voltage in the line alone
(c) both (a) and (b)
(d) physical configuration of conductors in space

88. Transmission lines are classified as short, medium and long depending on the
(a) length of line
(b) charging current or no load current
(c) capacitance of line
(d) both (a) and (b) above

89. A series compensated transmission line has better
(a) transient stability
(b) steady state stability
(c) short circuit capacity
(d) reactive capacity

90. Reactive power can be injected into a transmission line by using
(a) series capacitors
(b) shunt capacitors and reactors
(c) synchronous capacitors
(d) any of these

91. The earthing switch is generally installed on
(a) main board
(b) isolator frame
(c) circuit breaker frame
(d) none of these

92. Corona is observed on
(a) a.c. transmission lines only
(b) d.c. transmission lines only
(c) both a.c and d.c. transmission lines
(d) none of these

93. An advantage of corona on transmission lines is that
(a) it minimizes power loss
(b) it reflects electrical surges
(c) it works as a surge modifier during overloads
(d) none of these

94. Temperature increase produces which of the following effect on a transmission line?
(a) tension of the conductor and its sag increase
(b) tension of the conductor and its sag decrease
(c) tension of the conductor decreases and its sag increases
(d) tension of the conductor increases and its sag decreases

95. Transformer connection at the sending end of a transmission line is usually
(a) star-delta
(b) delta-delta
(c) delta-star
(d) star-star

96. High tension cables can be used for power transmission for voltages not exceeding
  (a) 11 kV (b) 22 kV
  (c) 33 kV (d) 110 kV

97. As the moisture content in the air increases, the disruptive critical voltage
  (a) increases
  (b) decreases
  (c) remains constant
  (d) may increase or decrease

98. The critical voltage of a transmission line may be increased by
  (a) increasing the conductor diameter
  (b) increasing the air spacing between the conductors
  (c) both (a) and (b) above
  (d) none of these

99. Void formation in the dielectric material of an underground cable may be controlled by
  (a) using a high permitivity solid dielectric
  (b) providing a strong metallic sheath outside the cable
  (c) filling oil at high pressure as dielectric
  (d) none of these

100. Bundle conductors are used to reduce the effect of
  (a) inductance of the circuit
  (b) capacitance of the circuit
  (c) corona and power loss due to corona
  (d) both (a) and (b) above

101. When the conductors of a 3-phase transmission line are not spaced equilaterally, transmission is done to
  (a) decrease the line inductance per phase
  (b) balance the 3 phases of the circuit
  (c) minimize the effect of adjoining communication circuit
  (d) none of these

102. Size of the earth wire is determined by
  (a) the ampere capacity of the service
  (b) the atmospheric conditions
  (c) the voltage of the service wires
  (d) none of these

103. As per Indian Standards, the cross-sectional area of the neutral wire in a 3-phase 4 wire system is
  (a) twice that of a phase conductor
  (b) equal to that of a phase conductor
  (c) half that of a phase conductor
  (d) one-fourth that of a phase conductor

104. In short overhead transmission line (upto 80 km), we may neglect
  (a) series resistance
  (b) shunt conductance
  (c) shunt capacitance
  (d) both shunt coductance and capacitance

105. If the voltage as well as reactance of a transmission line is doubled, the maximum steady state power limit of the line
  (a) remains unaltered
  (b) doubles
  (c) becomes 4 times
  (d) becomes 8 times

106. Rise of temperature of transmission line
  (a) increases the stress and decreases the length
  (b) increases the stress and increases the length
  (c) decreases the stress and increases the length
  (d) decreases the stress and decreases the length

107. A short transmission line has equivalent circuit consisting of
  (a) series resistance R and series inductance L
  (b) series resistance R and shunt capacitance C
  (c) series resistance R and shunt capacitance G
  (d) series inductance L and shunt capacitance G

108. Proximity effect is due to current flowing in the
  (a) earth
  (b) sheath
  (c) neighbouring conductor
  (d) all of these

109. Insulation resistance of a cable decreases with
  (a) decrease in he length of the insulation of cable
  (b) increase in the length of the insulation of cable
  (c) increase in electric stress
  (d) increase in temperature

110. The amount of active power transmitted over a transmission line is proportional to
  (a) sending end voltage V_S
  (b) receiving end voltage V_R
  (c) torque angle δ between V_S and V_R
  (d) difference voltage $(V_S - V_R)$

111. The characteristic impedance of a lossless cable is typically
  (a) 40 to 60 Ω
  (b) 100 to 120 Ω
  (c) 400 to 600 Ω
  (d) 1000 to 1500 Ω

112. The power loss in a long transmission line at no load equals

(a) 0

(b) $\dfrac{1}{4}I_0^2\,R$

(c) $\dfrac{1}{3}I_0^2\,R$

(d) $\dfrac{1}{2}I_0^2\,R$

113. For a power system, to be stable, the phase constant β of its transmission line should be

(a) $\dfrac{R_L R_O}{R_O + R_L}$

(b) $\dfrac{R_L - R_O}{R_L + R_O}$

(c) $\dfrac{R_L + R_O}{R_L - R_O}$

(d) $\dfrac{R_L R_O}{R_O R_L}$

114. For the same voltage boost, the reactive power capacity is more for a

(a) Shunt capacitor.

(b) Series capacitor.

(c) It is same for both series and shunt.

(d) None of the above.

115. To increase the power transmitting capacity of a transmission line we

(a) increase its line capacitance

(b) increase its line inductance

(c) decrease its line capacitance

(d) none of these

116. Guy is attached to a transmission line pole to

(a) reduce the sag

(b) hold the telephone lines

(c) strengthen the pole

(d) none of these

117. During rains, the direct capacitance of suspension type insulator

(a) decreases

(b) increases

(c) remain unchanged

(d) may increase or decrease

118. While calculating the fault current, the reactances of the machines connected to the power system are taken to be

(a) zero

(b) constant

(c) increasing with load

(d) decreasing with load

119. Compared to the normal impedance, the fault impedance of a circuit is

(a) the same

(b) higher

(c) lower

(d) may be lower or higher

120. Visual corona takes place in parallel wires at a voltage

(a) higher than disruptive critical voltage

(b) higher than Curie voltage

(c) equal to disruptive voltage

(d) none of these

121. Corona loss is maximum when using

(a) ACSR

(b) stranded wire

(c) unstranded wire

(d) transposed wire

122. Corona always causes

(a) system faults

(b) radio interference

(c) insulation failure

(d) none of these

123. If fault occurs near an impedance relay, the V I ratio is

(a) constant for all the locations of fault

(b) lower than the value if fault occurs away from the relay

(c) higher than the value if fault occurs away from the relay

(d) may be lower or higher than the value if fault occurs away from the relay

124. The fault MVA is given by

(a) $\dfrac{\text{Base MVA}}{\text{P.U. Xeq}}$

(b) $\text{Base MVA} \times \text{P.U. Xeq}$

(c) $\dfrac{\text{Base MVA}}{(\text{P.U. Xeq})^2}$

(d) none of these

where Xeq is the fault impedance at the point where fault has occurred

125. The peak short circuit current equals
(a) $\sqrt{2}$ ac component
(b) $1.8 \times \sqrt{2}$ ac component
(c) $\sqrt{3} \times \sqrt{2}$ ac component
(d) $2 \times \sqrt{2}$ ac component

126. For most reliable distribution supply, the configuration used is
(a) radial main
(b) ring main
(c) parabolic main
(d) balancing main

127. Breakdown of insulation of a cable can be avoided economically by the use of
(a) insulating material with different dielectric
(b) intersheath
(c) both (a) and (b) above
(d) none of these

128. Which of the following system is preferred for good efficiency and high economy in distribution system ?
(a) single phase system
(b) 2 phase 3 wire system
(c) 3 phase 3 wire system
(d) 3 phase 4 wire system

129. If the neutral of 3-phase star assembly is grounded, then for line currents Ia, Ib and Ic the current in the neutral wire is
(a) 0
(b) $I_a + I_b + I_c$
(c) $\dfrac{I_a + I_b + I_c}{2}$
(d) $\sqrt{2(I_a + I_b + I_c)}$

130. Any voltage surge travelling on the transmission line first enters
(a) step down transformer
(b) lightning arrestor
(c) switch gear
(d) over voltage relay

131. ACSR is used for transmission of power in preference to copper conductors because
(a) it is lighter
(b) it is more economical
(c) it has higher current carrying capacity
(d) it can stand higher surge voltages

132. Two transmission lines each having surge impedance of 75Ω are separated by cable link. For zero reflection, the surge impedance of the cable should be
(a) 0Ω
(b) 75Ω
(c) 150Ω
(d) 300Ω

133. For a 400 kV transmission line, the switching over voltage crest in kV is
(a) 400
(b) $400\sqrt{2}$
(c) 825
(d) 1155

134. For a 400 kV transmission line, the number of standard disc used in practice are
(a) 8
(b) 12
(c) 16
(d) 24

135. Compared to the insulation level of the station equipment, the line insulation is
(a) the same
(b) greater
(c) less
(d) not directly related

136. The sag of a transmission line is affected by
(a) its own weight and weight of the ice formed
(b) temperature and wind condition
(c) both (a) and (b) above
(d) none of these

137. In a transmission line, the shunt conductance results due to
(a) axial current in the conductor
(b) radial current in the conductor
(c) leakage over the insulator
(d) short circuiting of line by the load

138. Due to skin effect, resistance of the conductor
 (*a*) decreases
 (*b*) increases
 (*c*) remains same
 (*d*) uncertain

139. Considerable power is taken up for charging
 (*a*) D.C. transmission
 (*b*) A.C. transmission
 (*c*) electron transmission
 (*d*) none of these

140. As the transmission voltage increases, percentage resistance drop
 (*a*) increases
 (*b*) decreases
 (*c*) remain same
 (*d*) increase in random manner

141. The primary parameters of transmission line are
 (*a*) series inductance
 (*b*) shunt capacitance
 (*c*) series and shunt resistance
 (*d*) all of these

142. If a long transmission line is very lightly loaded or left open then the receiving end voltage rises. This effect is called
 (*a*) Joules effect
 (*b*) Einstein's effect
 (*c*) Raman effect
 (*d*) Ferranti effect

143. Transposition of power lines is done to
 (*a*) reduce copper losses
 (*b*) prevent short circuit between two lines
 (*c*) prevent interference with telephone lines
 (*d*) all of these

144. Capacitance current of a transmission system is usually reckoned in the case of
 (*a*) short line
 (*b*) medium line
 (*c*) long line
 (*d*) none of these

145. For a short line, receiving end voltage is more than sending end for
 (*a*) lagging power factor
 (*b*) leading power factor
 (*c*) unity power factor
 (*d*) zero power factor

146. Bundled conductors are used to
 (*a*) reduce radio interference
 (*b*) reduce reactance
 (*c*) both (*a*) and (*b*)
 (*d*) none of these

147. In a short line
 (*a*) shunting effects are neglected
 (*b*) shunting effects are included
 (*c*) may include or neglect
 (*d*) none of these

148. Charging current of a line is more at
 (*a*) mid point
 (*b*) one third of line
 (*c*) receiving end
 (*d*) sending end

149. For bulk power transmission over a long distance, economical method is transmission of
 (*a*) lower voltage
 (*b*) higher current
 (*c*) higher voltage
 (*d*) none of these

150. Angle between sending and receiving end voltage is called
 (*a*) load angle   (*b*) power angle
 (*c*) torque angle   (*d*) all of these

151. Two terminal network representing a 3 phase line is called
 (*a*) active network   (*b*) passive network
 (*c*) either (*a*) or (*b*)   (*d*) none of these

152. Real part of propagation constant of a transmission line is called
 (*a*) phase constant
 (*b*) gain constant
 (*c*) attenuation constant
 (*d*) none of these

153. In short lines, regulation and pressure drop are
 (*a*) vectorially equal
 (*b*) equal in phase
 (*c*) numerically equal
 (*d*) none of these

154. Secondary transmission and distribution system are of
 (*a*) radial structure   (*b*) ring structure
 (*c*) mesh structure   (*d*) none of these

155. Typical load always consumes
- (a) active power
- (b) reactive power
- (c) inverse power
- (d) none of these

156. Unit for energy transmission under steady state condition is called
- (a) static transmission capacity
- (b) static distribution
- (c) either (a) or (b)
- (d) none of these

157. In power systems, regulating transformers are used to control
- (a) current flow
- (b) load flow
- (c) electrons flow
- (d) none of these

158. Synchronous machines can be controlled by
- (a) terminal voltage and rotor current
- (b) terminal voltage and phase angle
- (c) rotor current and reactance
- (d) terminal voltage and reactance

Overhead Lines, Mechanical Design and Corona

159. Characteristic impedance of a telephone line is of the order of
- (a) $50\,\Omega$
- (b) $60\,\Omega$
- (c) $75\,\Omega$
- (d) $100\,\Omega$

160. Difference between surge impedance and characteristic impedence is that in surge impendance
- (a) line resistance is considered
- (b) line resistance is assumed to be zero
- (c) line capacitance is assumed to be zero
- (d) line impedance is assumed to be zero

161. Increase of temperature in transmission line
- (a) increases stress & decreases length
- (b) increases stress & length
- (c) decreases stress & length
- (d) decreases stress & increases length

162. Now-a-days copper is replaced by aluminium in lines because of
- (a) heavy weight of copper
- (b) high cost of copper
- (c) less conductivity of copper
- (d) scarcity of copper

163. If height of transmission tower is increased, line inductance
- (a) increases
- (b) decreases
- (c) remains same
- (d) uncertain

164. Voltage gradient is highest at the
- (a) centre of the conductor
- (b) surface of the conductor
- (c) 1/3 of the conductor
- (d) none of these

165. With impurities in copper, conductivity
- (a) increases
- (b) decreases
- (c) does not affect
- (d) uncertain

166. Shunt conductance in power transmission is due to leakage over
- (a) insulator
- (b) conductors
- (c) poles
- (d) ground

167. Entire line performance can be determined by
- (a) sending end power circle diagram
- (b) receiving end power circle diagram
- (c) universal power circle diagram
- (d) none of these

168. Booster transformer is located at
- (a) sending end
- (b) receiving end
- (c) mid point of line
- (d) anywhere on the line

169. Concrete poles are used because of their
- (a) longer life
- (b) less maintenance cost
- (c) both (a) and (b)
- (d) none of these

170. Voltage control method used in transmission system is by
- (a) tap changing transformers
- (b) injection of reactive power
- (c) booster transformer
- (d) all of these

171. Vertical loading in pole results on account of
- (a) dead weight of the equipment
- (b) conductor tension at angles in lines
- (c) interference in transmission lines
- (d) vibration of conductors

172. Transformer at sending end of a line is usually
  (*a*) Star-star   (*b*) Star-delta
  (*c*) Delta-star   (*d*) Delta-delta

173. In a d.c. 3 wire transmission system, cross-section of the neutral is generally
  (*a*) 1/2 of the outer conductor
  (*b*) 1/3 of the outer couductor
  (*c*) 1/4 of the outer conductor
  (*d*) none of these

174. Guy is fastened to a pole to
  (*a*) strengthen the pole
  (*b*) hold telephone cables
  (*c*) keep the wires from sagging
  (*d*) none of these

175. As transmission voltage increases, volume of the conductor
  (*a*) increases
  (*b*) decreases
  (*c*) remain same
  (*d*) increases proportionately

176. With 10% increase in span of the line, sag increases by
  (*a*) 18%   (*b*) 19%
  (*c*) 20%   (*d*) 21%

177. Spacing of the conductors is determined by
  (*a*) machanical considerations
  (*b*) electrical considerations
  (*c*) both (a) and (b)
  (*d*) none of these

178. Power transmission capacity of the transmission line is
  (*a*) proportional to voltage
  (*b*) proportional to square of operating voltage
  (*c*) inversely proportional to voltage
  (*d*) inversely proportional to square of voltage

179. Topmost wire in a transmission line carrying distribution line is
  (*a*) phase wire   (*b*) neutral wire
  (*c*) earth wire   (*d*) all of these

180. Corona loss occurs in
  (*a*) transmission lines
  (*b*) distribution transformer
  (*c*) generator
  (*d*) cables

181. Capacitance of a transmission line is a result of
  (*a*) potential difference between the conductors
  (*b*) current in the conductors
  (*c*) both (a) and (b)
  (*d*) none of these

182. Corona always results in
  (*a*) insulation failure   (*b*) faults in line
  (*c*) radio interference (*d*) all of these

183. Inductance due to conductor's own current is called
  (*a*) self inductance
  (*b*) mutual inductance
  (*c*) internal inductance
  (*d*) none of these

184. Inductance and capacitance of a transmission line depend upon
  (*a*) current in the line
  (*b*) voltage of the line
  (*c*) volume of the line
  (*d*) physical configuration

185. Transfer reactance of a line is reduced by
  (*a*) series compensation
  (*b*) shunt compensation
  (*c*) mixed series & shunt compensation
  (*d*) it can not be compensated

186. Corona loss is more in
  (*a*) stranded wire
  (*b*) unstranded wire
  (*c*) naked wire
  (*d*) equal in all wires

187. Corona
  (*a*) minimizes the power losses
  (*b*) reflects electrical surges
  (*c*) works as surge modifier during over voltages
  (*d*) all of these

188. Corona introduces
  (*a*) lagging current
  (*b*) leading current
  (*c*) high current
  (*d*) harmonic current

189. Power loss due to corona in winter is
  (*a*) same as in summer
  (*b*) less than in summer
  (*c*) more than in summer
  (*d*) none of these

190. By corona, surge voltage
  - (a) attenuates
  - (b) amplifies
  - (c) has no effect
  - (d) none of these

191. Ground wire is provided in an overhead line to
  - (a) provide more mechanical strength to the line
  - (b) provide a return path for all zero sequence currents
  - (c) work as lightening conductor
  - (d) all of these

192. Corona power loss can be reduced by
  - (a) increasing the wire diameter
  - (b) decreasing the wire diameter
  - (c) using insulated wire
  - (d) none of these

193. An infinite bus bar has a surge impedance equal to
  - (a) zero
  - (b) infinite
  - (c) surge impedance of the transmission line connected to it
  - (d) all of these

194. Critical voltage of the line can be increased by increasing
  - (a) spacing
  - (b) diameter
  - (c) both (a) and (b)
  - (d) none of these

195. Cross-sectional area of the neutral wire in a 3 phase, 4 wire system is equal to
  - (a) that of phase conductor
  - (b) 1/2 times that of phase conductor
  - (c) 1/4 times that of phase conductor
  - (d) 2 times that of phase conductor

OVERHEAD LINE INSULATORS

196. For high voltage applications, the insulator used is
  - (a) pin type
  - (b) suspension type
  - (c) strain type
  - (d) all of these

197. Insulators are used on overhead line to insulate the wire from
  - (a) the pole
  - (b) each other
  - (c) both (a) and (b)
  - (d) none of these

198. Insulators are required to withstand
  - (a) electrical stresses
  - (b) mechanical stresses
  - (c) both (a) and (b)
  - (d) none of these

199. Lines above 50 kV uses
  - (a) pin type insulator
  - (b) suspension type insulator
  - (c) strain type insulator
  - (d) any of them

200. Insulator disc subjected to maximum stress is
  - (a) near the conductor
  - (b) near the cross arm
  - (c) in the middle of string
  - (d) are expriences equal stress

201. In case of wet suspension type insulator
  - (a) string efficiency is increased
  - (b) string efficiency is decreased
  - (c) capacitance between units is decreased
  - (d) capacitance between units is increased

202. For improving string efficiency, ratio of capacity to earth to capacity per insulator should
  - (a) decrease
  - (b) increase
  - (c) remain same
  - (d) uncertain

203. Number of insulators used for a 230 kV line is
  - (a) 13
  - (b) 14
  - (c) 15
  - (d) 16

204. A guard ring is used to
  - (a) decrease potential across each units
  - (b) increase potential across each units
  - (c) make potential across each unit equal
  - (d) none of these

205. In string type insulator, if number of discs are increased the string efficiency
  - (a) decreases
  - (b) increases
  - (c) remains same
  - (d) uncertain]

Under Ground Cables

206. Under groung cables are generally not used for more than a distance of
  - (a) 50 km
  - (b) 75 km
  - (c) 90 km
  - (d) 100 km

207. For greater flexibility, degree of stranding for a cable when compared with overhead lines should be
  - (a) lesser
  - (b) higher
  - (c) same
  - (d) none of these

208. In underground cables, maximum stress is at the
(a) surface of the conductor
(b) sheath surface of the cable
(c) centre of the conductor
(d) between sheath and the conductor

209. Cables are sheathed to
(a) protect the insulation
(b) increase the rate of heat dissipation
(c) increase the cable capacity
(d) protect the cable from mechanical stresses

210. Cables are pulled into a conduit and spliced in a
(a) pole
(b) manhole
(c) feeder pillar
(d) all of these

211. Capacitance grading of a cable mean that the cable
(a) uses different dielectrics
(b) uses different intersheaths
(c) is classified according to its capacitance
(d) none of these

212. In H.S.L. type cables
(a) each case has its own lead sheath
(b) screen is perforated and each core has separate lead sheath
(c) each core is surrounded by a metallised and perforated paper which is kept at earth potential
(d) none of these

213. Cable with varnished cambric insulation has
(a) high dielectric strength
(b) high insulation resistance
(c) high mechanical stresses bearing capacity
(d) all of these

214. Induced currents in the sheaths are
(a) sheath eddy current
(b) sheath circuit eddy current
(c) induction current
(d) none of these

215. Grading of cables is done to
(a) increase its conduction efficiency
(b) increase its strength
(c) achieve a uniform stress distribution
(d) all of these

216. Pressure cables are filled with
(a) oil
(b) air
(c) nitrogen
(d) helium

217. Pressure in pressure cables is approximately
(a) 5 to 7 atm
(b) 7 to 9 atm
(c) 9 to 12 atm
(d) 12 to 15 atm

218. If inductance calculating method for overhead lines is applied to the underground cables also, then result will involve an error because of the
(a) sheath effects
(b) skin and proximity effects
(c) both (a) and (b)
(d) none of these

219. Formation of voids in the dielectric of a cable is due to effect of
(a) loading cycles in service
(b) increased pressure
(c) extra potential difference
(d) all of these

220. Sheath loss is a function of
(a) $(\text{frequency})^2$
(b) maximum voltage
(c) power factor
(d) corona loss

221. Cables should not be operated too hot because
(a) sheath may burst due to oil expansion
(b) decreased viscosity at high temperature cause oil to drain off from the higher levels
(c) due to unequal expansion the voids may be created
(d) all of these

222. For oil impregnated cables, maximum operating temperature is
(a) 10°C
(b) 25°C
(c) 45°C
(d) 65°C

223. Transformers and network pretectors used in underground cable system may be
(a) submersible type
(b) non-submersible type
(c) combined (a) and (b)
(d) none of these

224. Safe value of current carrying capacity of cables is determined by
  (*a*) maximum voltage
  (*b*) maximum temperature
  (*c*) power factor
  (*d*) maximum pressure

225. Test for conductor failure in cables can be done by comparing
  (*a*) resistances of the conductors
  (*b*) capacitance of the insulated conductors
  (*c*) maximum pressure on conductors
  (*d*) none of these

226. Dielectric losses in the insulation in case of cable is negligible in
  (*a*) d.c. transmission
  (*b*) a.c. transmission
  (*c*) both (*a*) and (*b*)
  (*d*) none of these

227. Underground cables have large charging current which
  (*a*) lags the voltage by 90°
  (*b*) leads the voltage by 90°
  (*c*) is in phase with voltage
  (*d*) is out of phase by 180° with voltage

228. All high voltage cables usually operate at a power factor
  (*a*) small but lagging
  (*b*) close to unity
  (*c*) small but leading
  (*d*) large and lagging

Distribution System

229. Low voltage a.c. distribution is
  (*a*) 220 V between phases
  (*b*) 400 V between phases
  (*c*) 3.3 kV between phases
  (*d*) none of these

230. Light points available in the houses are
  (*a*) power source
  (*b*) current source
  (*c*) voltage source
  (*d*) all of these

231. Systems getting supply from one end only are
  (*a*) ring type   (*b*) mesh type
  (*c*) radial type   (*d*) all of these

232. System which suffers from maximum voltage fluctuations is
  (*a*) ring type   (*b*) radial type
  (*c*) mesh type   (*d*) none of these

233. In d.c. transmission, voltage between feeder and distributor is changed by using
  (*a*) transformers
  (*b*) generator
  (*c*) rotating machines
  (*d*) mercury arc rectifiers

234. Bus coupler is needed in
  (*a*) main and transfer bus arrangement
  (*b*) double bus breaker arrangement
  (*c*) single bus arrangement
  (*d*) all of these

235. Outdoor sub-stations are preferred for voltages above
  (*a*) 3.3 kV   (*b*) 11 kV
  (*c*) 33 kV   (*d*) 66 kV

236. Synchronous motors installed at sub-stations give
  (*a*) unity power factor
  (*b*) lagging power factor
  (*c*) leading power factor
  (*d*) none of these

237. Outdoor busbars are of
  (*a*) strain type
  (*b*) rigid type
  (*c*) strain or rigid type
  (*d*) none of these

E.H.V. Transmission

238. By increasing potential of a conductor
  (*a*) potential between conductor and ground decreases
  (*b*) corona loss is reduced
  (*c*) insulation required is less
  (*d*) its potential gradient increases

239. Rectification at the ends of E.H.V. d.c. transmission is done by using
  (*a*) shunt generators
  (*b*) power capacitors
  (*c*) SCR
  (*d*) motor-generator set

240. EHV system is beyond

   (*a*) 11 kV   (*b*) 33 kV

   (*c*) 132 kV   (*d*) 200 kV

241. Series reactors have

   (*a*) low reactance

   (*b*) low resistance

   (*c*) low impedance

   (*d*) high resistance

242. E.H.V. cables are filled with oil under pressure of gas because

   (*a*) pressure provides the necessary strength

   (*b*) pressure provides the necessary voltage bearing capacity

   (*c*) pressure will avoid the formation of voids

   (*d*) all of these

243. For E.H.V. transmission bundled conductors are preferred because

   (*a*) of less cost, line inductance & corona loss

   (*b*) they are easy to fabricate

   (*c*) only bundled conductors can withstand high voltages

   (*d*) all of these

244. On a lightly loaded transmission line

   (*a*) receiving end voltage can exceed sending end voltage

   (*b*) receiving end voltage can't exceed sending end voltage

   (*c*) capacitive charging current is reduced

   (*d*) none of these

ANSWERS

1. (*d*)	**2.** (*b*)	**3.** (*c*)	**4.** (*a*)	**5.** (*d*)	**6.** (*b*)	**7.** (*c*)	**8.** (*d*)	**9.** (*c*)	**10.** (*d*)
11. (*a*)	**12.** (*c*)	**13.** (*a*)	**14.** (*d*)	**15.** (*d*)	**16.** (*c*)	**17.** (*a*)	**18.** (*b*)	**19.** (*d*)	**20.** (*d*)
21. (*a*)	**22.** (*b*)	**23.** (*c*)	**24.** (*b*)	**25.** (*c*)	**26.** (*a*)	**27.** (*b*)	**28.** (*a*)	**29.** (*c*)	**30.** (*c*)
31. (*d*)	**32.** (*d*)	**33.** (*d*)	**34.** (*c*)	**35.** (*b*)	**36.** (*a*)	**37.** (*b*)	**38.** (*b*)	**39.** (*a*)	**40.** (*c*)
41. (*a*)	**42.** (*c*)	**43.** (*a*)	**44.** (*c*)	**45.** (*a*)	**46.** (*d*)	**47.** (*b*)	**48.** (*b*)	**49.** (*c*)	**50.** (*d*)
51. (*c*)	**52.** (*a*)	**53.** (*a*)	**54.** (*b*)	**55.** (*b*)	**56.** (*c*)	**57.** (*c*)	**58.** (*a*)	**59.** (*a*)	**60.** (*c*)
61. (*c*)	**62.** (*d*)	**63.** (*d*)	**64.** (*c*)	**65.** (*c*)	**66.** (*c*)	**67.** (*b*)	**68.** (*c*)	**69.** (*a*)	**70.** (*a*)
71. (*a*)	**72.** (*d*)	**73.** (*b*)	**74.** (*b*)	**75.** (*a*)	**76.** (*c*)	**77.** (*b*)	**78.** (*a*)	**79.** (*c*)	**80.** (*a*)
81. (*a*)	**82.** (*c*)	**83.** (*b*)	**84.** (*b*)	**85.** (*a*)	**86.** (*c*)	**87.** (*d*)	**88.** (*d*)	**89.** (*a*)	**90.** (*d*)
91. (*b*)	**92.** (*c*)	**93.** (*c*)	**94.** (*c*)	**95.** (*a*)	**96.** (*c*)	**97.** (*b*)	**98.** (*c*)	**99.** (*c*)	**100.** (*c*)
101. (*b*)	**102.** (*a*)	**103.** (*d*)	**104.** (*d*)	**105.** (*b*)	**106.** (*c*)	**107.** (*a*)	**108.** (*c*)	**109.** (*b*)	**110.** (*c*)
111. (*a*)	**112.** (*c*)	**113.** (*b*)	**114.** (*a*)	**115.** (*a*)	**116.** (*c*)	**117.** (*a*)	**118.** (*b*)	**119.** (*c*)	**120.** (*a*)
121. (*c*)	**122.** (*b*)	**123.** (*b*)	**124.** (*a*)	**125.** (*b*)	**126.** (*b*)	**127.** (*c*)	**128.** (*c*)	**129.** (*b*)	**130.** (*b*)
131. (*b*)	**132.** (*b*)	**133.** (*d*)	**134.** (*d*)	**135.** (*d*)	**136.** (*c*)	**137.** (*c*)	**138.** (*b*)	**139.** (*b*)	**140.** (*b*)
141. (*d*)	**142.** (*d*)	**143.** (*c*)	**144.** (*c*)	**145.** (*b*)	**146.** (*b*)	**147.** (*a*)	**148.** (*d*)	**149.** (*c*)	**150.** (*d*)
151. (*b*)	**152.** (*c*)	**153.** (*c*)	**154.** (*a*)	**155.** (*b*)	**156.** (*a*)	**157.** (*b*)	**158.** (*c*)	**159.** (*c*)	**160.** (*a*)
161. (*d*)	**162.** (*d*)	**163.** (*c*)	**164.** (*b*)	**165.** (*b*)	**166.** (*a*)	**167.** (*c*)	**168.** (*c*)	**169.** (*c*)	**170.** (*d*)
171. (*a*)	**172.** (*b*)	**173.** (*a*)	**174.** (*a*)	**175.** (*b*)	**176.** (*d*)	**177.** (*a*)	**178.** (*b*)	**179.** (*c*)	**180.** (*b*)
181. (*a*)	**182.** (*c*)	**183.** (*c*)	**184.** (*d*)	**185.** (*a*)	**186.** (*b*)	**187.** (*c*)	**188.** (*d*)	**189.** (*c*)	**190.** (*a*)
191. (*d*)	**192.** (*b*)	**193.** (*a*)	**194.** (*c*)	**195.** (*c*)	**196.** (*b*)	**197.** (*c*)	**198.** (*c*)	**199.** (*b*)	**200.** (*a*)
201. (*d*)	**202.** (*a*)	**203.** (*d*)	**204.** (*c*)	**205.** (*a*)	**206.** (*d*)	**207.** (*b*)	**208.** (*a*)	**209.** (*a*)	**210.** (*b*)
211. (*a*)	**212.** (*c*)	**213.** (*b*)	**214.** (*a*)	**215.** (*c*)	**216.** (*c*)	**217.** (*d*)	**218.** (*c*)	**219.** (*a*)	**220.** (*a*)
221. (*d*)	**222.** (*d*)	**223.** (*c*)	**224.** (*b*)	**225.** (*b*)	**226.** (*a*)	**227.** (*b*)	**228.** (*c*)	**229.** (*b*)	**230.** (*c*)
231. (*c*)	**232.** (*b*)	**233.** (*c*)	**234.** (*a*)	**235.** (*c*)	**236.** (*c*)	**237.** (*c*)	**238.** (*d*)	**239.** (*c*)	**240.** (*d*)
241. (*b*)	**242.** (*c*)	**243.** (*a*)	**244.** (*a*)						

■■

Power System Protection

SWITCHES

A switch is used in an electric circuit as a device for making or breaking the electric circuit. switches may be classified as.

(*i*) *Oil switches* : These are usually used in very high voltage heavy current circuits.

(*ii*) *Air switches* : These are further classified into

    (*a*) Air-break switches

    (*b*) Isolators

    (*c*) Disconnected switches

BUS- BAR ARRANGEMENTS

Bus-bars are arranged to achieve

(*i*)   adequate operating flexibility

(*ii*) sufficient reliability

(*iii*) minimum cost.

The cost can be minimised by reducing the number of circuit breakers to a minimum but complication of the protective gear are increased.

Some bus-bar arrangements.

(1) *Single bus-bar arrangement.* In this arrangement a set of bus-bars is used for complete power station and to this bus-bar are connected all generators, transformers and feeders through circuit breakers and isolating switches. Such a bus-bar arrangement is cheaper in initial as well as in maintenance cost and simple in operation and relaying.

(2) *Single bus- bar system with sectionalization.* With increased number of generators and outgoing feeders connected to the bus-bars, it becomes essential to provide arrangement for sectionalizing the bus-bars so that a fault on any one section of the bus-bars may not cause a complete shutdown. This is achieved by providing a circuit breaker and isolating switches between the sections.

(3) *Ring bus-bar system.* In this arrangement each feeder is supplied from two paths, so that in case of failure of a section, supply is not interrupted.

(4) *Duplicate bus-bars system.* Duplicate bus-bar system with sectionalization is usually adopted in order to maintain continuity of supply. Such a system consists of two-bus-bar couplers and sectionalizing breaker converts the duplicate bus-bars into a ring system having greater flexibility.

(5) *Double main and transfer bus-bar arrangement.* This arrangement incorporates all advantages of the double bus as well as transfer bus-scheme. The scheme needs a bus-coupler for the on load transfer of circuits from one main bus to the other and a transfer coupler for taking out circuit breaker of various circuits for maintenance.

FUSES

Fuse is a wire of short length or thin strip of material having low melting point and is inserted in an electric circuit as a protective device to the flow of excessive current through the circuit. The time for blowing out of fuse depends upon the magnitude of excessive current- larger the current, the more rapidly the fuse will blow.

Advantages.

(*i*)   Provides cheapest type of protection

(*ii*) Needs no maintenance

(*iii*) Affords current limiting effect under short-circuit conditions

(*iv*) Interrupts enormous short-circuit currents without noise, flame, gas or smoke.

Disadvantages.

(*i*)   Time is lost in rewiring or replacing of fuse after operation

(*ii*) Discrimination between fuses in series cannot be obtained unless there is considerable difference in the relative sizes of the fuses concerned.

Functions of fuse wire.

(*i*)   To carry the normal working current safely without heating

(*ii*) To break the circuit when the current exceeds the limited current.

The materials used for fuse wires must be of low melting points, low ohmic loss, high conductivity and free from deterioration. An alloy of lead and tin (lead 37% and tin 63%) is used for small current rating fuses and beyond 20 A rating circuits copper wire fuses are used.

Types of Fuses.

A fuse unit essentially consists of a metal fuse element, a set of contacts between which it is fixed and a body to support and isolate them. Many types of fuses also have some means for extinguishing the arc which appears when the fuse element melts.

Commonly used fuses are

(*i*) *Round type fuse* : It is not in common use.

(*ii*) *Rewirable or kitkat fuse* : It is used in domestic installations of voltage rating upto 400 V and of current rating upto 300A.

(*iii*) *Low voltage HRC fuses* : It is used on *l* t distribution against overload and short-circuit condition.

(*iv*) *High voltage HRC fuses* : It is used for the back up protection to circuit breakers whose short-circuit capacity has been increased owing to extension of generating plant or interconnection to a value beyond their rated MVA

(*v*) *Time delay fuses (or slow acting fuses)* : It is used as a backup protection for motors having long starting operations.

Selection of Fuse.

In order to ensure that the fuses will correctly and reliably protect any given section or element of any electrical circuit, their characteristics and ratings must be selected in accordance with the requirements of rated voltage, maximum current rupturing capacity and rated current.

PROTECTIVE RELAY

Protective relays and relaying systems detect abnormal condition like fault in electrical circuits and operate automatic switch gear to isolate faulty equipments from the system as quickly as possible.

Protective relay functions in association with the switch gear to avert the consequences of faults. The switch gear must be capable of interrupting both normal currents as well as fault currents.

The protective relay on the other hand must be able to recognize an abnormal condition in the power system and take suitable steps to ensure its removal with least possible disturbance to normal operation.

Fault Statistics.

Frequency of fault occurrence in different links of a power system :

Equipments	% total
OH lines	50
Cables	10
Switch gear	15
Transformer	12
CTs and PTs	2
Control equipments	3
Miscellaneous	8

Frequency of different kinds of fault occurring in overhead lines :

Types of fault	% occurrence
(*i*) L – G	85%
(*ii*) L – L	8%
(*iii*) L–L–G	5%
(*iv*) L–L–L	2 or less

L – L – L fault occur due to the carelessness of operating personnel.

Zone of protection.

Various zones in the power system are arranged to overlap so that no part of the system remains unprotected.

Essential Qualities of protection.

Every protection system which isolates a purely element is required to satisfy four basic requirements

(*i*)   *Reliability* : circuit breaker should be reliable.

(*ii*) *Selectivity* : faulty selection is selected and other sections must be left intact.

(*iii*) Fastness of operation.

(*iv*) *Discrimination* : between fault and overload.

Primary or Back up protection.

If a fault in given zone is not cleared by the main or the primary protection scheme some form of backup protection is provided to do the next best thing.

e.g. over current or distant protection.

Energizing quantity.

The electrical quantity i.e. current or voltage either alone or in conjunction with other electrical quantities required for functioning of relay.

Characteristic quantity.

The quantity to which the relay is designed to respond e.g. current in over-current relay, impedance etc.

Setting.

The actual value of the energizing or characteristic quantity which the relay is designed to operate under given conditions.

Pick up.

A relay is said to pick up when it moves from the off position to the ON position. The value of the characteristic quantity above which this change occurs is known as pick up value.

Drop out or reset.

Drop out means relay moves from the on-position to the off-position. The value of the characteristic quantity below which this change occurs is known as drop out or reset value.

Operating time.

Time during which stored operating energy is dissipated after the characteristic quantity has been suddenly restored from a specified value to the value which it had at the initial position of the relay.

Over shoot time.

The time during which stored operating energy is dessipated after the characteristic quantity has been suddenly restored from a specified value to the value which it had at the initial position of the relay.

Characteristic angle.

The phase angle at which the performance of the relay is declared.

Characteristics of a relay.

This is the locus of the pick up or reset when drawn on a graph.

Reinforcing relay.

Relay which is energised by the contacts of the main relay and with its contact in parallel with those of the main relay and with its contact in parallel with those of the main relay relieves them to their current carrying duty. The seal in contacts are usually of higher current rating than those of main relay.

Auxiliary relay.

Relays which operate in response to the opening or closing of its operating circuit to assist another relay in the performance of its function.

Reach.

Remote limit of the zone of protection provided by the relay used mostly in connection with distant relays to indicate how far along a line the tripping zone of the relay extends.

Over reach or Under reach.

Errors in relay measurements resulting in wrong operation or failure to operate respectively.

METHODS OF DISCRIMINATION.

These methods are basically of two types

(1) location of fault.

(2) the type of fault.

(1) Methods Discriminative to Fault Location.

(*i*) **Discrimination by time :** Provide time lag feature. It is possible to trip the breaker nearest to the fault prior to those farther off the point of fault.

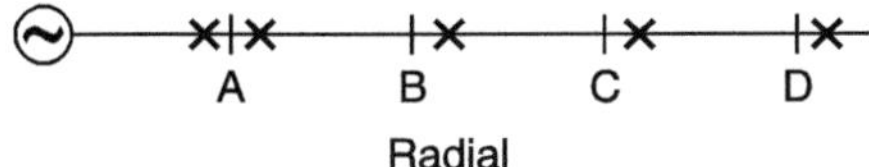

D – no added time lag

C – 0.4 sec. added time lag

B – 0.8 sec. added time lag

A – 1.2 sec. added time lag.

(*ii*) **Discrimination by current magnitude :** This depends on the current magnitudes as the magnitude of the fault current vary with the location of fault.

(*iii*) **Discrimination by time and direction:** In ring main which forms a closed loop it is not possible to isolate the faulty section with the help of time alone, hence in this case directional feature is also included.

(*iv*) **Discrimination by distance measurement :** The fault nearer the source which are more severe take longer time to clear in the case of time discrimination systems. The measurement of distance is achieved in various way by what is known as distance relay.

(*v*) **Current balance discrimination :** This is used for protection of individual elements in the power system.

This form of protection is based on one of the following two principles :

(*a*) Circulating current principles :

Circulating current principles compares the currents at the two ends of the protected section.

(*b*) Opposed voltage principles :

For external fault balance of current is not disturbed.

(2) Method discriminative to the type of fault.

(*a*) **Zero phase sequence networks :** Zero sequence current flow only when earth faults take place.

No zero sequence currents for load current or phase-phase fault.

Hence zero sequence relay can be used for detection of earth fault.

(*b*) **Negative phase sequence network :** The presence of negative phase sequence current represents some form of unbalanced condition such as phase to phase faults other the symmetrical three phase faults, broken conductor faults etc.

RELAY CLASSIFICATION

(1) According to the function in the protective scheme

(i) *Main :* Main relays are the protective elements which respond to any change in the actuating quantity e.g. current, voltage etc.

(ii) *Auxiliary relays :* These are controlled by the other relays to perform some auxiliary function such that introduction of time delay.

(iii) Signal relays

(2) According to the nature of actuating quantity to which the relay responds

(i) current realy

(ii) voltage

(iii) power

(iv) impedance

(3) According to the connection of sensing elements

(i) primary relays

(ii) secondary relays (connected through CT or PT).

(4) According to method by which the relays act upon the circuit breaker

(a) Electromagnetic relay

(b) Static relays.

Principle types of electromagnetic relays.

(i) Attracted armature relay

(ii) Induction type relay.

(i) Attracted armature type.

An electromagnetic force is produced by the magnetic flux which in turn is produced by the operating quantity.

(ii) Induction Relay.

Torque is produced in these relay when one alternating flux reacts with the current induced in the rotor by another alternating flux displaced in time and space but having the same frequency.

OVER CURRENT RELAY

The induction cup relay is employed to achieve this type of relay. Operating time of all over current relays tend to become asympotic to a definite minimum value with increase in the value of current.

In induction type of relay the distance of the armature carrying the bridge contacts to the relay contacts can be adjusted with the help of the time multiplier setting.

Taps are provided on the input of the operating quantity which can be adjusted with the help of inserting the plug. This is known as the *plug multiplier setting.*

Instantaneous Over-current Relays.

In this type of relay it operates instantly without any international time delay.

e.g. non-polarized attracted armature type. This relay is used when fault is very close to source.

Directional Relay.

Directional feature is introduced with silent pole magnet, having in addition a directional unit consisting of capacitance or resistance-capacitance circuit. Directional control unit controls the angle between two fluxes by varying R-X parameter of the lower electromagnet.

Distance Relay.

Distance relay response is some function of ratio between volts and amperes and for any given value of the ratio there may exist an infinite number of values of volts and amperes.

In other words, it is easy to think of impedance, reactance or resistance or combination of three of which the relay responds.

Principal types of distance relays.

(i) *Impedance relay :* for medium lines

(ii) *Reactance relay :* for very short lines

(iii) *Admittance relay (mho) :* for phase fault of longer line

(iv) Ohm relay

(v) Offset mho relay.

FEEDER (TRANSMISSION LINE) PROTECTION

Types of protection and their selection

(1) Over-current protection

    (i) Non-directional

    (ii) Directional

(2) Distance protection

(3) Pilot protection

    (i) Wire pilot protection

    (ii) Carrier pilot protection

    (iii) Microwave pilot protection

For various type of protections to be achieved types of relay used are

- *For back up protection* – time graded over-current relays.

- *For very short lines* – Reactance relay.

- *For medium lines* – Impedance relay.
- *For phase fault of longer line* – Mho relay.

Pilot protection is used for fault occurring within individual zones of equipments. Microwave pilot protections are used for long inter-connected lines.

Over current protection.

Over-current protection of feeder may be divided into two categories

(*i*) Non directional time/current grading.

(*ii*) Directional time/current grading.

Time grading system.

Time grading is achieved by the help of definite-time relays.

Current-Graded Scheme .

This system is based on the fact that the short circuit current along the length of the protected circuit decreases as the distance from the source to the fault location increases. In current grading each relay would be set to pick up at a progressively higher current towards the source. But the problem is that the relay cannot differentiate between the faults which are very close to or either side of relay, since difference in current is very small. Hence we use IDMT relays with combination of instantaneous over current relays.

Current/Time Graded System

Current/time grading is possible with inverse time over-current relays. Most widely used relay is IDMT relay. In IDMT relay current limit and time limit can be set within the design limit.

There are two adjustable basic setting on all inverse time relays, one is time multiplier setting (TMS) and other is current setting known as plug setting Multiplier (PSM).

Earth-Fault Protection.

Earth fault current is less than the phase to phase fault current. Earth fault protection can be provided with normal over-current relay, if the minimum earth fault current is sufficient in magnitude.

The relay used for earth-fault protection is different from the once provided for phase fault. It has the peculiarity that it is set independent of load current and thus setting below normal load current can be achieved.

Over-current earth fault protection can be provided with only one over-current relay. A current will flow through the relay winding only when a fault involving earth occurs.

Reach of a distance relay.

A distance relay is set to operate to a particular value of impedance, for an impedance greater than this set value the relay should not operate. This impedance or the corresponding distance is known as the reach of the relay. The tendency of a distance relay to operate at impedance larger than its setting value is known as over reach. Similarly the tendency of the relay to restrain at the set value of impedance or impedances lower than the set value is known as under reach.

- A distance relay may be under-reach because of the introduction of fault resistance.
- A distance relay may be over-reach due to the offset current present in the fault current.

TRANSFORMER PROTECTION

Faults in the transformer is of following three

(*i*)   Fault in auxiliary equipments

(*ii*)   Fault in transformer winding and connection

(*iii*) Over load and external short circuits.

(*i*) **Faults in auxiliary equipments.**

Auxiliary equipments of the transformer are

(*a*) Transformer oil

(*b*) Gas cushion

(*c*) Oil pumps and forced air fans

(*d*) Core and winding insulation.

(*ii*) **Winding Faults.**

There may be faults between adjacent turns or parts of coils such as phase to phase faults. Another fault may be fault to ground or across complete winding such as phase to earth-faults on the HV and LV external terminals.

(*iii*) **Over-loads and external short circuits.**

Over-loads may be sustained for long periods, being limited only by the permitted temperature rise in the winding and the cooling medium. Excessive overloading will result in deterioration of insulation and subsequent failure.

DIFFERENTIAL PROTECTION OF TRANSFORMER.

Differential protection is the most important type of protection used for internal phase to phase and phase to earth faults and is generally applied to transformer having rating of 5 MVA and above.

The differential protection of transformer is also known as Merz-price protection for the transformer.

Drawbacks of the differential scheme.

(*i*)   *Unmatched CT characteristics* : Difference in CTs characteristics due to different ratios may cause appropriate difference in the respective secondary currents, whenever through fault occur.

(*ii*) *Ratio change as a result of tapping* : Tap changing is common in the transformer. Compensating for this effect by varying the tapping on differential protection, CTs is impractical. To overcome false operation biased differential relay are used.

(*iii*) *Magnetizing inrush current* : When transformer is energised, the transient inrush of magnetic current flowing into the transformer may be as great as ten times full load current and it decays relatively slowly. Hence magnetic inrush current may cause false operation. To overcome this the relay may be given a setting higher inrush current.

Gas Actuated Relay-Buchholz Relay.

The heat produced by internal fault or overloading of transformer causes the transformer oil to decompose and produce a gas which can be made to detect the winding fault. Buchholz relay is the simplest form which is commonly used in all transformers produced with conservator.

CIRCUIT BREAKER

Circuit Breaker rating.

The rating of a circuit breaker refer to the characteristic values that defines the working condition for which the circuit breaker is designed and built. Circuit breaker must be capable of carrying continuously the full load current without excessive temperature rise and should be capable of withstanding the electrodynamic forces. The circuit breaker should also be in position to interrupt fault current safely.

Rated voltage.

The rated maximum voltage of a circuit breaker is the highest rms voltage above nominal system voltage for which the circuit breaker is designed and this is the upper limit for operation.

Rated current.

The rated current of a circuit breaker is the designated limit of current in rms amperes which it shall be capable of carrying continuously without exceeding the limit of observable temperature rise.

Rated frequency.

The frequency at which the circuit breaker is designed to operate standard frequency is 50 Hz.

Rated breaking capacity, symmetrical and asymmetrical.

After the fault the current starts decaying from a high initial value to a sustained value.

In addition owing to relaying time the circuit breaker starts to open its arcing contacts only some time later, after initiation of short circuit current. The actual current interrupted by circuit breaker is less than the initial value of short circuit current because of arcing.

Breaking current of a pole of a circuit breaker is the current in that pole at the instant of contact-separation. It an be expressed by two values.

(*i*)   **Symmetrical breaking current :** This is the rms value of ac component of the circuit in the pole at the instant of contact-separation.

(*ii*) **Asymmetrical breaking current :** This is the rms value of the total current comprising the ac and dc components of the current in that pole at the instant of contact separation.

Breaking capacity symmetrical or asymmetrical is the value of respective breaking current which the circuit breaker is capable of breaking at a stated recovery voltage and a stated reference restriking voltage under prescribing condition.

OBJECTIVE TYPE QUESTIONS

Power System protection; Circuit Breakers; Relays, Reactors

1. Arc voltage produced in ac circuit breaker is always
   - (a) in phase opposition to the arc current
   - (b) in phase with the arc current
   - (c) leading the arc current by 90°
   - (d) lagging the arc current by 45°

2. The dielectric strength of air at 25°C and 76 cm of mercury is
   - (a) 2.11 kV rms/cm
   - (b) 21.1 kV rms/m
   - (c) 211 kV rms/cm
   - (d) 2110 kV rms/m

3. Which of thermal protection switch is provided in power line system to protect against ?
   - (a) overload
   - (b) temperature rise
   - (c) short circuit
   - (d) over voltage

4. The following circuit breaker does not use pneumatic operating mechanism
   - (a) air break circuit breaker
   - (b) air blast circuit breaker
   - (c) bulk oil circuit breaker
   - (d) SF_6 circuit breaker

5. Fault diverters are basically
   - (a) circuit breakers
   - (b) fast switches
   - (c) relays
   - (d) fuses

6. In a power system, the rate of rise of restriking voltage depends upon
   - (a) switching condition only
   - (b) circuit power factor only
   - (c) both (a) and (b) above
   - (d) none of these

7. The voltage across the circuit breaker pole after final current zero is
   - (a) restriking voltage
   - (b) recovery voltage
   - (c) supply voltage
   - (d) none of these

8. Bulk oil circuit breaker is suitable for voltages upto
   - (a) 4 kV
   - (b) 10 kV
   - (c) 25 kV
   - (d) 36 kV

9. For remote operation, circuit breaker must be equipped with
   - (a) shunt trip
   - (b) inverse shunt trip
   - (c) time delay trip
   - (d) both (b) and (c) above

10. Lightining arrestor should be located
    - (a) away from the circuit breaker
    - (b) near the circuit breaker
    - (c) away from the transformer
    - (d) near the transformer

11. Which of the following circuit breaker is generally used in applications in railways?
    - (a) bulk oil circuit breakers
    - (b) mimumum oil circuit breakers
    - (c) air break circuit breakers
    - (d) none of these

12. The following medium is employed for extinction of arc in air break circuit breakers ?
    - (a) oil
    - (b) air
    - (c) water
    - (d) none of these

13. In a circuit breaker, the arcing contents are made of
    - (a) aluminium
    - (b) copper tungsten alloy
    - (c) electrolytic copper
    - (d) tungsten

14. Which of the following circuit breakers takes minimum time for installation ?
    - (a) bulk oil circuit breaker
    - (b) minimum oil circuit breaker
    - (c) air blast circuit breaker
    - (d) SF_6 circuit breaker

15. Circuit breakers are essentially
    - (a) current carrying contacts called electrodes
    - (b) arc extinguishers
    - (c) circuits to break the system
    - (d) transformers to isolate two systems

16. In a circuit breaker, arc is initiated by the process of
    - (a) thermal emission
    - (b) field emission
    - (c) alternators
    - (d) transmission lines

17. Buchholz relay is used for the protection of
    (a) switch yard
    (b) transformers
    (c) alternators
    (d) transmission lines

18. The basic problem in a circuit breaker is to
    (a) maintain the arc
    (b) extinguish the arc
    (c) emit ionization electrons
    (d) none of these

19. In oil and air blast circuit breakers, the current zero interruption is attained by
    (a) lengthening of arc
    (b) cooling and blast effect
    (c) deionizing the oil with forced air
    (d) both (a) and (b) above

20. Air blasty circuit breaker is operated at a pressure of
    (a) 5 to 10 kg/cm^2 (b) 10 to 15 kg/cm^2
    (c) 15 to 20 kg/cm^2 (d) 20 to 30 kg/cm^2

21. The voltage appearing across the contacts after the opening of the circuit breaker is called
    (a) surge voltage   (b) recovery voltage
    (c) arc voltage   (d) break open voltage

22. Buchholz relays are used for transformers of ratings above
    (a) 100 kV   (b) 200 kV
    (c) 500 kV   (d) 1000 kV

23. Air blast circuit breakers are preferred for
    (a) short duty   (b) intermittent duty
    (c) repeated duty   (d) none of these

24. The power factor of the arc in a circuit breaker is
    (a) zero leading
    (b) zero lagging
    (c) unity
    (d) any value from zero to unity

25. For a 400 kV system, the capacity of lightning arrester should be
    (a) 1 kA   (b) 5 kA
    (c) 10 kA   (d) 50 kA

26. A high speed circuit breaker can complete its operation in
    (a) 2 to 3 cycles   (b) 3 to 8 cycles
    (c) 6 to 12 cycles   (d) 10 to 20 cycles

27. Which of following are the desirable qualities of protective relays ?
    (a) speed sensitivity
    (b) stability, reliability
    (c) selectivity, adequacy
    (d) none of these

28. Basic quantity measured in a distance relay is
    (a) impedance   (b) voltage difference
    (c) current difference   (d) none of these

29. Drop out to cutoff ratio for most relays is of the order of
    (a) 0.2 to 0.3   (b) 0.3 to 0.4
    (c) 0.4 to 0.6   (d) 0.6 to 1.0

30. If the operation of a relay does not involve any change in air gap, then the ratio of rest to pick up is usually
    (a) low
    (b) medium
    (c) high
    (d) independent of the change in air gap

31. Plug setting of a relay can be altered by varying
    (a) number of ampere-turns
    (b) air gap of magnetic path
    (c) adjustable back up stop
    (d) none of these

32. Directional relays respond to the
    (a) flow of current
    (b) voltage polarities
    (c) flow of power
    (d) all of these

33. Which of the following is not an instanta-neous relay ?
    (a) induction disc type
    (b) hinged armature type
    (c) balanced beam type
    (d) polarized type

34. Which of the following is an instantaneous relay?
    (a) thermocouple type
    (b) induction type
    (c) permanent magnet moving coil type
    (d) shaded pole type

35. Which of the following is a directional relay?
    (a) mho relay
    (b) reactance relay
    (c) impedance relay
    (d) both (a) and (b)

36. Protective relays are devices which detect abnormal conditions in electrical circuits by measuring
(a) current during abnormal condition
(b) voltage during abnormal condition
(c) both (a) and (b) simultaneously
(d) constantly the electrical quantities which differ during normal and abnormal conditions

37. A distance relay measures
(a) current difference
(b) voltage difference
(c) impedance difference
(d) distance between two CT's

38. Various power system faults in increasing order of severity are
(a) LG, LL, LLG, LLLG
(b) LLLG, LLG, LG, LL
(c) LLG, LLLG, LL, LG
(d) LL, LG, LLLG, LLG

39. Which of the following type of reactors are popularly used in power systems ?
(a) compensation reactors
(b) current limiting reactors
(c) suppression or Peterson reactors
(d) all of these

40. Shunt reactors are connected with transmission lines for
(a) limiting fault current
(b) limiting fault voltage
(c) absorbing reactive power
(d) absorbing high voltage surges

41. Minimum faults occur in which of the following power system equipment ?
(a) transformer   (b) switch gear
(c) CT, PT   (d) alternator

42. Interruption due to fault and maintenance is minimum in
(a) main and transfer bus arrangement
(b) single bus arrangement
(c) sectionalized single bus arrangement
(d) double bus, double breaker arrangement

43. When a line-to-line fault occurs, the short circuit current of an alternator depends upon its
(a) short circuit reactance
(b) synchronous reactance
(c) transient reactance
(d) subtransient reactance

44. Resistance offered by series reactor is usually
(a) low   (b) medium
(c) high   (d) very high

45. Time interval from instant of contact separation to time of arc extinction is called
(a) closing time
(b) opening time
(c) arcing time
(d) none of these

46. Maximum short circuit current occurs due to
(a) line-to-line fault
(b) line-to-line circuit
(c) dead short circuit
(d) both (a) and (b) occurring simultaneously

47. Which of following are used to reduce short circuit fault currents
(a) reactors
(b) resistors
(c) capacitors
(d) parallel combination of all these

48. Oil immersed type reactor has the advantage of
(a) smaller size with large thermal capacity
(b) higher safety against flashover
(c) limiting the fault voltage
(d) both (a) and (b) above

49. Which of the following method of protection is used to achieve earth fault operation ?
(a) core balance method
(b) frame leakage method
(c) relay connected with neutral to ground
(d) none of these

50. Large internal faults below oil level are protected by
(a) earth fault and positive sequence relay
(b) Merz Price percentage differential relay
(c) horn gap and temperature relay
(d) mho and ohm relays

51. For an arc length of l metres carrying fault current of I amperes, the arc resistance in ohms is

(a) $\dfrac{2.9 \times 10^3\, l}{I^{1.4}}$ (b) $\dfrac{2.9 \times 10^4\, l}{I^{1.4}}$

(c) $\dfrac{3.1 \times 10^4\, l}{I^2}$ (d) $\dfrac{3.1 \times 10^4\, l}{I}$

52. Generator internal fault protection is usually based on the principle of
(a) differential protection
(b) cross-differential protection
(c) negative sequence protection
(d) all of these

53. The phase comparison relay has the merit that
(a) its operation does not depend upon the direction of power flow
(b) correct relay action can be obtained by using series capacitors on the line
(c) it can operate even for low value of fault current
(d) none of these

54. The advantage of grounding a power system is that
(a) earth fault current can be used to operate relays
(b) "arcing ground" phenomenon is avoided
(c) it provides symmetry to the line impedances
(d) both (a) and (b) above

55. Pilot wire protection is basically used for the protection of
(a) transmission lines
(b) alternators
(c) switch gears
(d) transformers

56. Which of the following carrier frequency is used in a carrier current protection scheme?
(a) 500 kHz to 5 kHz
(b) 5 kHz to 50 kHz
(c) 50 kHz to 500 kHz
(d) 500 kHz to 5 MHz

57. Power system insulation problem involves
(a) selection of "basic insulation level" insulation levels of system equipment and lightning arrestor
(b) determination of line insulation
(c) capacitance to earth and subsequent grounding
(d) both (a) and (b) above

58. Typical gap length of rod type surge diverter used for 132 kV line is
(a) 10 cm   (b) 20 cm
(c) 35 cm   (d) 65 cm

59. Which of the following are the requirements of protection of power station buildings against direct strokes ?
(a) interception alone
(b) interception and conduction
(c) interception, conduction and dissipation
(d) conduction and dissipation

60. A relay is said to be a high speed relay if it operation time is
(a) 1 to 2 cycles   (b) 2 to 3 cycles
(c) 3 to 5 cycles   (d) 5 to 7 cycles

61. Maximum demand of a consumer is 2kW and his daily energy consumption is 20 units. His load factor will be
(a) 10%   (b) 52%
(c) 41.6%   (d) None of above

62. Advantage of hydro-electric power station is
(a) low operating cost
(b) free from pollution problems
(c) no fuel transportation problems
(d) all of the above.

63. A sodium graphite reactor uses
(a) sodium as moderator and graphite as coolant
(b) sodium as coolant and graphite as moderator
(c) a mixture of sodium and graphite as coolant
(d) a mixture of sodium and graphite as moderator.

64. No moving parts are required in
(a) MHD generator
(b) Tidal power plant
(c) Thermioic conversion
(d) OTEC power plant.

65. A fast breeder reactor
(a) operates with fast neutrons and produces less fissionable material than it consumes
(b) operates with fast neutrons and produces more fissionable material than it consumes
(c) operates with slow neutrons and produces more fissionable material than it consumes.
(d) operates with slow neutrons and produces more fissonable material than it consumes.

66. Gas turbines can be brought to the bus bar from cold in about
(a) 2 minutes   (b) 30 minutes
(c) 1 Hour   (d) 2 Hours

67. Efficiency of a plant is secondary consideration for
  (a) base load power plants
  (b) peak load power plants
  (c) both peak load as well as base load power plants
  (d) neither peak load nor base load power plants

68. In hydrothermal source of geothermal energy
  (a) hot water or steam is available
  (b) hot gases are available
  (c) molten lava is available
  (d) none of the above.

69. A module is a
  (a) newly installed solar cell
  (b) series parallel arrangement of solar cells
  (c) a series of solar cells when not used for power generation
  (d) none of the above.

70. Connected load of a consumer is 2 kW and his maximum demand is 1.5 kW. The load factor of the consumer will be
  (a) 0.75   (b) 0.375
  (c) 1.33   (d) none of the above

71. Pumped storage plant in India
  (a) does not exist
  (b) exists in Kadamparai (Tamil Nadu)
  (c) exists in Gandhi Sagar dam (Kota)
  (d) is being installed in Haryana.

72. Tidal energy mainly makes use of
  (a) kinetic energy of water
  (b) potential energy of water
  (c) both kinetic as well as potential energy of water
  (d) none of the above.

73. In a super-heater
  (a) pressure rises, temperature drops
  (b) pressure rises, temperature remains constant
  (c) pressure remains constant and temperature rises
  (d) both pressure and temperature remains constant.

74. Equipment used for pulverising the coal is known as
  (a) Ball mill   (b) Hopper
  (c) Burner   (d) Stoker

75. A gas turbine works on
  (a) Carnot cycle   (b) Brayton cycle
  (c) Dual cycle   (d) Rankine cycle

76. Out of the following which one is not a unconventional source of energy ?
  (a) Tidal power
  (b) Geothermal energy
  (c) Nuclear energy
  (d) Wind power

77. Maximum efficiency of an open cycle gas turbine is nearly
  (a) 30%   (b) 40%
  (c) 50%   (d) 60%

78. A 100 MW thermal power plant will consume nearly how many tonnes of coal in one hour ?
  (a) 50 tonnes   (b) 150 tonnes
  (c) 1500 tonnes   (d) 15,000 tonnes

79. Most of the generators in thermal power plants run at
  (a) 3000 rpm   (b) 1500 rpm
  (c) 1000 rpm   (d) 750 rpm

80. A cooling tower can be seen in
  (a) gas turbine plant
  (b) nuclear power plant
  (c) hydroelectric power plant
  (d) thermal power plant.

81. Which of the following is considered as superior quality of coal ?
  (a) Bituminous coal
  (b) Peat
  (c) Lignite
  (d) Coke

B. Economics of Operation

82. In order to have lower cost of electrical energy generation :
  (a) The load factor and diversity factor should be low.
  (b) The load factor should be low but diversity factor should be high.
  (c) The load factor should be high but diversity factor low.
  (d) The load factor and diversity factors should be high.

83. The cost of generation is theoretically minimum if :

(a) The system constraints are considered.

(b) The operational constraints are considered.

(c) both (a) and (b)

(d) The constraints are not considered.

84. If the penalty factor of a plant is unity, its incremental transmission loss is

(a) 1.0

(b) – 1.0

(c) Zero

(d) None of the above

85. The loss coefficients for a two-bus system are

(a) $B_{11} = 0.02$, $B_{22} = 0.05$, $B_{12} = 0.01$, $B_{21} = 0.015$

(b) $B_{11} = 0.02$, $B_{22} = 0.04$, $B_{12} = -0.01$, $B_{21} = 0.01$

(c) $B_{11} = 0.03$, $B_{22} = 0.005$, $B_{12} = 0.001$, $B_{21} = -0.001$

(d) $B_{11} = 0.03$, $B_{22} = 0.05$, $B_{12} = 0.001$, $B_{21} = -0.001$.

86. If the penalty factor for bus 1 in a two-bus system is 1.25 and if the incremental cost of production at bus 1 is Rs. 200 per MWhr, the cost of received power at bus 2 is

(a) Rs. 250/M Whr.

(b) Rs. 62.5/MWhr.

(c) Rs. 160/MWhr.

(d) None of the above.

87. For economic operation, the generator with highet positive incremental transmission loss will operate at

(a) The lowest positive incremental cost of production.

(b) The lowest negative incremental cost of production.

(c) The highest positive incremental cost of production.

(d) None of the above.

88. The incremental transmission loss of a plant is

(a) Positive always.

(b) Negative always.

(c) Can be positive or negative.

(d) None of the above.

89. If the loading of the line corresponds to the surge impedance loading the voltage at the receiving end is

(a) Greater than sending end

(b) Less than sending end

(c) Equal to the sending end

(d) None of the above is necessary.

90. If r is the radius of the conductor and R the radius of the sheath of the cable, the cable operates stably from the view point of dielectric strength if

(a) $\dfrac{r}{R} > 1.0$

(b) $\dfrac{r}{R} < 1.0$

(c) $\dfrac{r}{R} < 0.632$

(d) $\dfrac{r}{R} < 0.368$

91. Shunt compensation in a EHV line is resorted to

(a) Improve the stability.

(b) Reduce the fault level.

(c) Improve the voltage profile.

(d) none of the above

92. Most economic load on an overhead line is

(a) Greater than the natural load.

(b) Less than the natural load.

(c) Equal to the natural load.

(d) None of the above is necessary.

93. The p.u. impedance value of an alternator corresponding to base values 13.2 kV and 30 MVA is 0.2 p.u. The p.u. value for the base values 13.8 kV and 50 MVA will be

(a) 0.306 p.u.

(b) 0.33 p.u.

(c) 0.318 p.u.

(d) 0.328 p.u.

94. Insulation of the modern EHV lines is designed based on

(a) lighting voltage

(b) switching voltage

(c) Corona

(d) RI

95. Impulse ratio of a gap of given geometry and dimension is

(a) Greater with solid than with air dielectric.

(b) Greater with air than with solid dielectric.

(c) Same for both solid and air dielectric.

96. The impulse ratio of a rod gap is

(a) Unity.

(b) Between 1.2 and 1.5.

(c) Between 1.6 and 1.8.

(d) Between 2 and 2.2.

97. Effect of bonding the cable is

(a) To increase the effective resistance and inductance.

(b) To increase the effective resistance but reduce inductance.

(c) To decrease the effective resistance and inductance.

(d) To decrease the effective resistance but increase the inductance.

98. For effective application of counterpoise it should be buried into the ground to a depth of

(a) 1 metre.

(b) 2 metres.

(c) Just enough to avoid theft.

(d) None of the above.

99. Corona loss is less when the shape of the conductor is

(a) Circular.   (b) Flat.

(c) Oval.   (d) Independent of shape.

100. A system is said to be effectively grounded if its

(a) Neutral is grounded directly.

(b) Ratio of $\dfrac{X_0}{X_1} > 3.0$.

(c) Ratio of $\dfrac{X_0}{X_1} > 2.0$.

(d) Ratio of $\dfrac{X_0}{X_1} < 3.0$.

101. Velocity of travelling wave through a cable of relative per mittivity 9 is

(a) 9×10^8 metres/sec.

(b) 3×10^8 metres/sec.

(c) 10^8 metres/sec.

(d) 2×10^8 metres/sec.

102. Voltage at the two ends of a line are 132 kV and its reactance is 40 ohms. The capacity of the line is

(a) 435.6 MW.   (b) 217.8 MW.

(c) 251.5 MW.   (d) 500 MW.

103. For a lumped inductive load, with increase in supply frequency

(a) P and Q increase.

(b) P increases, Q decreases.

(c) P decreases, Q increases.

(d) P and Q decrease.

104. Corona loss on a particular system at 50 Hz is 1 kW/phase per km. The corona loss on the same system with supply frequency 25 Hz will be

(a) 1 kW/phase/km.

(b) 0.5 kW/phase/km.

(c) 0.667 kw/phase/km.

(d) None of the above.

105. Most economic load on an underground cable will be

(a) Greater than its surge loading.

(b) Less than the surge loading.

(c) Equal to the surge loading.

(d) None of the above is necessary.

106. Self GMD method is used to evaluate

(a) Inductance.

(b) Capacitance.

(c) Inductance and capacitance both

(d) None of the above

107. Surge impedance of 50 miles long underground cable is 50 ohms. For a 25 miles length it will be

(a) 25 ohms   (b) 50 ohms

(c) 100 ohms   (d) None of the above

108. Capacitance and inductance per unit length of a line operating at 110 kV are 0.01 mF and 2 mH. The surge impedance loading of the line will be

(a) 40 MVA   (b) 30 MVA

(c) 27 MVA   (d) None of the above

109. Sending end voltage of a feeder with reactance 0.2 p.u. is 1.2 p.u. If the reactive power supplied at the receiving end of the feeder is 0.3 p.u., the approximate drop of volts in the feeder will be

(a) 0.2 p.u.   (b) 0.06 p.u.

(c) 0.05 p.u.   (d) 0.072 p.u.

110. Presence of earth in case of overhead lines

(a) Increases the capacitance.

(b) Increases the inductance.

(c) Decreases the capacitance.

(d) Decreases the inductance.

111. Effect of increase in temperature in overhead transmission lines is to

(a) increase the stress and length.

(b) Decrease the stress and length.

(c) Decrease the stress but increase the length.

(d) None of the above.

112. Ferranti effect on long overhead lines is experienced when it is
 (*a*) Lightly loaded.
 (*b*) On full load at unity p.f.
 (*c*) On full load at 0.8 p.f. lag.
 (*d*) In all these cases.

113. In-rush current of a transformer at no load is maximum if the supply voltage is switched on
 (*a*) At zero voltage value.
 (*b*) At peak voltage value.
 (*c*) At V / 2 value.
 (*d*) At $\sqrt{3}/2$ V value.

114. If the inductance and capacitance of a system are 1.0 H and 0.01 μF respectively and the instantaneous value of current interrupted is 10 amp, voltage across the breaker contacts will be
 (*a*) 50 kV   (*b*) 100 kV
 (*c*) 60 kV   (*d*) 57 kV

115. In case of a 3-phase short circuit in a system, the power fed into the system is
 (*a*) Mostly reactive.
 (*b*) Mostly active.
 (*c*) Active and reactive both equal.
 (*d*) Reactive only.

116. Standard impulse testing of a power transformer requires
 (*a*) Two applications of chopped wave followed by one application of a full wave.
 (*b*) One aplication of chopped wave followed by one application of a full wave.
 (*c*) One application of chopped wave followed by two applications of a full wave.
 (*d*) None of the above.

117. Phase modifier is normally installed in the case of
 (*a*) Short transmission lines.
 (*b*) Medium length lines.
 (*c*) Long length lines.
 (*d*) For all length lines.

118. In order to eliminate sheath losses, a successful method is
 (*a*) To transpose the cable along with cross bonding.
 (*b*) Transpose the cables only.
 (*c*) Cross bonding the cables is enough.
 (*d*) None of the above is effective.

119. Stringing chart is useful for
 (*a*) Finding the sag in the conductor.
 (*b*) In the design of tower.
 (*c*) In the design of insulator string.
 (*d*) Finding the distance between the tower.

120. For an existing a.c. transmission line the string efficiency is 80. Now of d.c. voltage is supplied for the same set up, the string efficiency will be
 (*a*) 80%
 (*b*) More than 80%
 (*c*) Less than 80%
 (*d*) 100%

121. Coefficient of reflection for current for an open ended line is
 (*a*) 1.0   (*b*) 0.5
 (*c*) -1.0 (*d*) Zero.

122. Leakage resistance of a 50 km long cable is 1 MΩ. For a 100 km long cable it will be
 (*a*) 1 MΩ
 (*b*) 2 MΩ
 (*c*) 0.66 MΩ
 (*d*) None of the above

123. A voltmeter gives 120 oscillations per minute when connected to the rotor. The stator frequency is 50 Hz. The slip of the motor is
 (*a*) 2%   (*b*) 4%
 (*c*) 5%   (*d*) 2.5%

124. Solution of coodination equations takes into account
 (*a*) All the system constraints.
 (*b*) All the operational constraints.
 (*c*) All the system and operation constraints.
 (*d*) None of the above.

125. Charging reactance of 50 km length of line is 1500 Ω. The charging reactance for 100 km length of line will be
 (*a*) 1500 Ω (*b*) 3000 Ω
 (*c*) 750 Ω (*d*) 600 Ω

126. In a two plant system, the load is connected at plant no 2. The loss coefficients
 (*a*) B_{11}, B_{12}, B_{22} are nonzero.
 (*b*) B_{11} and B_{22} are nonzero but B_{12} is zero.
 (*c*) B_{11} and B_{12} are nonzero but B_{22} is zero.
 (*d*) B_{11} is nonzero but B_{12} and B_{22} are zero.

127. Capacitance of a 3-core cable between any two conductors with sheath earthed is 2 μF. The capacitance per phase will be

   (*a*) 1 μF

   (*b*) 4 μF

   (*c*) 0.667 μF

   (*d*) 1.414 μF

128. For a synchronous phase modifier the load angle is

   (*a*) 0°

   (*b*) 25°

   (*c*) 30°

   (*d*) None of the above

129. The insulation resistance of a cable of length 10 km is 1 MΩ, its resistance for 50 km length will be

   (*a*) 1 MΩ

   (*b*) 5 MΩ

   (*c*) 0.2 MΩ

   (*d*) None of the above

130. Three insulating materials with breakdown strengths of 250 kV/cm, 200 kV/cm, 150 kV/cm and permittivities of 2.5, 3.0 and 3.5 are used in a single core cable. If the factor of safety for the materials is 5, the location of the materials with respect to the core of the cable will be

   (*a*) 2.5, 3.0, 3.5   (*b*) 3.0, 2.5, 3.5

   (*c*) 3.5, 3.0, 2.5   (*d*) 3.5, 2.5, 3.0

131. Three insulating materials with same maximum working stress and permittivities 2.5, 3.0, 4.0 are used in a single core cable. The location of the materials with respect to the core of the cable will be

   (*a*) 2.5, 3.0, 4.0   (*b*) 3.0, 2.5, 4.0

   (*c*) 4.0, 3.0, 2.5   (*d*) 4.0, 2.5, 3.0

132. Select the correct statement

   (*a*) The negative and zero sequence voltages are maximum at the fault point and decrease towards the neutral.

   (*b*) The negative and zero sequence voltages are minimum at the fault point and increase towards the neutral.

   (*c*) The negative sequence is maximum and zero sequence minimum at the fault point and decrease and increase respectively towards the neutral.

   (*d*) None of the above.

133. For the system shown in diagram below, a line-to-ground fault on the line side of the trans-former is equivalent to

   (*a*) A line-to-ground fault on the generator side of the transformer.

   (*b*) A line-to-line fault on the generator side of the transformer.

   (*c*) A double line-to-ground on the generator side of the transformer.

   (*d*) A 3-phase fault on the generator side of the transformer.

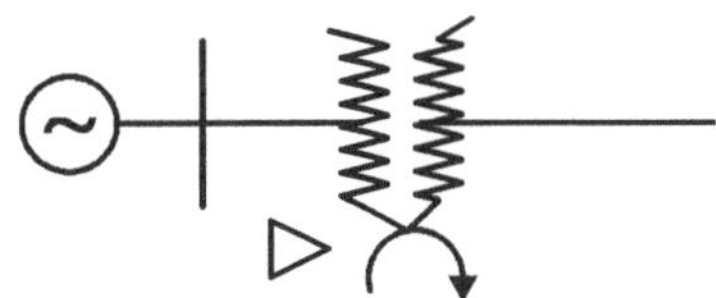

134. Size of conductor on modern EHV lines is obtained based on

   (*a*) Voltage drop

   (*b*) Current density

   (*c*) Corona

   (*d*) above (*a*) and (*b*)

135. At a particular unbalanced node, the real powers specified are

     Leaving the node 20 MW, 25 MW

     Entering the node 60 MW, 30 MW

   Balancing power will be

   (*a*) 30 MW leaving the node.

   (*b*) 45 MW leaving the node.

   (*c*) 45 MW entering the node.

   (*d*) 22.5 MW entering the node and 22.5 MW leaving the node.

136. Positive sequence component of voltage at the point of fault is zero when it is a

   (*a*) 3-phase fault

   (*b*) L-L fault

   (*c*) L-L-G fault

   (*d*) L-G fault

137. If I_{a1} is the positive sequence current of an alternator and Z_1, Z_2 and Z_0 are the sequence impedances of the alternator. The drop produced by the current Ia_1 will be

   (*a*) $I_{a1} Z_1$

   (*b*) $I_{a1} (Z_1 + Z_2)$

   (*c*) $I_{a1} (Z_1 + Z_2 + Z_0)$

   (*d*) $I_{a1} (Z_2 + Z_0)$

138. Tick out the correct one
  (a) The insulators and lightning arresters should have high impulse ratio.
  (b) The insulators and lightning arresters should have low impulse.
  (c) The insulator should have high impulse ratio and lightning arrester low.
  (d) The lightning arrester should have high impulse ratio but insulator low.

139. An overhead line with surge impedance 400 ohms is terminated through a resistance R. A surge travelling over the line does not suffer any reflection at the junction if the value of R is
  (a) 20 ohms
  (b) 200 ohms
  (c) 800 ohms
  (d) None of the above

140. In case of a large size alternator the voltage control becomes serious if
  (a) SCR is high.
  (b) SCR is low.
  (c) Voltage control is independent of SCR.
  (d) none of the above.

C. Power System Protection

141. Current chopping tendency is minimised by using the F6 gas at relatively
  (a) High pressure and low velocity.
  (b) High pressure and high velocity.
  (c) Low pressure and low velocity.
  (d) Low pressure and high velocity.

142. Order of the lightning discharge current is
  (a) 10,000 amp
  (b) 100 amp
  (c) 1 amp
  (d) 1 microampere

143. For the same rupturing capacity, the actual current to be inter-rupted by an HRC fuse is
  (a) Much less than any CB.
  (b) Much more than any CB.
  (c) Equal to the CB.
  (d) None of the above is necessary.

144. Arcing on transmission lines is prevented by connecting a suitable
  (a) Circuit breaker.
  (b) Protective relay.
  (c) Inductor in the neutral.
  (d) Capacitor in the neutral.

145. For rural electrification in a country like India with complex network it is preferable to use
  (a) Air break C.B.   (b) Oil C.B.
  (c) Vacuum C.B.   (d) M.O. C.B.

146. Chances of arc interruption in subsequent current zeros
  (a) Increases in case of ABCD but decreases in OCB.
  (b) Decreases in case of ABCB but increases in OCB.
  (c) Decreass in both the cases.
  (d) Increases in both the cases.

147. Stability of arc in vacuum depends upon
  (a) The contact material only.
  (b) The contact material and its vapour pressure.
  (c) The circuit parameters only.
  (d) The combination of (b) and (c).

148. Resistance switching is normally resorted in case of
  (a) Bulk oil circuit breakers.
  (b) Minimum oil circuit breakers.
  (c) Air blast circuit breakers.
  (d) All types of breakers.

149. Mho relay is normally used for the protection of
  (a) Long transmission lines.
  (b) Medium length lines.
  (c) Short length lines.
  (d) No length criterion.

150. Number of pilot wires required for protecting 3-phase transmission lines using translay system of protection is
  (a) 6   (b) 4
  (c) 3   (d) 2

151. A Mho relay is a
  (a) Voltage restrained directional relay.
  (b) Voltage controlled over current relay.
  (c) Directional restrained over current relay.
  (d) Directional restrained over voltage relay.

152. Shape of the disc of an induction disc relay is
  (a) Circular
  (b) Spiral
  (c) Elliptic
  (d) Elliptic

153. A 3-phase braker is rated at 2000 MVA, 33 kV, its making current will be

(a) 35 kA   (b) 49 kA

(c) 70 kA   (d) 89 kA.

154. An overhead line with series compensation is protected using

(a) Impedance relay   (b) Reactance relay

(c) Mho relay   (d) None of the above

155. Shunt fault is characterized by

(a) Increase in current, frequency and p.f.

(b) Increase in current reduction in frequency and p.f.

(c) Increase in current and frequency but reduction in p.f.

(d) None of the above.

156. Where voltages are high and current to be interrupted is low the breaker preferred is

(a) Air blast C.B.

(b) Oil C.B.

(c) Vacuum C.B.

(d) Any one of the above.

157. If the time of operation of a relay for unity TMS is 10 secs., the time of operation for 0.5 TMS will be

(a) 20 secs.   (b) 5 secs.

(c) 10 secs.   (d) None of the above

158. If the phase angle of the voltage coil of a directional relay is 50° the maximum torque angle of the relay is

(a) 130°   (b) 100°

(c) 25°   (d) None of the above

159. A reactance relay is

(a) Voltage restrained directional relay.

(b) Directional restrained over-current relay.

(c) Voltage restrained over-current relay.

(d) None of the above.

160. For measuring positive, negative and zero sequence voltages in a system, the reference is taken as

(a) Neutral of the system only.

(b) Ground only.

(c) For zero sequence neutral and for positive and negative the ground.

(d) None of the above.

161. Per cent bias for a generator protection lies between

(a) 5 to 40

(b) 40 to 45

(c) 45 to 20

(d) None of the above

162. Minimum oil circuit breaker has less volume of oil because

(a) There is insulation between contacts.

(b) The oil between the breaker contacts has greater strength.

(c) Solid insulation is provided for insulating the contacts from earth.

(d) None of the above

163. Carrier current protection scheme is normally used for

(a) HV transmission lines only.

(b) HV cables only.

(c) HV transmission and cables.

(d) None of the above.

164. To limit current chopping in vacuum circuit breakers, the contact material used has

(a) High vapour pressure and low conductivity properties.

(b) High vapour pressure and high conductivity properties.

(c) Low vapour pressure and high conductivity properties.

(d) Low vapour pressure and low conductivity properties.

165. A fault is more severe from the view point of RRRV if it is a

(a) Short line fault.

(b) Medium length line fault.

(c) Long line fault.

(d) None of the above.

166. Match the it ems in List I to items in List-II and select the correct answer from the codes given below the lists

Items	Application
A. Surge arrester	P. Reduction of charging current
B. Circuit breaker	Q. Over voltage protection
C. Series capacitor	R. Increase of power transfer
D. Shunt reactor	S. Over current protection.

Codes

(*a*) A—P, B—Q, C—R, D—S
(*b*) A—Q, B—S, C—R, D—P
(*c*) A—R, B—P, C—Q, D—S
(*d*) A—S, B—R, C—Q, D—P

167. Positive, negative and zero sequence impedances of a solidly grounded system under steady state condition always follow the relations
 (*a*) $Z_1 > Z_2 > Z_0$
 (*b*) $Z_1 < Z_2 < Z_0$
 (*c*) $Z_0 < Z_1 < Z_2$
 (*d*) None of the above

168. Phase comparators in case of static relays and electro-mechanical relays normally are
 (*a*) Sine and cosine comparators respectively.
 (*b*) Cosine and sine comparators respectively.
 (*c*) Both are cosine comparators.
 (*d*) Both are sine comparators.

169. For reducing tower footing resistance it is better to use
 (*a*) Chemical and ground rods only.
 (*b*) Chemical and counterpoise only.
 (*c*) Ground rod and counterpoise only.
 (*d*) Chemical, ground rods and counterpoise.

170. Rate of rise of restriking voltage depends
 (*a*) type of circuit breaker.
 (*b*) inductance of the system only.
 (*c*) capacitance of the system only.
 (*d*) inductance and capacitance of the system.

171. Breakdown strength of air at STP is 24 kV/cm. Its breakdown strength at 30°C and 72 cm of Hg will be
 (*a*) 24.25 kV/cm.　　(*b*) 20.2 kV/cm.
 (*c*) 23 kV.　　(*d*) 49.5 kV/cm.

172. Capacitor switching is easily done with
 (*a*) Air blast circuit breaker.
 (*b*) Oil C.B.
 (*c*) Vacuum C.B.
 (*d*) Any one of the above.

173. The normal practice to specify the making current of a circuit breaker is in terms of
 (*a*) r.m.s. value
 (*b*) Peak value
 (*c*) Average value
 (*d*) Both r.m.s. and peak value.

174. Chances of arc interruption in subsequent current zero
 (*a*) Increases in case of OCB.
 (*b*) Decreases in case of OCB
 (*c*) Interruption is always at first current zero (in OCB)
 (*d*) None of the above.

175. If the inductance and capacitance of a system are 4 H and 0.04 μF respectively and the instantaneous value of current interrupted is 40 amps, the value of shunt resistance across the breaker for critical damping is
 (*a*) 400 kΩ　　(*b*) 40 kΩ
 (*c*) 5 kΩ　　(*d*) 4 kΩ

176. For effective use of a counterpoise wire
 (*a*) Its leakage resistance should be greater than the surge impedance.
 (*b*) Three-phase and two-earth fault relays are required.
 (*c*) Two-phase and two-earth fault relays are required.
 (*d*) Two-phase and one-earth fault relays are required.

177. If the fault current is 2000 amps, the relay setting 50% and the C.T. ratio is 400/5, then the plug setting multiplier will be
 (*a*) 25 amps　　(*b*) 45 amps
 (*c*) 50 amps　　(*d*) None of the above

178. For protection of parallel feeders fed from one end the relays required are
 (*a*) Non-directional relays at the source end and directional relays at the load end.
 (*b*) Non-directional relays at both the ends.
 (*c*) Directional relays at the source end and non-directional at the load end.
 (*d*) Directional relays at both the ends.

179. High voltage d.c. testing for HV machines is resorted because
 (*a*) Certain conclusions regarding the continuous ageing of an insulation can be drawn.
 (*b*) The stress distribution is a representation of the service condition.
 (*c*) Standardization on the magnitude of voltage to be applied is available.
 (*d*) The stresses do not damage the coil end insulation.

180. If a combination of HRC fuse and circuit breaker is used, the C.B. operates for
(a) Low overload currents.
(b) Short circuit current.
(c) Under all abnormal current.
(d) The combination is never used in practice.

181. Most suitable C.B. for short line fault without switching resistor is
(a) Air blast C.B.
(b) M.O.C.B.
(c) SF_6 Breaker
(d) None of the above

182. A large-size alternator is protected against overloads by providing
(a) Overcurrent relays.
(b) Temperature sensitive relays.
(c) Thermal relays.
(d) A combination of (a) and (b).
(e) A combination of (b) and (c).

183. Impedance relays can be used for
(a) phase faults only
(b) earth faults only
(c) both phase and earth faults
(d) none of these

184. System frequency and system voltage respectively control
(a) active power, reactive power
(b) active power, active power
(c) reactive power, reactive power
(d) reactive power, active power

185. Surge impedance of 400W implies
(a) open circuit impedance of 400 Ω
(b) line can be theoretically loaded upto 400Ω
(c) line can be practically loaded upto 400Ω
(d) short circuit impedance of 400Ω

186. Power system uses
(a) suppression coils
(b) current limiting resistors
(c) compensation reactors
(d) all of these

187. Reactance used in case of generator is
(a) synchronous reactance
(b) transient reactance
(c) sub-tranisent reactance
(d) all of these

188. In a generator, 3ϕ, short circuit current is limited by
(a) transient reactance
(b) synchronous reactance
(c) sub-tranisent reactance
(d) all of these

189. 3ϕ, short circuit current will be
(a) infinite at infinite time
(b) maximum at infinite time
(c) zero at infinite time
(d) 10 mA at infinite time

190. Negative sequence component of a voltage is equal to
(a) zero sequence component
(b) positive sequence component
(c) complex conjugate of the positive sequence component
(d) complex conjugate of the zero sequence component

191. For L — G fault, all networks are in
(a) series   (b) parallel
(c) star   (d) delta

192. Series reactor should have
(a) high resistance   (b) low resistance
(c) high impedance   (d) low impedance

193. For L — L fault, network consists of
(a) positive sequence   (b) negative sequence
(c) zero sequence   (d) both (a) and (b)

CIRCUIT BREAKERS

194. Ionization in circuit breakers is facilitated by
(a) increase of field stregth
(b) increase of mean free path
(c) high temperature
(d) all of these

195. Arc interruption is done by
(a) high resistance interruption
(b) low resistance interruption
(c) both (a) and (b)
(d) none of these

196. Part of circuit breaker helpful in breaking the current is
(a) Trip coil   (b) Contacts
(c) Handle   (d) Medium

197. Desired tripping of a circuit breaker is
(a) manually
(b) automatically
(c) that it should give warning
(d) none of these

198. For single frequency transients, ratio of peak restriking voltage to time between voltage zero and peak voltage is called
(a) restriking voltage
(b) recovery voltage
(c) rate of rise restriking voltage
(d) active recovery voltage

199. In a circuit breaker, to facilitate arc quenching, dielectric strength can be increased by
(a) lengthening of the gap
(b) cooling
(c) blast effect
(d) all of these

200. An ideal circuit breaker should offer
(a) zero & infinite impedance before & after interruption respectively
(b) infinite & zero impedance before & after interruption respectively
(c) equal impedance before & after interruption
(d) none of these

201. Instantaneous voltage in a circuit breaker depends upon
(a) restriking voltage
(b) rate of rise restriking voltage
(c) power factor
(d) frequency

202. Recovery voltage is the value of the r.m.s. voltage that re-appears across the poles of a circuit breaker before
(a) restriking voltage
(b) final arc distinction
(c) rise of voltage
(d) all of these

203. Which of the following is not a protective gear?
(a) Fuse
(b) Circuit breaker
(c) Relay
(d) None of these

204. Arcing time is the time between
(a) separation of circuit breaker and extinction of arc
(b) separation of circuit breaker and rise of recovery voltage
(c) normal current interrption and arc extinction
(d) none of these

205. Time between energisation of trip coil and separation of contacts is called
(a) closing time
(b) opening time
(c) both (a) and (b)
(d) none of these

206. Rate of rise restriking voltage depends upon
(a) active recovery voltage
(b) natural frequency of oscillations
(c) both (a) and (b)
(d) rating of circuit breaker

207. Interrupting a low inductive current may lead to
(a) very high restriking voltage
(b) very high current
(c) rupture of circuit breaker
(d) current chopping

208. Current chopping can be avoided by
(a) resistance switching
(b) inductive switching
(c) capacitive switching
(d) diode switching

209. Time between separation of contacts and energisation of trip coil is called
(a) opening time   (b) closing time
(c) arching time   (d) decaying time

210. Difficulty of performing the circuit breaking operation is a function of
(a) circuit voltage
(b) magnitude of the current
(c) electrical constants of the circuit
(d) none of these

211. When contacts of circuit breaker opens
(a) arc is produced
(b) voltage rises
(c) breaker fails
(d) arc chamber is broken

212. A.C. air break circuit breakers are used for
(a) very high voltage
(b) very low voltage
(c) medium voltage
(d) medium and low voltage

213. Air blast circuit breakers are preferred for
(a) short duty
(b) intermittant duty
(c) repeated duty
(d) all of these

214. Phenomenon of arc interrrpution takes place at
(a) zero voltage
(b) zero current
(c) high current
(d) high voltage

215. Over voltage may be due to
(a) lightning impulse waveform
(b) 50 Hz a.c.
(c) peak value of 50 Hz a.c.
(d) all of these

216. In oil circuit breakers, dielectric strength of oil should be
(a) high   (b) low
(c) medium   (d) none of these

217. Main disadvantage (s) of oil circuit breaker is that it
(a) is easily inflammable
(b) may form an explosive mixture with air
(c) requires maintenance
(d) all of these

218. Breaker should adjust itself to
(a) fault magnitude and time
(b) increased arc and time of quenching
(c) R R R V
(d) none of these

219. At higher currents, the switchgear exhibit
(a) corona effect
(b) skin effect
(c) mechanical stresses
(d) poor regulation

220. Plain circuit breakers can't be used for voltage above
(a) 400 V   (b) 3.3 kV
(c) 11 kV   (d) 33 kV

221. Quantity of oil in bulk oil circuit breakers increases with
(a) decrease in voltage
(b) increase in voltage
(c) pressure of arc
(d) mechanical stresses

222. Rating of circuit breaker depends upon
(a) breaking capacity
(b) making capacity
(c) short time capacity
(d) all of these

223. Symmetrical breaking current is
(a) peak value of a.c. component
(b) average value of a. c. component
(c) r.m.s. value of a.c. component
(d) all of these

224. In vacuum breakers, current wave
(a) reaches its maximum value
(b) attains its r.m.s value
(c) is chopped
(d) attains its average value

FUSE

225. Fusing factor should be
(a) equal to zero   (b) equal to one
(c) less than now   (d) more than one

226. Fuse wire should possess
(a) high specfic resistance and high melting point
(b) high specific resistance and low melting point
(c) low specific resistance and low melting point
(d) low specific resistance and high melting point

227. If strands are twisted, then fusing current will
(a) increase
(b) reduce
(c) remain same
(d) may increase or decrease

228. Fusing factor is defined as the ratio between
(a) maximum fusing current and rated voltage
(b) maximum fusing current and rated current
(c) minimum fusing current and rated current
(d) minimum fusing current and rated voltage

229. Fuses can serve upto a current of
(a) 25 A   (b) 50 A
(c) 75 A   (d) 100 A

230. Cut-off current in a fuse is the
   (a) maximum value actually reached
   (b) r.m.s value actually reached
   (c) average value actually reached
   (d) none of these

231. Best practicable material for a fuse wires is
   (a) Aluminium   (b) Copper
   (c) Iron   (d) Tin

232. H.R.C. fuses has
   (a) high rating of current
   (b) high rupturing capacity
   (c) high resistance capacity
   (d) none of these

233. Cartridge type fuse can be used upto a voltage of
   (a) 400 V   (b) 11 kV
   (c) 20 kV   (d) 33 kV

234. Liquid type H.R.C. fuses are used upto a voltage of
   (a) 33 kV   (b) 66 kV
   (c) 132 kV   (d) 200 kV

235. Selection of fuse is based on
   (a) steady load   (b) fluctuating load
   (c) a & b   (d) none of these

PROTECTIVE RELAYS

236. A single phasing relay can be used with
   (a) 1ϕ motor   (b) $2^r \phi$ motor
   (c) 3ϕ motor   (d) all of these

237. A relay is used to
   (a) break the fault current
   (b) sense the fault
   (c) sense the fault and direct to trip the circuit breaker
   (d) all of these

238. In impedance relay, current element torque should be
   (a) equal to voltage element torque
   (b) greater than voltage element torque
   (c) less than voltage element torque
   (d) none of these

239. Over current fault is most likely in
   (a) tranformer
   (b) overhead line equipment
   (c) alternator
   (d) motors

240. Good relay should possess
   (a) speed & reliability
   (b) speed & sensitivity
   (c) adequateness & selectivity
   (d) all of these

241. Relay gets its operating energy from
   (a) transformer   (b) alternator
   (c) overhead lines   (d) C.T., P.T.

242. An impedance relay is used for
   (a) earth faults   (b) interphase faults
   (c) both (a) and (b)   (d) none of these

243. Earthing transformer is used to
   (a) improve neutral wire's current capacity
   (b) avoid overheating of transformer
   (c) provide artificial earthing
   (d) avoid harmonics

244. Basic relay connection requirement is that the relay must operate for
   (a) load   (b) internal faults
   (c) both (a) and (b)   (d) none of these

245. MHO relay is inherently a
   (a) directional type
   (b) non-directional type
   (c) unidirectional type
   (d) none of these

246. Instantaneous relay should operate within
   (a) 0.0001 sec   (b) 0.001 sec
   (c) 0.01 sec   (d) 0.1 sec

247. Buchholz relay is used to protect against
   (a) inter-turn fault
   (b) external faults
   (c) rotor faults
   (d) every internal faults

248. Distance relays re generally
   (a) impedance type
   (b) MHO type
   (c) reactance type
   (d) all of these

249. Plug setting of a relay can be changed by changing
   (a) air gap
   (b) back up stop
   (c) number of ampere turns
   (d) all of these

250. Percentage differential protection is used to prevent against
(a) inter-turn faults (b) external faults
(c) heavy loads (d) magnetizing current

251. Relays for transmission line protection are
(a) in three zones
(b) in two zones
(c) independent of zone
(d) none of these

252. Induction cup relays responds to
(a) current (b) voltage
(c) power (d) impedance

253. Split-phase relay responds to
(a) over load faults (b) over voltage
(c) inter turn faults (d) all of these

254. Directional relays responds to
(a) power (b) current
(c) voltage (d) reactance

255. In carrier current protection, wave trap is used is for trapping
(a) high frequency waves entering in generating units
(b) power frequency waves
(c) both (a) and (b)
(d) none of these

256. For phase fault on long line, which relay is used?
(a) MHO relays (b) reactance relays
(c) impedance relays (d) all of these

257. For protection against synchronising power surges, which relay is used?
(a) split-phase relays (b) impedance relays
(c) reactance relays (d) MHO relays

258. Under voltage relays are used for
(a) motors (b) alternators
(c) bus bars (d) all of these

259. More faults occur in
(a) generators (b) under ground cables
(c) transformers (d) over head lines

260. Instantaneous relay is
(a) hinged armature type
(b) polarized type
(c) balanced beam type
(d) all of these

261. Back up protection is needed for
(a) over voltage (b) over current
(c) short circuits (d) all of these

262. An instantaneous relay is
(a) permanent moving magnet
(b) induction cup
(c) shaded pole
(d) moving coil

263. Relays which act directly on C.B. are called
(a) auxiliary relays
(b) main relays
(c) both (a) and (b)
(d) none of these

264. Time classification of relays includes
(a) instantaneous relays
(b) definite time lag
(c) inverse time lag
(d) all of these

265. Single phase preventers are used for
(a) transformers
(b) transmission lines
(c) motors
(d) underground cables

266. Operating current in relay is
(a) a.c. only (b) d.c. only
(c) both (a) and (b) (d) none of these

267. For motor protection, which relay is used?
(a) Thermocouple type relays
(b) Bimetallic relays
(c) Electronic relays
(d) All of these

268. Pilot wire protection is for
(a) overhead lines (b) transformer
(c) motors (d) cables

269. In an impedance relay, fault current is maximum if fault occurs near the
(a) relay
(b) centre of the line
(c) transformer
(d) none of these

270. Actual tripping of a static relay is obtained by
(a) SCR (b) thyristors
(c) UJT (d) none of these

271. It is possible to work on ungrounded systems of 11 kV for a length of
    (*a*) 10 Kms   (*b*) 50 Kms
    (*c*) 90 Kms   (*d*) 110 Kms

272. Advantage of grounded neutral is
    (*a*) persistent arcing grounds are eliminated
    (*b*) earth faults are utilized to disconnect the fault
    (*c*) both (*a*) and (*b*)
    (*d*) none of these

273. Neutral can be grounded by
    (*a*) solid grounding
    (*b*) resistance grounding
    (*c*) reactance grounding
    (*d*) all of these

Overvoltage Lightning Protection

274. Lightning arrestors are
    (*a*) surge reflectors   (*b*) surge divertors
    (*c*) surge absorbers   (*d*) surge attenuators

275. Location of lightning arrestor is
    (*a*) after the transformer
    (*b*) after the distributor
    (*c*) before the transformer
    (*d*) none of these

276. Thyrite is used in lightning arrestors because of its
    (*a*) straight line characteristic
    (*b*) non-linear characteristic
    (*c*) none of these
    (*d*) all of these

ANSWERS

1. (*b*)	**2.** (*b*)	**3.** (*a*)	**4.** (*c*)	**5.** (*b*)	**6.** (*c*)	**7.** (*b*)	**8.** (*d*)	**9.** (*a*)	**10.** (*d*)
11. (*c*)	**12.** (*b*)	**13.** (*b*)	**14.** (*d*)	**15.** (*a*)	**16.** (*d*)	**17.** (*b*)	**18.** (*b*)	**19.** (*d*)	**20.** (*d*)
21. (*b*)	**22.** (*c*)	**23.** (*c*)	**24.** (*c*)	**25.** (*c*)	**26.** (*b*)	**27.** (*d*)	**28.** (*a*)	**29.** (*d*)	**30.** (*c*)
31. (*a*)	**32.** (*c*)	**33.** (*a*)	**34.** (*c*)	**35.** (*d*)	**36.** (*d*)	**37.** (*c*)	**38.** (*a*)	**39.** (*d*)	**40.** (*c*)
41. (*d*)	**42.** (*d*)	**43.** (*b*)	**44.** (*a*)	**45.** (*b*)	**46.** (*d*)	**47.** (*a*)	**48.** (*b*)	**49.** (*a*)	**50.** (*c*)
51. (*a*)	**52.** (*a*)	**53.** (*c*)	**54.** (*c*)	**55.** (*d*)	**56.** (*a*)	**57.** (*a*)	**58.** (*c*)	**59.** (*c*)	**60.** (*a*)
61. (*c*)	**62.** (*d*)	**63.** (*b*)	**64.** (*c*)	**65.** (*b*)	**66.** (*a*)	**67.** (*b*)	**68.** (*a*)	**69.** (*b*)	**70.** (*d*)
71. (*b*)	**72.** (*b*)	**73.** (*c*)	**74.** (*a*)	**75.** (*b*)	**76.** (*c*)	**77.** (*a*)	**78.** (*a*)	**79.** (*a*)	**80.** (*d*)
81. (*a*)	**82.** (*d*)	**83.** (*d*)	**84.** (*c*)	**85.** (*c*)	**86.** (*a*)	**87.** (*a*)	**88.** (*c*)	**89.** (*c*)	**90.** (*d*)
91. (*c*)	**92.** (*a*)	**93.** (*a*)	**94.** (*b*)	**95.** (*a*)	**96.** (*b*)	**97.** (*b*)	**98.** (*c*)	**99.** (*a*)	**100.** (*d*)
101. (*c*)	**102.** (*a*)	**103.** (*c*)	**104.** (*c*)	**105.** (*b*)	**106.** (*a*)	**107.** (*b*)	**108.** (*c*)	**109.** (*c*)	**110.** (*a*)
111. (*c*)	**112.** (*a*)	**113.** (*a*)	**114.** (*b*)	**115.** (*a*)	**116.** (*a*)	**117.** (*c*)	**118.** (*a*)	**119.** (*a*)	**120.** (*d*)
121. (*c*)	**122.** (*d*)	**123.** (*b*)	**124.** (*d*)	**125.** (*c*)	**126.** (*d*)	**127.** (*b*)	**128.** (*a*)	**129.** (*c*)	**130.** (*a*)
131. (*c*)	**132.** (*a*)	**133.** (*b*)	**134.** (*c*)	**135.** (*b*)	**136.** (*a*)	**137.** (*a*)	**138.** (*c*)	**139.** (*d*)	**140.** (*b*)
141. (*c*)	**142.** (*a*)	**143.** (*a*)	**144.** (*c*)	**145.** (*c*)	**146.** (*b*)	**147.** (*d*)	**148.** (*c*)	**149.** (*a*)	**150.** (*d*)
151. (*a*)	**152.** (*b*)	**153.** (*d*)	**154.** (*d*)	**155.** (*b*)	**156.** (*c*)	**157.** (*b*)	**158.** (*d*)	**159.** (*b*)	**160.** (*d*)
161. (*a*)	**162.** (*c*)	**163.** (*a*)	**164.** (*a*)	**165.** (*a*)	**166.** (*b*)	**167.** (*a*)	**168.** (*b*)	**169.** (*c*)	**170.** (*d*)
171. (*d*)	**172.** (*c*)	**173.** (*b*)	**174.** (*a*)	**175.** (*c*)	**176.** (*b*)	**177.** (*d*)	**178.** (*a*)	**179.** (*a*)	**180.** (*a*)
181. (*c*)	**182.** (*b*)	**183.** (*c*)	**184.** (*a*)	**185.** (*b*)	**186.** (*d*)	**187.** (*d*)	**188.** (*b*)	**189.** (*c*)	**190.** (*c*)
191. (*a*)	**192.** (*b*)	**193.** (*d*)	**194.** (*d*)	**195.** (*c*)	**196.** (*b*)	**197.** (*b*)	**198.** (*c*)	**199.** (*d*)	**200.** (*a*)
201. (*c*)	**202.** (*b*)	**203.** (*d*)	**204.** (*a*)	**205.** (*d*)	**206.** (*c*)	**207.** (*d*)	**208.** (*a*)	**209.** (*a*)	**210.** (*c*)
211. (*a*)	**212.** (*d*)	**213.** (*c*)	**214.** (*b*)	**215.** (*d*)	**216.** (*a*)	**217.** (*d*)	**218.** (*a*)	**219.** (*b*)	**220.** (*c*)
221. (*b*)	**222.** (*d*)	**223.** (*c*)	**224.** (*c*)	**225.** (*d*)	**226.** (*d*)	**227.** (*b*)	**228.** (*c*)	**229.** (*d*)	**230.** (*a*)
231. (*b*)	**232.** (*b*)	**233.** (*d*)	**234.** (*c*)	**235.** (*c*)	**236.** (*c*)	**237.** (*c*)	**238.** (*a*)	**239.** (*b*)	**240.** (*d*)
241. (*d*)	**242.** (*c*)	**243.** (*c*)	**244.** (*b*)	**245.** (*a*)	**246.** (*c*)	**247.** (*d*)	**248.** (*b*)	**249.** (*c*)	**250.** (*d*)
251. (*a*)	**252.** (*d*)	**253.** (*c*)	**254.** (*a*)	**255.** (*a*)	**256.** (*c*)	**257.** (*d*)	**258.** (*d*)	**259.** (*d*)	**260.** (*a*)
261. (*c*)	**262.** (*a*)	**263.** (*b*)	**264.** (*d*)	**265.** (*c*)	**266.** (*c*)	**267.** (*d*)	**268.** (*a*)	**269.** (*a*)	**270.** (*d*)
271. (*d*)	**272.** (*c*)	**273.** (*d*)	**274.** (*b*)	**275.** (*c*)	**276.** (*b*)				

Control Systems

Servomechanism : It is a feedback control system in which the output is mechanical position, velocity or acceleration.

Open loop control system : In these output has no effect upon the control action.

Closed loop control system : In these output signal has direct effect upon the control action.

$$\text{Mason's gain formula is } P = \frac{1}{\Delta} \sum_k P_k \Delta_k$$

(*a*) If all the roots of the characteristic equation have negative real parts, the system is stable.

(*b*) If any root of the characteristic equation has a positive real parts or if there is a repeated root on the jω - axis, the system is unstable.

(*c*) If the condition (*a*) is satisfied except for the presence of one or more nonrepeated roots on the jω-axis, the system is marginally stable.

The positiveness of the co-efficients of the characteristic equation is necessary as well as sufficient condition for stability of the system of first and second order.

Routh and Hurwitz's criterion are equivalent of each other.

Root locus method : In this roots of the characteristic equation are plotted for all values of a system parameter.

For frequency response, there are three commonly used representations of sinusoidal transfer functions.

(*a*) Bode plot or logarithmic plot

(*b*) Polar plot

(*c*) Phase plot or log-magnitude plot

Relation between location of roots of the characteristic equation and open loop frequency response can be studied by Nyquist stability criterion.

The relation between constant M and N circles to log-magnitude and phase angle is called *Nicholas chart*.

OBJECTIVE TYPE QUESTIONS

1. Effect of feedback on the plant is to

  (*a*) control system transient response

  (*b*) reduce the sensitivity to plant parameter variations

  (*c*) both (*a*) and (*b*)

  (*d*) none of these

2. In an open loop system

  (*a*) output control the input signal

  (*b*) output has no control over input signal

  (*c*) some other variables control the input signal

  (*d*) neither output nor any other variable has any effect on input

3. Electrical resistance is analogous to

  (*a*) intertia   (*b*) dampers

  (*c*) spring   (*d*) fluid capacity

4. Output of the feedback control system should be a function of

  (*a*) input   (*b*) reference and output

  (*c*) feedback signal   (*d*) none of these

5. Transient response in the system is basically due to

  (*a*) stored energy   (*b*) forces

  (*c*) friction   (*d*) coupling

6. Transfer function of a system is defined as the ratio of output to input in

  (*a*) Z-transform   (*b*) Fourier transform

  (*c*) Laplace transform (*d*) All of these

7. Transfer function of a system can be used to study its

  (*a*) steady state behaviour

  (*b*) transient behaviour

  (*c*) both (*a*) and (*b*)

  (*d*) none of these

8. Automatic control system in which output is a variable is called

  (*a*) closed loop system

  (*b*) servomechanism

  (*c*) automatic regulating system

  (*d*) process control system

9. With feedback system sensitivity to parameter

(a) decreases   (b) increases

(c) becomes zero   (d) becomes infinite

10. With feedback system, tranient response

(a) decays constantly   (b) decays slowly

(c) decays quickly   (d) rises fast

11. In control system non-linearity caused by gear trains is

(a) Backlash   (b) Dead space

(c) Coulomb friction   (d) Saturation

12. Time sharing of an expansive control system can be achieved by using a/an

(a) a.c. control system

(b) analog control system

(c) sampled data control system

(d) none of these

13. Laplace transform is not applicable to non-linear system because

(a) non-linear systems are time varying

(b) time domain analysis is easier than frequency domain analysis

(c) initial conditions are not zero in non linear systems

(d) superposition law is not applicable to non-linear system

14. Linear differential transformer is an

(a) electromechanical device

(b) electric device

(c) electromagnetic device

(d) electrostatic device

15. Which of the following is not a desirable feature of a modern control system ?

(a) no oscillation

(b) accuracy

(c) quick response

(d) correct power level

16. Device used for conversion of coordinates is

(a) Syschros

(b) Microsyn

(c) Synchro resolver

(d) Synchro transformer

17. Most common use of the synchros is as

(a) error detector

(b) transmission of angular data

(c) transmission of arithmetic data

(d) for synchronisation

18. In a closed loop system, source power is modulated with

(a) error signal

(b) reference signal

(c) actuating signal

(d) feed back signal

19. Non-linearity in the servo system due to saturation is caused by

(a) servo motor   (b) gear trains

(c) relays   (d) none of these

20. Microsyn is the name given to

(a) potentiometer

(b) magnetic amplifier

(c) resolver

(d) rotary differential transformer

21. Differential is used in synchro differential unit for generators only

(a) indicating difference of rotation angle of two synchro generators only

(b) indicating sum of rotation angle of the synchor genes rators only

(c) both (a) and (b)

(d) none of these

22. Value of $i(0^+)$ for the system whose transfer function is given by the equation

$$I(s) = \frac{2s+3}{(s+1)(s+3)} \text{ is}$$

(a) 0   (b) 1

(c) 2   (d) 3

23. If transfer function of the system is $\dfrac{1}{TS+1}$, then steady state error to the unit step input is

(a) 1   (b) zero

(c) T   (d) infinite

24. Power amplification in a magnetic amplifier can be increased

(a) by negative feed back

(b) by positive feed back

(c) with higher inductane of a.c. coil

(d) none of these

25. Friction coefficient is usually kept low to

(a) minimize velocity-lag error

(b) maximize velocity-lag error

(c) minimize time constant

(d) maximize speed of response

26. If for second order system damping factor is less than one, then system response will be
   (a) Under damped   (b) Over damped
   (c) Critically damped (d) None of these

27. In the derivative error compensation
   (a) damping decreases and settling time increases
   (b) damping increases and settling time increases
   (c) damping decreases and settling time decreases
   (d) damping increases and settling time decreases

28. Second-derivative input signal adjust
   (a) time constant of the system
   (b) time constant and supress the oscillations
   (c) damping of the system
   (d) gain of the system

29. For unity damping factor, the system will be
   (a) under damped   (b) critically damped
   (c) over damped   (d) oscillatory

30. System generally preferred is
   (a) under damped   (b) critically damped
   (c) over damped   (d) oscillatory

31. For second order linear system, settling time is
   (a) $\dfrac{1}{4}$ of the time constant
   (b) $\dfrac{1}{2}$ of the time constant
   (c) 4 times the time constant
   (d) 2 times the time constant

32. For a desirable transient response of a second order system damping ratio must be between
   (a) 0.4 and 0.8   (b) 0.8 and 1.0
   (c) 1.0 and 1.2   (d) 1.2 and 1.4

33. If overshoot is excessive, then damping ratio is
   (a) equal to 0.4
   (b) less than 0.4
   (c) more than 0.4
   (d) infinity

34. Physical meaning of zero initial condition is that the
   (a) system is at rest and stores no energy
   (b) system is at rest but stores energy
   (c) reference input to working system is zero
   (d) system is working but stores no energy

35. A low value of friction coefficient
   (a) minimize the velocity lag error
   (b) maximize the velocity lag error
   (c) minimize the time constant of the system
   (d) maximize the time constant of the system

36. If gain of the system is increased, then
   (a) roots move away from the zeros
   (b) roots move towards the origin of the S-plot
   (c) roots move away from the poles
   (d) none of these

37. If gain of the critically damped system is increased, the system will behave as
   (a) under damped   (b) over damped
   (c) critically damped   (d) oscillatory

38. Settling time is inversely proportional to product of the damping ratio and
   (a) time constant
   (b) maximum overshoot
   (c) peak time
   (d) undamped natural frequency of the system

39. If gain of the system is zero, then the roots
   (a) coincide with the poles
   (b) move away from the zeros
   (c) move away from the poles
   (d) none of these

40. 0 type system has
   (a) zero steady state error
   (b) small steady state error
   (c) high gain constant
   (d) high error with high K

41. At resonance peak, ratio of output to input is
   (a) zero   (b) lowest
   (c) highest   (d) none of these

42. Relation between Fourier integral and Laplace transform is through
   (a) time domain
   (b) frequency domain
   (c) both (a) and (b)
   (d) none of these

43. Steady state error is always zero in response to the displacement input for
   (a) type 0 system
   (b) type 1 system
   (c) type 2 system
   (d) type (N > 1) system for N = 0, 1, 2....N

44. If steady state state error for type 1 system for unit ramp input is kept constant, then constant output is

(a) distance   (b) velocity

(c) acceleration   (d) power

45. For type 2 system, position error arises at steady state when input is

(a) ramp

(b) step displacement

(c) constant acceleration

(d) none of these

46. To decrease the type number of system

(a) first integrator and then diffrentiator is inserted

(b) first diffentiator and then integrator is inserted

(c) only diffrentiator is inserted in the forward path

(d) only integrator is inserted in the forward path

47. If feeback is introduced in the system the transient response

(a) does not very   (b) decays very fast

(c) decays slowly   (d) dies off

48. The frequency range over which response of the system is within acceptable units is called the system

(a) band width

(b) modulation frequency

(c) demodulation frequency

(d) carrier frequency

49. Lead compensation in the system add

(a) zeros   (b) poles

(c) both (a) and (b)   (d) none of these

50. In type 1 system steady state accleration error is

(a) 0   (b) 1

(c) infinity   (d) none of these

51. Lead lag compensation improve

(a) transient response of the system

(b) steady state response of the system

(c) both (a) and (b)

(d) none of these

52. If open loop transfer function of a system is

$$G(s)H(s) = \frac{K}{S(1 + T_1 S)(1 + T_2 S)}$$

then system will be

(a) unstable   (b) conditionally stable

(c) stable   (d) marginally stable

53. To decrease time constant of the servomechanism

(a) decrease torque of servomotor

(b) increase damping of the system

(c) increase intertia of the system

(d) decrease inertia of the system

54. Servomechanism is called a proportional error device when output of the system is function of

(a) error

(b) error and its first derivative

(c) first derivative of erro

(d) none of these

55. Which of the following motor is suitable for servomechanism ?

(a) a.c. series motor

(b) 1 φ induction motor

(c) 2 φ induction motor

(d) 3 φ induction motor

56. Servomechanism with step-displacement input is

(a) Type 0 system   (b) Type 1 system

(c) Type 2 system   (d) Type 3 system

57. Main difference between servomotor and standard motor is that

(a) servomotor has low inertia and higher starting torque

(b) servomotor has low inertia and low starting torque

(c) servomotor has high inertia and high starting torque

(d) none of these

58. Self balancing instrument uses

(a) D.C. servomotor

(b) A.C. servomotor

(c) tachometer

(d) magnetic amplifier

59. If poles of the system are lying on the imaginary axis in s-plane, then system will be

(a) stable

(b) marginally stable

(c) conditionally stable

(d) unstable

60. According to Hurwitz criterion the characteristic equation

$$s^4 + 8 s^3 + 18 s^2 + 16 s + 5 = 0 \text{ is}$$

(a) unstable

(b) marginally stable

(c) conditionally stable

(d) unstable

61. A system is called absolutely stable is any oscillations set up in the system are
(a) damped out
(b) self-sustaining and tend to last indefinitely
(c) negative peaked only
(d) none of these

62. Best method to determine stability and transient response of the system is
(a) Bode plot   (b) Signal flow graph
(c) Nyquist plot   (d) Root locus

63. If poles of system are lying on the imaginary axis in s-plane, the system will be
(a) unstable
(b) marginally stable
(c) conditionally stable
(d) unstable

64. The number of pure integrations in the system transfer function determine
(a) degree of stability
(b) stability of the system
(c) transient performance of the system
(d) steady state performance

65. Which system conveniently see the impact of poles and zeros on phase and gain margin ?
(a) Root locus
(b) Nyquist plot
(c) Routh-Hurwitz criterion
(d) Bode plot

66. Factor which cannot be can cancelled from numerator and denominator of $G(s)\,E(s)$ in
(a) Bode plot   (b) Nyquist plot
(c) higher frequencies (d) none of these

67. If value of gain is increased, then roots of the system will move to
(a) origin
(b) lower frequencies
(c) higher frequencies
(d) none of these

68. Intersection of root locus branches with the imaginary axis can be determined by the use of
(a) polar plot   (b) routh's criterion
(c) nyquist criterion (d) none of these

69. If gain is zero, then
(a) roots move away from zeros
(b) roots coincide with poles
(c) roots move away from poles
(d) none of these

70. To increase damping of a pair of complex roots compensator used is
(a) phase lag
(b) phase lead
(c) phase lag lead
(d) one with 60° lead circuit

71. For type 3 system, lowest frequency asymptote will have the slope of
(a) 15 db/octave   (b) -16 db/octave
(c) 17 db/octave   (d) -18 db/octave

72. If a pole is added to a system it causes
(a) lag compensation
(b) lead compensation
(c) lead-lag compensation
(d) none of these

73. For steady state transient inprovement, compensator used is
(a) lead copensator
(b) lag compensator
(c) lead lag compensator
(d) none of these

74. Which gives the information between number of poles and zeros of the closed loop transfer function ?
(a) Routh Hurwitz criterion
(b) Bode diagram
(c) Root locus method
(d) Nyquist plot

75. To study time delay of the system which of the following is used ?
(a) Nyquist plot
(b) Bode plot
(c) Routh Hurwitz method
(d) Nicholas chart

76. Closed loop ples are
(a) zeros of $1 + G(S).\,H(s)$
(b) zeros of $G(s)\,H(s)$
(c) poles of $G(s)\,H(s)$
(d) poles of $1 + G(s)\,H(s)$

77. Maximum over shoot is the function of
(a) damping ratio
(b) natural frequency of ocillation
(c) both (a) and (b)
(d) damped frequency of ocillation

78. Feed back control systems are basically

   (*a*) low pass filter

   (*b*) high pass filter

   (*c*) band pass filter

   (*d*) band stop filter

79. A linear system obeys the principle of

   (*a*) homogenity

   (*b*) reciprocity

   (*c*) superposition and homogenity

   (*d*) none of these

80. If poles are more than zeros in G(S) F(S), then number of root locus segment is equal to

   (*a*) number of poles

   (*b*) number of zeros

   (*c*) sum of poles and zeros

   (*d*) difference of poles and zeros

81. For G(S) F(S) = $\dfrac{k(S+z)}{S+p}$, $(z < p)$ the plot is

   (*a*) one pole on the imaginary axis

   (*b*) one zero on the right hand side of the plane

   (*c*) one pole and one zero on the left hand side of plane

   (*d*) 2 poles and 2 zeros on the left hand side of plane

82. Number of root-locus segments which do not terminate on the zeros is equal to

   (*a*) number of poles

   (*b*) number of zeros

   (*c*) sum of poles and zeros

   (*d*) difference of poles and zeros

83. In a root locus plot, the increase in k will

   (*a*) increase damping ratio

   (*b*) decrease damping ratio

   (*c*) not change damping ratio

   (*d*) none of these

84. In a root locus plot, increase in k will

   (*a*) increase overshoot of the response

   (*b*) derease overshoot of the response

   (*c*) not change overshoot of the response

   (*d*) none of these

85. In a root locus plot, increase in k will

   (*a*) result in decrease in the damped and undamped natural frequencies

   (*b*) result in increase in the damped and undamped natural frequencies

   (*c*) not change the damped and undamped natural frequencies

   (*d*) none of these

86. In root plot if k is greater than critical value, then increasing k will

   (*a*) increase valuve of the real part of closed loop

   (*b*) decrease value of the real part of closed loop

   (*c*) not change value of the real part of closed loop

   (*d*) none of these

87. Plot of the constant gain loci of the system is

   (*a*) asymptote

   (*b*) circle with centre at the origin

   (*c*) parabola

   (*d*) ellipse

88. In root locus technique, angle between adjacent asymptote is

   (*a*) $180°/(m+n)$ (*b*) $360°/(m+n)$

   (*c*) $360°/(m-n)$ (*d*) $180°/(m-n)$

89. Frequency response mean

   (*a*) transient response of a system to a sinusoidal input

   (*b*) steady state response of a system to a sinusoidal input

   (*c*) oscillatory response of a system to a sinusoidal input

   (*d*) none of these

90. Bode plot approach is applied to

   (*a*) minimum phase network

   (*b*) non minimum phase network

   (*c*) any network

   (*d*) none of these

91. The type of transfer function used in Bode plot is

   (*a*) $G(s)$ (*b*) $G(j)$

   (*c*) $G(jw)$ (*d*) $G(js)$

92. Bode analysis method can be applied

   (*a*) if transfer function has no poles and zeros on R.H. of s-plane

   (*b*) if transfer function has no poles on R.H. of s-plane

   (*c*) if tranfer function has no zero on R.H. of s-plane

   (*d*) to all transfer functions

93. A complex-conjugate pair of poles near the jw axis will produce a
   (a) high oscillatory mode of transient response
   (b) steady state mode of response
   (c) sinusoidal mode of response
   (d) none of these

94. Frequency range over which response of the system is within acceptable limits is called system
   (a) modulation frequency
   (b) demodulation frequency
   (c) carrier frequency
   (d) band width

95. Polar plots for +ve and −ve frequencies
   (a) are always symmetrical
   (b) can never be symmetrical
   (c) may be symmetrical
   (d) none of these

96. Slope in Bode plot is expressed as
   (a) $-6\,db$/decade   (b) $-6\,db$/octave
   (c) $-8\,db$/octave   (d) $-7\,db$/octave

97. Transfer founction, when the Bode diagram is plotted should be of the form
   (a) $(1 + T)$ (b) $(1 + S)$
   (c) (Ts) (d) $(1 + Ts)$

98. In Nyquist criterion roots of the characteristic equation are given by
   (a) zeros of open loop transfer function
   (b) zeros of closed loop transfer function
   (c) poles of closed loop transfer function
   (d) poles of open loop tsansfer function

99. Nyquist stability criterion requires polar plot of
   (a) characteristic equation
   (b) closed loop transfer function
   (c) open loop transfer function
   (d) none of these

100. Gain margin expressed in decibels is
   (a) positive if Kg greater than 1 and negative for Kg less than 1
   (b) negative if Kg is greater than 1 and positive for Kg less than 1
   (c) always zero
   (d) infinity for Kg equal to 1

101. By adding a pole at $s = 0$, Nyquist plot of the system will
   (a) shift 90° clockwise
   (b) shift 90° anticlockwise
   (c) shift 180°
   (d) not change at all

102. Gain margin of a first or second order system is
   (a) zero
   (b) 1
   (c) 100
   (d) infinite

103. For relative stability of the system which of the following is sufficient ?
   (a) Gain margin
   (b) Phase margin
   (c) Both (a) and (b)
   (d) None of these

104. For all frequencies, a unit circle in the Nyquist plot trans forms into
   (a) db line of amplitude plot in Bode diagram
   (b) 1 db line of amplitude plot in Bode diagram
   (c) either (a) and (b)
   (d) none of these

105. Cut off frequency is the frequency at which magnitude of closed loop frequency response is
   (a) $1\,db$ below its zero frequency
   (b) $2\,db$ below its zero frequency
   (c) $3\,db$ below its zero frequency
   (d) $4\,db$ below its zero frequency

106. Bandwidth gives an indication of
   (a) characteristic equation of the system
   (b) speed of response of a control system
   (c) transfer function of the control system
   (d) transients in the system

107. Cut off rate is the slope of log-magnitude curve
   (a) at the start of curve
   (b) at the end of of curve
   (c) near the cut off frequency
   (d) none of these

ANSWERS

1. (c)	**2.** (d)	**3.** (b)	**4.** (b)	**5.** (a)	**6.** (c)	**7.** (c)	**8.** (d)	**9.** (a)	**10.** (c)
11. (a)	**12.** (c)	**13.** (d)	**14.** (a)	**15.** (a)	**16.** (c)	**17.** (d)	**18.** (a)	**19.** (a)	**20.** (c)
21. (a)	**22.** (c)	**23.** (b)	**24.** (d)	**25.** (a)	**26.** (a)	**27.** (d)	**28.** (b)	**29.** (b)	**30.** (a)
31. (c)	**32.** (a)	**33.** (b)	**34.** (a)	**35.** (a)	**36.** (c)	**37.** (a)	**38.** (b)	**39.** (a)	**40.** (b)
41. (c)	**42.** (c)	**43.** (d)	**44.** (b)	**45.** (c)	**46.** (c)	**47.** (b)	**48.** (a)	**49.** (b)	**50.** (c)
51. (c)	**52.** (c)	**53.** (d)	**54.** (a)	**55.** (c)	**56.** (b)	**57.** (b)	**58.** (b)	**59.** (b)	**60.** (a)
61. (a)	**62.** (c)	**63.** (b)	**64.** (d)	**65.** (d)	**66.** (c)	**67.** (c)	**68.** (b)	**69.** (b)	**70.** (b)
71. (d)	**72.** (b)	**73.** (c)	**74.** (d)	**75.** (a)	**76.** (a)	**77.** (b)	**78.** (a)	**79.** (c)	**80.** (a)
81. (c)	**82.** (d)	**83.** (b)	**84.** (a)	**85.** (b)	**86.** (c)	**87.** (b)	**88.** (c)	**89.** (b)	**90.** (a)
91. (a)	**92.** (a)	**93.** (a)	**94.** (d)	**95.** (a)	**96.** (b)	**97.** (d)	**98.** (c)	**99.** (c)	**100.** (a)
101. (a)	**102.** (d)	**103.** (c)	**104.** (c)	**105.** (c)	**106.** (b)	**107.** (c)			

■■

Printed by Libri Plureos GmbH in Hamburg,
Germany